Prayers for the Gathered Community

PRAYERS FOR THE GATHERED COMMUNITY

RESOURCES FOR THE LITURGICAL YEAR

DON C. SKINNER

United Church Press
Cleveland, Ohio

United Church Press, Cleveland, Ohio 44115
© 1997 by Don C. Skinner

Printed in the United States of America on acid-free paper

| 02 | 01 | 00 | 99 | 98 | 97 | | 5 | 4 | 3 | 2 | 1 |

Library of Congress Cataloging-in-Publication Data
Skinner, Don C., 1932–
    Prayers for the gathered community : resources for the liturgical year /
Don C. Skinner.
      p.   cm.
    Includes bibliographical references and index.
    ISBN 0-8298-1217-2 (pbk. : alk. paper)
    1. Church year.   2. Prayers.   I. Title.
BV30.S54   1997
242'.3—dc21   97-23737
                                                              CIP

To the Ford Chapel Deacons, Allegheny College, 1985–1993

Ginny Adkins

Karen Anewalt

Joanne Baillie

Andy Barden

Kristin Barden

Rich Barnhart

David Bell

Wendy Brown

Paul Caswell

Lisa Drew

Paul Dunham

Megan Franley

David Gilson

Dale Harmon

Kim Harris

Jeanne Hartung

Jim Hodges

Rick Hughes

C. J. Jaques

Allison Jones

Sue Kidder

Stephanie Kinsey

T. J. Litwiler

Kevin Long

Michael Madonia

Dan Maloy

Helen Mason

Sheri Mathewson

Sean McAtee

Karen McFeeters

Nate McKnight

Jay Nelson

Myrna Newman

Elizabeth Weiss Ozorak

Rodger Parry

Christy Provost

Varvara Pyros

Ann Richmond

Josh Ringle

Jen Scott

Lisa Selnekovic

Don Shufran

Anne Stetler

Terry Steyer

Heidi Vossler

Barb Wilke

Heidi Wimpfheimer

Tom Wise

Contents

Preface

The core of what follows began as an effort, between 1985 and 1993, to meet the prayer needs of one congregation (and that a unique one). It was written for use by the students, faculty, and staff who made up the congregation of Ford Memorial Chapel at Allegheny College and periodic visitors who frequent a college campus—alumni, parents, trustees.

The group was unique in several regards. First, they represented the diversity of the whole church of Jesus Christ. They were nurtured in virtually every denomination typical of American society, from liberal to conservative, liturgical to charismatic. A few had no prior religious training. Our coming together never lacked for challenge!

Second, they were part of a community that prides itself on rigorous and critical assessment of all phases of human experience, including spirituality. In consequence, just about every belief students bring to college with them is challenged, but not because their professors set out to undermine faith. After thirty-five years in higher education, I feel comfortable stating that many college faculty, probably the majority, do not practice any organized religion. Others—a significant minority—possess great personal faith and are actively engaged in the life of the church. A very few are avowed atheists—some without having explored any real alternative. I encountered professors who were hostile, though not near as many as were merely indifferent! But I met none who used the classroom simply to attack religious belief. College faculty are called professors for a reason: they strive, many with passion, to explore the truths found in their disciplines and to communicate those truths to their students.

In consequence, students bathe in a flood of new ideas, authoritatively presented, that tax traditional beliefs precisely because those beliefs rest on a foundation too narrow to support the larger truths they must now carry. There is no need to undertake an agnosticism recruitment drive. Infantile spirituality (as distinct from childlike faith) is difficult to retain when your mind is growing so fast that the racket of snapping synapses keeps you awake at night. It is a time at once troubling and exhilarating; a time that tests, like few other experiences can, an individual's capacity to grow. And spiritual growth is not exempted. Mature minds require mature faith: new skins for new wine! A mind that has grappled with quantum physics is unlikely any longer to be comfortable with third-grade religiosity.

The upshot was that these people demanded solid preaching, penetrating questions, and cogent answers.

Third, they were bright. One point in our covenant as a worshiping community was that we were not expected to check our brains at the door of the chapel. Christian worship was presumed to be as rich intellectually as it was spiritually. Achieving this is not a simple task. They err grievously who assume that the transfer of classroom shop-talk to Sunday chapel is sufficient. The students were clear what they did *not* want: "We attend nine to twelve lectures a week," they noted. "What we do not need on Sunday is another lecture. We want a *sermon*."

But even that is not sufficient. Faithful execution of the dual task of being teacher and pastor to the academy requires liturgical material that is intellectually compelling, aesthetically pleasing, and spiritually engaging. Unable consistently to find liturgical material that both met those criteria and was germane to the church year, I began to compose my own. The response was immediate and favorable.

It was also a valuable lesson, demonstrating that "form" prayer need be neither drab nor pedantic—a point elaborated upon in the Introduction to this book. Poetically phrased and carefully crafted, such prayers answer a deeply felt yearning among Christians, gathered in corporate worship, for a coherent unison voice with which to express the mystery of the transcendent in human life.

I want also to lay to rest the perception that the content of college chapel services is removed from life in the "real world"; or worse, that campus worship is necessarily esoteric and unorthodox, with little relevance to parish congregations.

Our chapel services covered the full range of human concerns, not just those of the college campus. They were intended to realign us, each week, with the global Body of Christ. It is already too easy to retreat into the "ivory tower," even while I hasten to assert that that phrase is both overused and not terribly helpful. Life on a college campus is no more withdrawn from the "real world" than life in a hospital or police station, the chamber of commerce, or the chambers of government.

Campus life is one facet of the totality of life, in all its broad complexity. One may choose to use the campus as a refuge in which to hide, while ignoring the commonalities and magnitudes of the human situation. But it may also be used as a platform from which to assess, and respond to, events in local, national, or international life, including the life of the church.

In Ford Chapel, we gathered as the people of God, a faith community within the context of the academic community, and sought to use the chapel experience as a window on the world that we protest Christ calls us to serve. The material that follows was written while peering out that window, asking what it is that God intends us to be, to do, and to strive for. They are of equal value wherever the church gathers to celebrate the presence of God in human life.

Acknowledgments

Five people warrant special thanks for their support in making this book a reality.

The Rev. Dr. Charles Brown Ketcham, James Mills Thoburn Professor of Religious Studies at Allegheny College, now professor emeritus, was the first to urge me to systematize and publish these readings. He and his wife, Joyce, were sensitive and supportive advisers during my early tenure as chaplain at Allegheny.

To my good friends Dr. Ward and Vicki Jamison, my gratitude is deeper than I can convey in words. Their work with the students of Allegheny College embodies what we intend by the term "quality education." For eight years, no Sunday passed without special music performed by a student choir that Ward trained or a soloist from among Vicki's students. The task was not in their job descriptions, and they surely got no pay for it! Their only motive was their commitment to students and a refusal to do less. But their involvement was, and remains, personal as well as professional. They are a faithful sounding board off which I can bounce ideas, knowing the response will be candid and thoughtful.

Finally, expressions of gratitude to one's spouse are obligatory at a time like this. Most ministers, I suspect, owe their spouses that much even if no book is involved, simply for submitting to the same preaching week in, week out for a lifetime, when what they really long to do is go to church! In my case, the debt is larger. Patricia had no great desire to write a book but has patiently served as an astute critic, and her uncanny precision at proofing a manuscript has saved me from more embarrassment than I care to remember. Add a patience that is as close to eternal as anything I expect to experience this side of the grave, and it is clear that my debt to her is great. Even if I spend the rest of my life trying to make it up to her, I will fail. If it is true, as Jesus hinted, that rewards we receive in this life are deductible from what we may reasonably expect in the next, I think I'm in trouble.

Introduction

The church of Jesus Christ lives in two alternating and interlocking states: at the call of Christ, we gather in community, to celebrate the presence of God among us, to study Scripture, to assess our task in the world, and to devise a plan of action. At the command of Christ, we scatter out into our communities, to be "Christ to our neighbor," bringing the power of love to bear on a world too comfortable with evil, and embodying the good news of Jesus Christ in word and action. This physical movement, this contracting and expanding, is defined by the church's theological character.

To use a somewhat presumptuous metaphor, it is like the breathing of God in the world. With each inhaled breath, we are pulled in to be purified and recharged through Word and sacrament. With each exhaled breath, the power of Word and sacrament are loosed again to strive for the world's transformation.

No one has yet improved on the blueprint for the task of the *gathered* church that appears in Acts 2:42, a terse outline of the post-Pentecost conduct of the apostles: "They devoted themselves to the apostles' teaching and fellowship, to the breaking of bread and the prayers." It would be difficult to be more succinct than that!

This book addresses the last of these activities. It provides a coherent set of prayers that pastors and congregations can use as a resource for engaging in this central act of the church as gathered community, and does so with specific attention to the major themes and way stations that constitute the church year. Beginning with Advent, the church's "new year," my goal has been to provide pastors and congregations a complete set of prayers and readings for each Sunday and special day of the church calendar.

The reader will note a particular style in the writing, the cause of which should be made clear at the outset. Prayer does not, after all, take shape in a vacuum. How we express ourselves reflects the assumptions we bring to the act of praying—about the character of God, about ourselves, about our relationship to God and our relationship to our fellow human beings. Less acknowledged, perhaps, because seldom articulated, is that prayer reflects the expressive taste and literary sensibilities of those offering it—a point that is more divisive than we may be aware. In actuality, how we pray probably causes greater tension among Christians than what we pray about.

Clearly, we do not all agree on how to go about it. Some Christians brand prepared material, like what follows, as cold and lifeless. To be meaningful, they argue, prayer must be unplanned, arising spontaneously from the heart—yours, mine, or someone else's. As soon as a prayer is written down, the immediacy, the freshness, the urgency of one-on-one encounter with God is lost.

The view has scriptural support. Jesus urges us to pray in real words about real concerns. We are instructed to keep it simple: don't ramble all over the landscape, get to the point (Matthew 6:7). Still, I do not ascribe to the claim that only spontaneous prayer is legitimate prayer. The very claim undervalues the richness of prayer by insisting that only one style is sufficient, while Christian experience points to a diversity of style that is mind-boggling. The mother at her child's hospital bedside sobbing, "Oh, please! Oh please!" and nothing more, prays. Anxious friends who, not knowing what to say, merely visualize the one they care about embraced by God's love, pray. The ragtag corps of volunteers who appear out of nowhere after a tornado demolishes a town, laboring to restore hope to strangers sifting the debris of shattered lives, pray. And the congregation that rises as one and, in unison voice, thunders forth a declaration of thanksgiving, prays—and it matters not a bit that the words they use are printed in a bulletin. Only one thing matters: that the words faithfully voice their intent.

The point may be carried a step further. If we assume that spontaneity implies (after the *Oxford Universal Dictionary*) "voluntary and unconstrained action on the part of persons," then one may fairly contend that printed unison prayers may actually yield greater "spontaneity" than much that we term free-form prayer. This is true because the effort applied in advance not simply to pray the same words this week as last, next year as this, yields a richer vocabulary, greater expressiveness, and attention to ideas that might not even occur to us but for the forethought. It is also true because many of us, left to our own imagination, feel some degree of inadequacy. Indeed, some of us, in such a circumstance, become tongue-tied! But aided by a thoughtful and poetically crafted prayer, we feel ourselves armed with the whole panoply of language and find fresh voice for our yearning, a greater outlet for thought and emotion. A printed prayer may impose some constraint on the moment of prayer, but it frequently provokes deeper insight than attends *ad libitum* prayer—especially if the entire congregation participates in giving it voice.

In some traditions, community prayer is simply understood to be the aggregate of individual prayer, everyone present engaged together in a cacophony of praise and supplication. The result can be exciting and spiritually driving. Among those for whom it is not, responses vary. Some find it meaningless. Others experience discomfort, and downright embarrassment. For such as these, praying "together" means just that—addressing common concerns in communal voice and language. Again, the question ought to be, which form does the congregation feel best provides the voice it seeks?

The metaphor of the kite is useful here. Loosed from its constraining string, a kite sails off in whatever direction the air happens to be moving and, sooner or later, lands in a heap. Tethered to a string, the kite's power is harnessed, its movement focused. It is transformed into a thing of wonder and delight. So with prayer. Free flight is exciting and at times absolutely essential. But it can also be erratic and undisciplined. The gift of written, unison prayer lies in its capacity to focus the power of a group, to bring collective spiritual energy to bear on an issue of concern through the medium of unified language.

My further assumptions about prayer include the following. First, *prayer should be intelligible.* Many years ago, U.S. Supreme Court Justice Oliver Wendell Holmes observed cryptically, "The trouble with law is that ideas become encysted in phrases, and for a long time thereafter cease to stimulate controversy." We may say the same thing about God-talk. We in the churches invest heavily in religious jargon, never stopping to define what we mean. Worse, we use one undefined word to explain another! It is a sad fact that religious vocabulary can be a substitute for thinking. (To experience the point requires only that one attempt to compose and deliver a sermon absent a single "religious" term. Try it. It is a humbling exercise.) This is not to deprecate the use of religious language in prayer. Our Christian vocabulary is an essential part of our experience. It grounds us in our history. But the context of each "loaded" word must make its meaning clear. How shall we know, otherwise, what we are saying or whether we are saying what we mean, or saying anything at all!

It was the apostle Paul who legitimized glossolalia, "speaking in tongues," as a gift of the Spirit (see, e.g., his essay on diversity and unity in the church in 1 Corinthians 12). But he immediately cautioned concerning its validity and usefulness, first by declaring, in perhaps his most eloquent and beloved passage, that the most excellent gift of all is love (1 Corinthians 13) and charged that glossolalia is valueless unless someone present is capable of both understanding and interpreting what is said (1 Corinthians 14). Otherwise, the effort has no greater value than clanging a gong. In this formative treatise, Paul rather remarkably hints that our inability clearly to interpret what is spoken detracts from whatever meaning God might intend to give our words. Running our mouths senselessly, no matter how piously, still issues in gibberish. If the church's vision and task are not served, God will not dignify our words by making them meaningful.

Prayer is as much an act of feeling as of intellectual effort. Among the saddest divisions to tear the church, in my judgment, is the controversy over whether intellectual penetration or the free flow of feeling is better. The answer is, yes. To argue otherwise is to suggest that human beings are either all unfeeling intellect or brainless bundles of emotion. It takes no great power of observation to see that while some of us possess more of one than the other or are more comfortable with one than the other, we are all a blend of both. More, we need both. Prayer must draw on and feed both, else it does not embrace our full humanity. Neither mindless babble devoid of substance nor cerebral expostulation devoid of feeling will do. Prayer can, and ought to be, both intellectually driving and emotionally absorbing.

Prayer should serve the liturgy. It seems odd that this point should require making. But my experience in Protestant churches suggests that few of us understand what "liturgy" means. The conventional wisdom that liturgy is "a public service of worship" is certainly true. But such a definition fails dismally to grasp the wealth of meaning the term possesses. Our English word derives from the Latin *leiturgia,* which in turn springs from a Greek root *leitourgia,* a conflation of two words meaning "belonging to the people" and "work." Quite literally, liturgy is "the work of the people." Compare this with common practice in most churches, where people spend the majority of their time in a state bordering on lethargy, passively observing the actions of clergy. Beyond singing a couple of hymns and reciting the Prayer of Jesus, many congregations are given little opportunity to do anything at all. They surely are not working!

Taken into membership the day my wife and I joined our present church was a couple from another congregation in town. During the reception following, someone asked what was happening at their former church that caused them to change. "Nothing," came the telling response. "Nothing at all." Precisely. One sage observer noted that in most churches the minister is the actor, God the prompter, and the people the audience. In fact, the people ought to be the actor, the minister the prompter, and God the audience.

The material that follows is offered in support of the latter view and in the hope that it may help get something started. Of the nine prayers and responses provided for each Sunday, six are written specifically for unison or antiphonal reading: the invocation, call to praise, prayer of praise, confession, offertory dedication, and thanksgiving.

I am constrained to make a corollary point here. I suspect that we clergy keep the chancel to ourselves out of fear, not faith. It's a form of job security. How frequently we complain because our people do not take on a larger share of the work; yet we fail actively to engage them at the starting point, in the serious business of leading worship. Inviting laywomen and men to lead the people in the central act of our gathered life by reading Scripture and leading antiphonal readings and prayers is an important first step in training an informed and diligent laity. In my ideal church, the minister could fall ill and most worshipers wouldn't realize it for two weeks!

There are also things that prayer ought not to do. Herewith is a list of some I think most important:

1. Prayer ought not to whine. The prototype is Ezekiel, who, encountering a vision of the holy, fell to the ground, only to hear God complain: "Mortal, stand up on your feet, and I will speak with you" (Ezekiel 2:1). For heaven's sake, no groveling.

2. We should not ask to be excused from the consequences of our own stupidity. An acquaintance once told me about riding a ski tow to the top of the hill for the first time. Looking back down the hill—which inevitably appears much higher from the top—she found herself praying, "Lord, I know I got myself up here, but please help me to get down again in one piece!" No comment.
3. Prayer should not be trivialized by pleading things that are merely inconvenient. I was shocked once to hear a student credit God with helping him find his car keys. If the young man really prays that effectively, he ought, without further delay, to ask for world peace! On the other hand, if that incident reflects a general perception of what constitutes a need worthy of divine intervention, the church is in serious trouble.
4. Similarly, prayer should not ask over again for things we already possess. Jesus admonishes us that God knows what we need before we ask (Matthew 6:8). Prayer should concentrate on circumstances the outcome of which is both important and in doubt, in either the physical or spiritual sense.
5. Prayer should not seek the transformation of things that we ourselves are unwilling to work to change. There is an adage to the effect that we should pray as if everything depended upon God and work as if everything depends on us. To pray for God to act where we have the capability but fail to use it is to gainsay our claim to be the people of God. We empty the church of its authority and ourselves of relevance. Our model here is Isaiah who, confronted in the temple by God's terrible majesty and hearing the words, "Whom shall I send, and who will go for us?" replies, "Here am I, send me!" (Isaiah 6:8).

The prayers that follow attempt (insofar as attentiveness did not flag!) to honor these rules.

Finally, a word about inclusive language. As an educator and writer, I am appalled by the extent to which we tolerate shoddy writing simply because it attempts to be "inclusive." Even some who claim to be educators and ought to have some competence with words often fail dismally. Who has not read a directive something like "Each student desiring to go on the field trip must have his/her parents provide him/her with a permission slip stating that he/she is authorized to go." Such tortured syntax is both needless and inexcusable. It is possible to write in English without depending on gender-specific pronouns. For example: "Students desiring to participate in the field trip must provide the office with a note of authorization from a parent."

One has to wonder whether resistance to inclusive language is caused by the concept itself or the deplorable way it too often is applied. Human beings, as a general rule, resist change for emotional, not rational, reasons. They don't *like* it. And when change is introduced badly, no matter how useful or appropriate it may be, it generates resistance. This is especially true when those favoring change have a need to say so publicly, often aggressively. Encountering anger, they mistakenly assume it to be directed at their cause, not at themselves, and respond by ridiculing their detractors as narrow minded and obtuse.

At any point where the language of faith is in transition, people are easily threatened. We need, at such times, to encourage experimentation and to listen thoughtfully to the feedback. There is no place, at such a time, for petulance, unless we mean to fail. To deliberately or needlessly cause dissension in the church is to divide the body of Christ, a tactic that any serious Christian should employ with dread.

As in any such venture toward change, some offerings will be profound, others silly. We should not worry. The faith has endured and prospered for two millennia, not because we always had the right language, but because we often enough had the right spirit. Open hearts and minds and open discussion cannot but enrich us. Such is the case, for example, when church folk, troubled by what they perceive as a needless attack on traditional language, learn something most do not realize, because no one took the trouble to teach them: that it is incorrect to refer to the Holy Spirit as "he." The Hebrew word for spirit—*ruach*—is a feminine form. This "wind from God" who "swept over the face of the waters" at creation (Genesis 1:2), the "breath of life" breathed into the dust-fashioned Adam (Genesis 2:7), whom Isaiah declared would animate the shoot that would come forth from the stump of Jesse (Isaiah 11:1–2), who swept Jesus into the wilderness after his baptism (Matthew 4:1), and "filled the entire house where they were sitting" at Pentecost (Acts 2:2), is linguistically the "mother spirit," that quality of God that incorporates what we, in our penchant for categorizing things, call "feminine." Many such helpful insights await us when we open ourselves to one another in love.

It is not clear in any case that God is troubled by these points that prove so divisive among us; but that is not reason to dismiss them lightly. How people receive our words has much to do with how they receive our God. If by too slavish a defense of gender-specific terms we offend some whom Christ seeks to reach in love, we "load people with burdens hard to bear, and . . . do not lift a finger to help them" (Luke 11:46). On the other hand (and with apologies to the apostle Paul), we ought "not, for the sake of words, to destroy the work of God" (see Romans 14:20). The debate over language should be undertaken thoughtfully, with open minds and patient spirits.

In any case, I have tried, in composing the material in this book, to be as inclusive as possible. One way to do this while avoiding awkward style, a technique on which I depend in my own writing, is to take seriously Paul Tillich's counsel that God is not a subject (even less an object) about whom we can converse meaningfully; God is the One we must address. I have tried in these prayers and readings, insofar as humanly possible (and taking modest liberties with the biblical text), not to talk *about* God but to direct our words *to* God, to whom be the glory and the honor!

Finally, a word about the types of prayers included. Early in the formation of the Ford Chapel deacons, we spent some time reviewing the order of service previously employed, asking whether and how it ought to be changed. The discussion included a review of the six forms of prayer historically used by the Christian church: Praise, Confession, Supplication, Intercession, Thanksgiving, and Communion of Saints. As the dialogue progressed, a consensus began to emerge to build the service around these forms of prayer. Two benefits might result. First, it would ensure that we engaged regularly in each form and did not overlook an aspect of prayer that generations of thoughtful Christians found meaningful. Second, it would allow us to draw from all traditions, thus honoring the diversity of backgrounds represented in our congregation. For those interested, the resultant service order is reproduced in Appendix A.

Clearly absent from the collection following are two of the forms listed above: Supplication (prayer for ourselves) and Intercession (prayer for others). Their absence is deliberate. Such petitions, which constitute the bulk of what is often called the "pastoral prayer," of necessity ought to spring from the people's sense of their own immediate needs and the needs of others about whom they care. Topics ought to be relevant and timely. The more proximate the preparation of such prayers to the service during which they are used, the better. Indeed, of all points in the liturgy, this is the one where spontaneity is not only appropriate but indispensable. A book such as this cannot supply it nor should one try.

Included in what follows are materials that fit the other rubrics often included in a Protestant order of worship—invocations, calls to reconciliation (or confession), declarations of forgiveness (often called assurances of pardon), calls for the offering and offertory dedications. It is my hope that ministers and others planning services of worship "for the gathered community" will find here a useful resource to enrich the lives of their congregations.

Advent

Four Sundays preceding Christmas
Liturgical Color: Blue (formerly Purple)

The English word Advent comes from the Latin *adventus,* meaning "coming." Advent is the period during which the church prepares to embrace its vision of God's immediate participation in physical life. In historical terms, we prepare for the birth of Jesus. In theological terms, we prepare for Incarnation, "the Word [that] became flesh and lived among us . . . full of grace and truth" (John 1:14). It is the archetypal intersection of the physical and the spiritual, of the immediate and the transcendent. In Christian belief, the event inaugurates the fulfillment of the ancient promise: that God's choosing of the Hebrew nation will ultimately yield blessing to the entire world (Genesis 12:3).

Advent is therefore the church's "new year" celebration. It encompasses the four Sundays preceding Christmas. In contrast to current custom surrounding the secular new year, however, Advent is not a time of personal excess and vacuous resolutions; it is a period of sober (as opposed to somber) reflection and assessment. Since we have the benefit of knowing our history before we reenact it, we know in advance what—and whom—we expect: a moment in time when divine personhood became human event, an event at once tender and earth-shaking. Jesus is God's singular gift of self to the world, calling from us a richly mixed response of penitence and anticipation.

Advent is rooted in two interlocking scriptural themes, both centering on the "fullness of time": the historic expectation of Israel's post-Exilic restitution as a nation, voiced in messianic prophecy (e.g., Isaiah 40; Malachi 3:1–5) and the eschatological hope of the early church, as evidenced in the apocalyptic teachings of Jesus, John the Baptist, and others (e.g., Mark 13; Luke 3:1–17). Common themes among these passages require that we attend to Scripture's "both/and" vision of God:

both gentle and stern, both loving and holy. The God of Jewish and Christian scripture is both Judge and Redeemer. To view God as judge and not redeemer leaves us without hope. To view God as redeemer but not judge excuses us from meaningful standards of personal and corporate responsibility. Periods when the church emphasizes God as judge to the neglect of redemption are periods of mean spiritedness and fearmongering, a people without love. When God's redemptive action is emphasized to the neglect of divine righteousness, the church fosters vapid piety blind to the reality of evil, a people without awe.

This paradox is nowhere described more grippingly, nor with greater economy of words, than in Malachi's startling prophecy at the opening of chapter 4: "See, the day is coming, burning like an oven, when all the arrogant and all the evildoers will be stubble; the day that comes shall burn them up, says the God of hosts, so that it will leave them neither root nor branch. But for you who revere my name the sun of righteousness will rise, with healing in its wings. You shall go out leaping like calves from the stall. And you shall tread down the wicked, for they will be ashes under the souls of your feet, on the day when I act, says the God of hosts." No insipid vision this; no "sweet Jesus meek and mild." But also not a vindictive and petulant deity for whom only punishment brings satisfaction. This God delivers, with one gesture, destruction so consuming it scarcely leaves a residue, restoration so empowering that it constitutes rebirth.

The story is told that Karl Barth once entered a lecture hall on the chalkboard of which someone had written, "God is other people." Studying the phrase briefly, Barth picked up the chalk and inserted a comma between "other" and "people." By so deft a stroke, a world of difference is illuminated and the nature of Advent qualified: it is a time for enhanced awareness of who God is and who we are—and that the two are not the same!

The season first awakens in us a sure confidence in God's unwavering faithfulness, evidenced in the fulfillment of historic promises. But Advent also dramatizes the interdependence of humility and hope. We see, right from the start, that repentance is the prerequisite of redemption, confession the qualifying condition of forgiveness.

This is a touchy issue for many Protestant Christians, who resist the idea of "confession" on one of several grounds: either that they have "done nothing wrong" and therefore have nothing to confess, or that "confession is something Catholics do." Neither excuse is sufficient. Those who state they have done nothing wrong really mean that they are without sin—at least any *real* sin. (Lucky them!) If this be so, then we must inquire why they bother with a church that preaches universal human need for Christ's redeeming intervention. At the very least, they betray a profound ignorance of biblical theology, which may be more the fault of us clergy who have failed to teach them than any fault of their own. Those who worry that a posture of penitence is too Catholic are equally misinformed. The sacrament of reconciliation, as practiced in the contemporary Roman Catholic church, recognizes that it is one thing to admit, in private and to no one in particular, to unworthy thought and conduct, but something else to look another living being in the eye and say it right out loud. Hardest of all is to go face to face with the very person you have offended and admit it. In this encounter, the priestly role of the clergy is clearly delineated. The priest, at that moment, "stands in the place of God" and receives, person to person, the admission of sin and contrition. Those who have never found it necessary to sit down, close up and personal, to confess an act they would give just about anything to hide, and to ask to be forgiven have yet to understand the profoundly visceral nature of both sin and forgiveness. It is a facet of spirituality, in my judgment, on which few Protestant churches have yet done their homework.

The origins of Advent are unclear. The first authoritative reference occurred at the Synod of Larida (542 C.E.), although an earlier canon of the Council of Saragossa in 380, which mandated church attendance by the faithful between December 17 and Epiphany, may allude to Advent's evolution.

In recent years, there appears to be renewed interest in the symbol of the Advent Wreath, a custom the origin of which is also lost in antiquity. The wreath (a circle) was early used in northern Europe as a symbol of eternity. Its fabrication from evergreen branches reflected the belief that conifers—which generally do not lose their foliage in the fall—remained "alive" through the long winter, a symbol of the continuity of life in the face of seeming universal death. At some point the wreath was brought into the church, adorned with four candles that are lit progressively through the four Sundays of the season. Those troubled by this seeming corruption of Christian worship by a pagan symbol may take comfort from the directive of Pope Gregory I to the "other" Augustine (the missionary to the Celts and first archbishop of Canterbury, not the venerable bishop of Hippo) around 596 C.E.: "Sanctify to Christ the things of the pagans": find those things that are coherent with Christian spirituality, giving symbolic materiality to belief, and include them among the symbols of the church, the better to appeal to those you seek to reach in your role as Christ's ambassador. It was sound counsel. The willingness of the church to adopt symbols of the cultures it sought to evangelize and incorporate them into its liturgical life has often enriched the dramatic impact of worship in exciting and unexpected ways.

Material appropriate for an Advent wreath lighting appears at the end of this section. These brief liturgies, generally used to open the four services for Advent, provide an opportunity to incorporate lay leadership in the service, whether as families, church groups, or individuals.

A final word concerning the selection of hymns and carols for Advent: many churches pass over material composed specifically for this season of watchful waiting, and jump directly to the employment of Christmas carols. This is unfortunate, in large part because it drains Advent of its temper of expectancy and leads to a premature focus on Christmas. In this, the church is not distinguishable from shopping malls that haul out the Christmas decorations somewhere between Halloween and Thanksgiving. It is the liturgical equivalent of young couples who want to employ amniocentesis to determine the gender of their child about three months into pregnancy: they are no more prepared to be parents for the information and their child's birth has been drained of an essential ingredient of mystery and thus of part of its quality as miracle. When we skip the preliminaries and rush directly to the main event, is it so surprising that we arrive feeling unprepared? How could it be otherwise? Little wonder so many Christians are exhausted by Christmas before it arrives and can't wait later than December 26 to pack the evidence and return it to the attic!

Most hymnals contain at least a small selection of Advent carols. Some of these melodies "feel" difficult to sing, especially those rooted in plainsong, such as "O Come, O Come, Emmanuel" or "Let All Mortal Flesh Keep Silence." Or those tailored to an age when group singing was more consistently taught and rehearsed, like "Wake, Awake, for Night Is

Flying." They are not so difficult as they seem, however, only unfamiliar; and the congregation willing to devote a small amount of time and effort to becoming familiar with them will be enriched and rewarded. Other carols, such as "Come, O Long-Expected Jesus" or "Watcher, Tell Us of the Night," are more easily learned. And contemporary carols, such as "Carol of the Wreath" are now being composed with the candle-lighting liturgy in mind. They are easy to sing and suitable for guitar accompaniment. Several approaches may be used when incorporating carols in a wreath-lighting liturgy. A single verse or an entire carol may be sung. Some congregations prefer to sing the verses of a single carol in serial fashion, using a new verse each Sunday or repeating previously used verses and adding a new one through the four weeks of Advent.

Prayers and Liturgical Readings

First Sunday of Advent

—

Invocation

We come in humility, holy God; for how else should we come? Does one approach the birth of a child carelessly? Does the birth of our own children leave us unmoved and not choked with feeling? How much more, then, is our feeling intensified, our modesty enlarged, when we prepare to witness the birth of the child by whom salvation comes? So silence our mutterings and compel our notice and prepare us now and in the days ahead to receive you in this most precious child of heaven and earth.

Call to Praise (from Psalm 96:11–13)

Leader:	Let the heavens be glad,
People:	Let the earth rejoice;
Leader:	Let the sea roar
People:	And all that fills it;
Leader:	Let the field exalt
People:	And everything in it.
Leader:	Then shall all the trees of the forest sing for joy, for God is coming;

People: God is coming to judge the earth.
Leader: God will judge the worlds with righteousness,
People: And the peoples with truth.
Unison: Praise the name of God!

Prayer of Praise
Creator of time and history who, drawing us through the circle of the year, brings us again to this moment of beginning: we praise you for the returning drama of Advent, by which we rekindle our spirits and prepare afresh to receive your incarnate Word. With the whole company of those who gather in prayer and anticipation, we draw breath and wait to join the midnight angel's shout: "Glory to God in the highest, and on earth, peace!" Amen, may it be so!

Call to Reconciliation
Luke the evangelist records that when Mary, the mother of our Savior, visited her kinswoman Elizabeth and shared with her the remarkable news she had received from the angel Gabriel, she broke into a hymn of praise which we now title the Magnificat. Part of this sublime poem declares that God's "mercy is on them that fear him from generation to generation," and that God "has put down the mighty from their thrones, and exalted them of low degree." This passage hints at the role of humility as the foundation upon which alone we receive God's mercy. Hearing Mary's admonition, let us humbly acknowledge what separates us from God and from our sisters and brothers, and seek divine healing.

Prayer of Confession
The sunrise of your presence illumines the hidden places of our lives, Transcendent Judge, and fills us with fear. Comforting ourselves with the illusion that our private actions are unobserved, our unspoken thoughts secure in the silence of our minds, we are caught off-guard and are startled to meet you. The secret places of our lives are penetrated by your seeing; our most guarded words are within your hearing; our most private thoughts are subject to your discerning. Have mercy on us then, Sovereign, for as we cannot hide from you, neither can we redeem ourselves, but for the healing of your mercy and the power of your grace.

Declaration of Forgiveness (from Psalm 107:1–9)
Note: The assurances for Advent are adapted from Psalm 107, a work that bears a strong affinity of language to the messianic prophecies that help the church to prepare for the coming of Christ. It may be useful for the leader to inform the congregation of the origin of these texts before each is read. The congregational response is a means for the people to claim the text for themselves—by affirming God's compassion, to complete the cycle of reconciliation.

Leader: O give thanks to God, who is good, whose steadfast love endures forever! Let the redeemed say so, who have been bought back from trouble and gathered in from the lands, from the east and from the west, from the north and from the south. Some wandered in desert wastes, finding no way to a city to dwell in; hungry and thirsty, their souls fainted within them. Then they cried to heaven in their troubles, and God delivered them from their distress, leading them by a straight way, till they reached a city to dwell in. Let them give thanks for steadfast love and wonderful works on behalf of humanity, for God satisfies the thirsty and fills the hungry with good things.

People: Hearing this word of grace, we say together, Amen. Thanks be to God!

Call for the Offering
Many of us, one suspects, think of the offering as something we do at our own initiative. We demonstrate what we think of as our generosity by sharing with those in need. A closer look requires us to amend this view. We are not born generous, after all. We acquire altruism by imitating compassionate elders. They, in turn, learned it from those who preceded them. So where did it all begin? From a biblical viewpoint, it began with God. We learn to love, and to give, from the God who first loved and gave to us (1 John 4:10–11). We give in emulation of God's liberality, never more than during this season when we celebrate the greatest gift of all. Come then, let us be imitators of God and, by our generosity, signal to the world the motive of our charity.

Prayer of Dedication

God of grace, out of your love you send Jesus again into our world, not to condemn, but to save, and—in saving—to transform your people into agents of reconciliation. Because of your mercy, we are moved to respond in loving commitment. We give these gifts, therefore, that others may know our joy, and discover the true life that the Christchild offers us.

Prayer of Thanksgiving

In gratitude, holy God of history, we receive the gift of the drama of the church year now beginning again its sacred cycle, to chronicle before us, in memory and celebration, your life among us. By the recurrence of each event, we are reminded of what we too easily forget and are renewed by fresh awareness of our calling—to be agents of reconciliation on behalf of the Christ whose birth now overtakes us. Jubilant, we rejoice in the observance of events that draw us closer to family, friends, and community. Thank you, Author of the Word made flesh, that in giving yourself to us, you teach us how to give ourselves to one another.

Second Sunday of Advent

—

Invocation

Drain us now of distractions, O God, and free us from all that diverts our attention, so that all our senses can focus on the Christchild's coming. Show us again, in this most notable, yet most humble of births, the mingling of divine and human we call incarnation. In the coming birth of your child and ours, teach us the dimensions of holy mystery, deliver us from preoccupation with trivial things, and focus our hearts, with reverent diligence, on things eternal.

Call to Praise (from Isaiah 35:1–4)

Leader: The wilderness and the dry land shall be glad,
People: The desert shall rejoice and blossom;
Leader: Like a crocus it shall blossom abundantly,
People: And rejoice with joy and singing.
Leader: You with weak hands, be strengthened!
People: You whose knees shake, take courage!

Leader:	For our God comes with vengeance;
People:	With terrible recompense, God comes to save us!
Unison:	Amen! So let it be!

Prayer of Praise

From across the centuries, our God, we hear again your call to be a holy people, a company worthy to be called by the name of God Most High. In obedience to that call, we prepare ourselves to receive the gift of your newborn, the miracle who transforms us from no people to your people, from alienated individuals to reconciled community. Receive now our praise, that you deem us, of all your human creatures, worthy of so remarkable a transformation. In hopeful adoration, we watch for the innocence that travels from heaven's domain to earth's manger, here to teach us what we must do to be the people of God.

Call to Reconciliation

During Advent, we prepare ourselves to celebrate anew the birth of Jesus, who calls us to repentance, invites us to become citizens of the city of God, and bestows on us his name. We who call ourselves Christian, and are so called by others, have a responsibility to acknowledge that we bear this name not by our deserving, but by God's grace. This realization undergirds the office of confession: we affirm to ourselves and announce to the world that in Christ God makes a gift of restorative love that we do not deserve and cannot earn; and through that love, our lives are cleansed and renewed. Let us confess together.

Prayer of Confession

Your season of hope bursts upon us, hopeful Deity, but we are unprepared. From the watchtower the cry awakens us to the bridegroom's coming, but our lamps are not ready. Unattuned to Earth's music, we are deaf to angel songs. Preoccupied with the electrified glare of the season's gaudy displays, we are blind to starlight. Trapped in the midnight of our fear, we do not recognize the ascending dawn. What hope is there for us, except your unwillingness to abandon us to the night of our souls. Break in upon us—again—with the light of the ancient promise soon to be fulfilled in a child's birth. Then we will be a people chastened, forgiven, and blessed, and turn again to praise you.

Declaration of Forgiveness (from Psalm 107:1–3, 10–16)

Leader: O give thanks to God, who is good, whose steadfast love endures forever! Let the redeemed say so, who have been bought back from trouble and gathered in from the lands, from the east and from the west, from the north and from the south. Some sat in hopelessness and in gloom, prisoners in affliction and in iron, for they had rebelled against the word of God and spurned the counsel of the Most High. Then they cried to heaven in their trouble, and God delivered them from their distress and brought them out of gloom and broke their bonds asunder. Let them give thanks for steadfast love and wonderful works on behalf of the children of humanity, for God shatters the doors of bronze and cuts in two the bars of iron.

People: Hearing this word of grace, we say together, Amen. Thanks be to God!

Call for the Offering

As we give our morning offering, it is well to be reminded why we give it: not because we first loved God, but because God first loved us and came to us in the Word made flesh to teach and heal us; and to admonish us to provide for the teaching and healing of others. The gift of the manger has little value unless it is multiplied through us who, in response to it, may ourselves become gifts to a world in pain.

Prayer of Dedication

As we receive the gift of Christ soon to be born among us, merciful Sovereign, receive in response our gifts of thanksgiving; that our celebration of his coming may move beyond songs and shouts of joy and take on material substance for his people, whose need is ours to allay, whose loneliness is ours to relieve, whose hunger is ours to satisfy, through the love of Christ Jesus our Savior.

Prayer of Thanksgiving

The season of Advent makes vivid, O God, the contrasts that characterize our world and stands us anew on the ground of our gratitude: we remember the hunger beyond our doors and thank you for food; we are appalled by the homeless huddled atop steam grates and thank you for homes; we notice threadbare garments and thank you for clothing; we see the sick and broken and thank you for health; we observe the lonely and alone and thank you for family and friends; we see the prisoners and thank you for liberty. Hear our voice of gratitude, merciful God; but forbid that we be merely content to enjoy our blessings. Rather, drive us by the now-coming Christ to stretch out to these others; that because Christ's love works in us, they may find cause to thank you and to thank you again and again.

Third Sunday of Advent

—

Invocation

Beyond the prattle of daily life we heard you, Spirit who dwells within and about us, calling us apart to ponder the birth of hope that dawns before us even as we watch and wait. So we come, not entirely clear about what motivates us, confused in our loyalties, anxious about what you may require of us. Still we come, because we are told that this child reveals how deeply you love us. Now, by the heat of that love, melt our uncertainty and recast us as your own people. Bring us to our knees before the infant in whose powerlessness resides power beyond our imagining. Claim us, make clear our task, and send us out so possessed by your Spirit that all who meet us will know that we, indeed, have witnessed the first light of the dawn of salvation.

Call to Praise (from Isaiah 40:3-5)

Leader: A voice cries: "In the wilderness prepare the way of the Sovereign,

People: Make straight in the desert a highway for our God.

Leader: Every valley shall be lifted up,

People: Every mountain and hill be made low;

Leader: The uneven ground shall become level,

People: The rough places a plain.

Leader: The glory of God will be revealed,

People: And all flesh shall see it together,

Unison: For the mouth of God has spoken." We will praise our Creator's name!

Prayer of Praise

The mystery of your presence sanctifies our seasons, our God, giving substance to the symbols by which we remember again your tangible participation in our common life. Accord us respite from the trivialities and travails of a bewildering world and relief from our preoccupation with petty affairs and personal histories. Then we will praise you for refocused attention, as we attend to what truly matters, equip ourselves to recognize you in the child for whose birth we now prepare, and magnify your name for the mystery of peace coming among us. Let our praise serve you, redeeming God, as Jesus' birth revealed you, who alone are worthy of our time and our devotion.

Call to Reconciliation

Hanging on the cross, Jesus asked God to forgive those who were crucifying him, because they did not know what they were doing (Luke 23:34). This seems a strange event on which to reflect during Advent. But the concept is important: those who fail to recognize Jesus in the one event will not recognize him in the other, or receive the peace that comes only to those truly reconciled to God. It is because we know Christ on the cross that we recognize Jesus in the manger. If we were unaware of the significance of his death, his birth would not concern us. This is cause for great humility, that feeling which alone makes it possible for us to recognize Jesus when he comes. By turning to God now, with truly open hearts, asking to be released from all that separates us both from God and from one another, we become worthy to kneel by the manger and say, "This is the Christ." Join your voice with mine, then, in common confession.

Prayer of Confession

Ignoring our despair, bright God, you summon us to become a people of promise. Into the muddle of our gloom, you scatter the glow of hope's illumination. Challenged by your new-again story of redeeming birth, we muck around for shadows in which to hide, reducing the scope of its wonder to fit the limits of our imaginations. Forgive us for pinched expectations. Purge us of our preoccupation with secrets. Fire us with zeal to become bearers of light. Above all, merciful Sovereign, remind us that you understand our fear because you have known it; feel the anxieties of our flesh because you have carried them; know the way of our salvation because you have walked it. Then may we, overcoming despair and gloom and hopelessness, be transformed into agents of healing to a shattered world.

Declaration of Forgiveness (from Psalm 107:1–3, 16–21)

Leader: O give thanks to God, who is good, whose steadfast love endures forever! Let the redeemed say so, who have been bought back from trouble and gathered in from the lands, from the east and from the west, from the north and from the south. Some were sick through their sinful ways, and because of their iniquities suffered affliction. Loathing any kind of food, they drew near to the gates of death. Then they cried to heaven in their trouble, and God delivered them from their distress, sending forth the divine Word to heal them and deliver them from destruction. Let them give thanks for steadfast love and wonderful works on behalf of the children of humanity, offering sacrifices of thanksgiving and reciting God's deeds in songs of joy.

People: Hearing this word of grace, we say together, Amen. Thanks be to God!

Call for the Offering

We Christians are a people of miracles. Scripture is full of stories of events that made visible, to sensitive observers, the miraculous power of God. During Advent, we prepare to celebrate again the miracle by which all others are measured: the incorporation of the divine word in human flesh. With little difficulty, we acknowledge the unique character of these events. Less easy for us to recognize is that we are given the power to become miracles ourselves—to make manifest in the life of someone, somewhere, the healing power of God. That is the very definition of miracle. Consider, now, what great good we can do and resolve not to wait a moment longer to do it.

Prayer of Dedication

In this we know the quality of divine mercy, Holy One: not that we loved you first, but that you first loved us and gave your child for our redemption. So let it be with us, who seek through our lives to be embodiments of your mercy: to be among the first to reach out to those who are unloved and those who seem unlovable. Let these gifts be the next of many steps by which love is multiplied and all humankind comes, finally, within the reach of your embrace.

Prayer of Thanksgiving

Whose providence is equal to that of our God, who fills our lives with all that is needful and more? Whose mercy is like our Redeemer's, who reaches beyond our fear and covers our weakness? Whose love is equal to God's love in Christ, securing for us the promise of eternal life? Then let us, with fearless voices, hearts united, and minds attuned, raise the shout of thanksgiving to the Sovereign of history, whose ancient promise now comes to fulfillment, when nations shall know the majesty of Israel's God and all knees bow before their Maker. Amen, Holy Majesty, may it be so!

Fourth Sunday of Advent

Invocation

With rising anticipation we sense the impending fullness of time, the end of expectation and beginning of fulfillment. From the watchtower the voice is lifted to cry us awake. In the east the sky warms with the gathering dawn. Angel voices, as yet dimly heard, are raised in rehearsal, preparing the hymn that will press glad tidings of coming grace on a weary world. With growing excitement that proves among us, young or old, the infectiousness of wonder that attends the coming of Christmas, we make final preparation, plan the last menu, wrap the last present, hang the last decoration. Now pause we one more time, to watch and wait, hear your Word, sing your praise, secure your mercy. Come, Christ Jesus, for we are ready.

Call to Praise (from Isaiah 11:1–2, 6)

Leader: There shall come forth a shoot from the stump of Jesse,
People: A branch shall grow from its roots,
Leader: Upon whom God's Spirit will rest,

People: The spirit of wisdom and understanding,
Leader: The spirit of counsel and might,
People: The spirit of knowledge and the fear of God.
Leader: The wolf will dwell with the lamb,
People: And the leopard will lie down with the kid,
Leader: The calf and the lion and the fatling together,
People: And a little child shall lead them.
Unison: For so great a promise, we will rejoice in singing praise to God!

Prayer of Praise
Holy One, whose mercy is soon to lay among us in swaddling clothes, we glorify you for your Spirit's unswerving grace that will not let us go; that births Mary's child, angel-sung and shepherd adored, not only in the manger, but in each heart that is open to his coming. In awe, we revel in the mystery of your love shaped as the incarnate Word come to dwell among us, until your world is wholly embraced. Before the gift overtakes us, Sovereign, we praise you for it. O Come, Emmanuel! Be born in us!

Call to Reconciliation
Each of us, at some time in life, experiences turmoil of will and spirit: what we want is locked in battle with what we know God wants. The church addresses this tension in the office of reconciliation, when we seek God's intervention to help us resolve the conflict. This is a particularly appropriate concept during Advent: the arrival of Jesus is divine intervention, disclosing to a fractured world the possibility and promise of reconciliation. But it is not achieved through a power play. God does not issue an order, but offers a gift. The Word made flesh presents itself, invites us to admit our need, and waits—with undeserved patience— for our response. Let us respond together, bowing to the child whose very weakness is more healing than all the power we possess.

Prayer of Confession
You come to us, Triumphal One, in the spring of hope, but we are frozen in the winter of unbelief. You shatter the calm of our night with a burst of angel song, but we bury our faces and whine about needing

sleep. Offered the liberty to engage in prodigal acts of generosity, we cling to self-serving ways and condition ourselves for death. Your Word explodes on the world, a sunburst of hope that evaporates the fog of doubt; but we run and hide in our little sanctuaries, embracing the illusion that the familiar and customary can save us. O we are a dismal lot, unworthy of the glory that bursts around our heads even as we resist its coming. Come, Fulfilling One. Shatter our defenses, overwhelm our reluctance, fire our imaginations. Then shall we, like stunned shepherds, gain the courage to look up and see, to listen and come finally to the manger, where flesh is sanctified by holy passion and all humanity redeemed.

Declaration of Forgiveness (from Psalm 107:1–3, 39–43)

Leader: O give thanks to God, who is good, whose steadfast love endures forever! Let the redeemed say so, who have been bought back from trouble and gathered in from the lands, from the east and from the west, from the north and from the south. When we are diminished and brought low through oppression, trouble, and sorrow, God pours contempt on princes and makes them wander in a trackless waste but raises up the needy out of affliction and makes their families like flocks. The upright see and are glad; and all wickedness stops its mouth. Whoever is wise, give heed to these things, and let us consider the steadfast love of God.

People: Hearing this word of grace, we say together, Amen. Thanks be to God!

Call for the Offering

Let the quality of our act of offering be driven by the quality of God's mercy that intends, through the coming drama of Christ Jesus, to redeem Creation. Let the quality of the love that we expend here be defined by the quality of love that God expends on us, in the gift of the child whose advent we now observe. Let the theme of our stewardship, this Advent season and into the new year, be the measure of our gratitude for God's prodigal mercy toward us. Then we shall, indeed, welcome the newborn child!

Prayer of Dedication

We hear in the night the cry of those who keep watch: "Behold, our Sovereign comes: in the desert prepare a highway for our God"—a highway constructed not of cement and steel but of acts of mercy and love. We bring now, approaching Savior, our contribution to the building of your road. Through our work, let some valley be lifted up, some hill be made a plain, and all the people of God shouting with joy together.

Prayer of Thanksgiving

Deep calls unto deep, Creator God, proclaiming the day of the Savior's coming. From mountain peak to valley floor, the voice descends, reverberates, and echoes toward heaven. Church bells peal and choirs sing. Twinkling lights transform our towns into lands of enchantment and electronic devices give fresh voice to ancient and cherished melodies. In this season of coming wonder, the world holds its breath as deliverance draws near. So thank we our God for promises made and mercies fulfilled; for old wounds healed and renewal proclaimed; for justice bursting and righteousness rolling. Thank you, O God, who authors our seasons and redeems our celebration.

Advent Wreath Liturgies

Note: Antiphonal readings are more dramatic if the congregation is divided in halves (right-left, north-south, or whatever) as opposed to the traditional "responsive reading" format between leader and people. Varying style in this manner requires congregants to be more self-conscious about what is happening in worship. This approach has the further advantage of adding special intensity to the unison voice when it speaks the final line of each reading. Such variations may usefully be employed to highlight special seasons and events in the life of the church.

The First Candle (from Isaiah 2:2–4)

Leader: In days to come, the mountain of God's house shall be established as the highest of the mountains, raised above the hills;

People: All the nations shall stream to it.

Leader: Many peoples shall come and say: "Come, let us go up to the mountain of God,

People:	To the house of the God of Jacob;
Leader:	That we may be taught holy ways
People:	and stay in the holy paths."
Leader:	For out of Zion shall go forth instruction,
People:	The word of God from Jerusalem,
Leader:	To judge between the nations,
People:	and arbitrate for many peoples;
Leader:	They shall beat their swords into plowshares,
People:	And their spears into pruning hooks;
Leader:	Nation shall not lift up sword against nation,
People:	Neither shall they learn war any more.
Unison:	So let us praise the name of God, the giver of peace.

Lighting of the first candle.

Leader:	Reach into our celebration, Approaching Majesty, as we light the first candle of Advent and let it remind us of who you are and why you have called us here; that the weeks ahead may be for us a time of growing insight, co-equal with the growing light, a fitting tribute to lay before the newborn Christ for whose promised coming we now begin to prepare. And let all the people of God say,
People:	Amen.

Carol verse.

The Second Candle (from Isaiah 52:7–10)

Leader:	How beautiful on the mountains are the feet of the messenger who announces peace,
People:	Who brings good news and publishes peace,
Leader:	Who announces salvation,
People:	Who says to Zion, "Your God reigns!"
Leader:	Listen! Your sentinels lift up their voices,
People:	Together they sing for joy;
Leader:	For in plain sight they see God returning to Zion.
People:	Break forth together in singing, you ruins of Jerusalem;
Leader:	For God's people are comforted,

People: And redemption embraces Jerusalem.

Unison: God's sleeve has been rolled up before the eyes of the nations, and all the ends of the earth will see the salvation of our God!

Lighting of the second candle.

Leader: Instruct us, God of the coming light, that as we wait and watch for the coming of redemptive love into the life of the world, you also wait and watch with us, sharing our thoughts, anticipating our questions, feeling our rising expectations. Let this second candle remind us who we are—the people of God, witnesses to a world in pain. Let it remind us that we are who we are because your light lives also in us. And let all the people of God say,

People: Amen.

Carol verse.

The Third Candle (from Isaiah 58:6–9)

Leader: Is not this the fast that I choose: to loose the bonds of injustice,

People: To undo the thongs of the yoke,

Leader: To let the oppressed go free,

People: And to break every yoke?

Leader: Is it not to share your bread with the hungry,

People: And bring the homeless poor into your house;

Leader: When you see the naked, to cover them,

People: And not to hide yourself from your own kin?

Leader: Then shall your light break forth like the dawn,

People: And your healing shall spring up quickly;

Leader: Your vindicator shall go before you,

People: And the glory of God will be your rear guard.

Unison: Then you shall call, and God will answer; you shall cry for help, and God will say, here I am.

Lighting of the third candle.

Leader: The lighting of the third candle teaches us, O God of kinship and community, of those we call neighbor—in our congregation, in our town, in our world. We remember that Christ, asked to name the greatest commandment, voiced the ancient law of Israel: to love God and to love neighbor with all we are and all that is in us. Let this candle remind us that we are not called to ourselves, but to others; and that we will know our neighbor first and most clearly in the approaching child of Bethlehem. And let all the people of God say,

People: Amen.

Carol verse.

The Fourth Candle (from Isaiah 25:6–8)

Leader: On this mountain the Sovereign of hosts will make for all people a feast of rich foods, a feast of well-aged wines,

People: Of rich food filled with marrow, of well-aged wines strained clear.

Leader: And God will destroy on this mountain the shroud that is cast over all peoples,

People: the sheet that is spread over all nations,

Unison: And death will be swallowed up forever.

Leader: Then God will wipe away the tears from all faces,

People: And the disgrace of the people will be taken away from all the earth,

Unison: For the Holy One has spoken.

Leader: It will be said on that day, "Lo, this is our redeemer for whom we have waited, so that we might be saved.

People: This is the One for whom we have waited; let us be glad and rejoice in God's salvation."

Unison: For the hand of God will rest on this mountain.

Lighting of the fourth candle.

Leader: The lighting of the fourth candle instructs us, O God of reconciliation, that in Jesus we find our unity—within ourselves, with one another, with you. Let your love grow in us, a burgeoning force that reaches out to clasp the whole creation. For soon now, in the birth of Jesus the Christ, the old will pass away, behold, the new will come. Let this candle remind us that we are not of the old, but of the new, making freshly alive again, in symbol and sacrament, the gift of Christ. And let all the people of God say,

People: Amen!

Carol verse.

2

Christmas and Christmastide

Our word "Christmas" is a conflation of two Old English words, *Cristes Masse*—quite literally "the mass of Christ," i.e., celebration of the mass of the nativity of Christ. To Western Christians of the late twentieth century, the nature of Christmas seems self-evident: it is a birthday blowout. Its history, however, is tortuous and illustrates how events we take for granted sometimes required long and heated debate before becoming established in the early church.

Christmas was unknown to the New Testament church. The earliest Gospel, Mark, begins with the story of Jesus' baptism, not his birth. The birth narratives of Matthew and Luke came later. The evolution of Christmas as we know it followed a similar pattern. In church history, the celebration of Epiphany antedated the observance of Christmas; and before the fifth century, there was not even consensus on when Jesus' birth might have occurred. Suggested dates ranged from November 17 to May 20 and were based on a mind-boggling array of abstruse arguments. The author of *De Pascha computus*, for instance, in 243 C.E., wrote that he was informed by private revelation that Jesus was born on March 28. His argument is wonderfully circuitous: since the world was created perfect (flowers in bloom, trees in leaf), creation clearly took place in the spring. Since the moon was created full, the date must have been near the vernal equinox. And Genesis 1:16–19 states that the sun and moon were created on Wednesday (the fourth day). The historic date most consistent with all these events was March 28. It follows, therefore, that Christ, being the Sun of Righteousness, was born March 28!

Clement of Alexandria (born c. 150 C.E.) condemned such speculation as superstition (as well he might!). As late as 245 C.E., the great church leader Origen of Alexandria, in his Eighth Homily on Leviticus, repudiated the very idea of a birthday observance as sinful because it treated Christ as if he were a pharaoh (observance of the pharaoh's birthday being a long-standing Egyptian tradition). Even as this line of thinking lost adherence, however, celebration of Jesus' birth did not occur independently but as an adjunct to commemoration of his baptism. As late as 353 C.E., the Roman church appended the birth observance to the baptismal feast on January 6.

When changes did occur, they often resulted in civil unrest. Armenian historians wrote that when Justinian moved the observance of the Temple presentation of the infant Jesus from February 14 to February 2—making it consistent with December 25 as the date of Jesus' birth—a display of armed force was required to quell public rioting. This in the name of the Peaceful One!

The final ground for settling on December 25 appears to have been doctrinal and to have originated in the Western church for two reasons. Around 350–440 C.E., infant baptism rapidly replaced adult baptism as customary procedure. Setting Christmas at December 25 undergirded this liturgical shift by pointing to its theological root: to celebrate the physical birth of Jesus at all was a festal assertion that the divine logos was present in Jesus at birth and did not enter—as formerly argued—with the descent of the Spirit at his baptism. In consequence, Christmas thereafter displaced Epiphany as the central event of the season and the baptism diminished in liturgical importance while celebration of Jesus' birth increased.

At the same time, emphasis on the physical birth of Jesus provided a doctrinal counterpunch to the Marcionite, or Manichaean, heresy then current, the chief tenet of which was that Jesus was not really born at all, but was merely an apparition. At least, the Marcionites argued, he was not a real flesh-and-blood child of Mary. Against this view, the new emphasis on Christ's nativity affirmed incarnational theology in its fullest sense and indelibly shaped how Christmas has been observed since.

In our own observance of that birth, we engage in a bit of conflation of a different sort. Lightly stepping over inconsistencies in the Gospel accounts of the birth of Jesus, we combine mutually exclusive stories, tending in the process to diminish both their dramatic flow and their significance. The most popularly utilized account is provided by Luke

2:1–20, in which the shepherds, on angelic instruction, travel to the Bethlehem stable where they share center stage with the holy family. The other story, found in Matthew 2:1–15 (Mark and John give no account whatever of Jesus' birth), introduces the Magi, the "wise men" or "three kings," said to come from the East. Matthew makes no mention of shepherds nor Luke of Magi. Nor do Matthew's star-struck travelers visit the stable. Rather, "On entering the *house* they saw the child with Mary his mother, and they fell down and worshiped him" (Matthew 2:11, emphasis added). Joseph is not mentioned as present. We may also note that at no point does Matthew stipulate that the Magi were three in number.

The tendency of those who write the scripts for church pageants to wrap these events in a single package is understandable. Few congregations, one suspects, are inclined to mount multiple pageants! What generally occurs is a church-school triptych with epilogue:

1. Joseph and Mary arrive in the chancel with a doll (or light bulb!) wrapped in a blanket.
2. The angel's announcement propels the shepherds down the aisle to visit the child, leading kindergartners in sheep's clothing.
3. Three wisepersons in bathrobes parade majestically in and lay foil-wrapped gifts at the manger.
4. The congregation adjourns to the social hall to eat cookies and sing carols.

It is not my intention to ridicule such pageantry. It inhabits my fondest childhood memories of Christmas. Children first absorb this signal event in salvation history by witnessing its reenactment by peers and mentors in the congregational family. We drain the several Gospel accounts of their unique impact, however, if we allow a childlike view of the first Christmas to dominate the formation of *liturgy*. Displacing the Magi from Matthew's account and relocating them as a footnote to Luke's excludes the accompanying detail of the story essential to understanding why Matthew centers his birth account on the Magi's appearance and their significance to his interpretation of the Christ event.

Matthew's and Luke's accounts are not only scripturally distinct, they serve different purposes and should be accorded liturgical separation. Language relating to shepherds, angel choirs, and mangers adhere to Christmas. The Magi are an essential ingredient of Epiphany (as now observed), for reasons that will become more apparent in the introduction to that section.

Christmas is one of several events accompanied by a "season," historically known as a "tide"—a period during which the event continues to shape the unfolding of the liturgical drama. Christmastide is among the briefer examples, beginning the day after Christmas and extending twelve days, to the onset of Epiphany, January 6.

The following material may be used for a Christmas Day service, or for the Sundays following Christmas.

Prayers and Liturgical Readings

Christmas Day, or First Sunday after Christmas

—

Invocation
Most gracious God: we greet the dawning of this day with shouts of Noel! For now is born among us the bringer of peace, whose name affords us cause for joyful celebration and gives the nations the sure knowledge of redeeming love. Enter now our celebration. Laugh and sing with us and through us the hymns and carols of our jubilation. Override our inhibitions and self-conscious restraint, that our songs and prayers and shouts may resound without reserve, to the glory of your holy name and honor to the name of Jesus, our infant Savior.

Call to Praise (from Isaiah 9:2, 6–7)
Leader: The people who lived in shadows have seen a great light;
People: Those who dwell in a land of deep gloom, on them has light shined.
Leader: For to us a child is born,
People: To us a child is given;
Leader: And the government will be upon this child's shoulder,

People:	And the child's name shall be called "Wonderful Counselor, Mighty God, Everlasting Parent, Bringer of Peace."
Leader:	Of the increase of this government and of peace there will be no end.
People:	The zeal of the God of hosts will do this.

Prayer of Praise

Now sing we angel songs, echoing the shouts of heaven's host that cries the infant's birth. Now journey we in the shepherds' path, seeking the manger-bedded child in swaddling clothes. Now stand we wonder-struck before the mystery of heaven, Word incarnate in our flesh, burning with redemptive zeal. Now is made manifest among us Emmanuel— God-with-us—no longer the promise for which we hope, but the actuality that embraces us, startling our senses awake, restoring our zeal, reshaping our intentions. Now is history changed forever, with love the force that ever after drives all God-fearing souls to acts of courage and compassion. Praise be to God, our maker and redeemer, author of history, and shaper of this moment by which our history is defined.

Call to Reconciliation

The very innocence of the stable-born infant accuses us, before all-merciful God, of our reluctance to welcome the Christchild fully into our hearts, our minds, our homes. With loyalties divided, we receive the child with our hands and lips, yet hold our hearts and minds in reserve. This same child's innocence, however, hints at all the goodness and service to humanity that could be realized if we put our hesitation behind us: the hunger satisfied, the solace conferred, the pain relieved. Be reminded that God is never so eager to judge us as to heal us. But remember, too, that healing is possible only when we acknowledge the reality of the illness. Join your voice now with mine, as we confess our need, and pray that God will shower on us the same, selfless love that shines around the Christchild.

Prayer of Confession

As far as your holiness exceeds our capacity for goodness, O God, so far does your righteousness transcend our ability to grasp it. In dread, therefore, we come before the manger of Christ, confessing the shabbiness of our values, the shallowness of our goals, the transparency of our illusions. Unwilling to stretch ourselves to seize the vision of eternity new-born in our presence, we content ourselves with planning the holiday. Possessed of more than plenty in our homes, at our tables, in our wardrobes, we extend ourselves timidly on behalf of those for whom hunger and rags and hopelessness are the companions of daily suffering. Given opportunity on a scale that most of the world cannot imagine, we elect entertainment and distraction and devote ourselves to the gratification of personal appetite. Purge and discipline us by the shining infant who lies in purity before us and plant us on the bedrock of the Word now incarnate, through whom alone we are able to see truth.

Declaration of Forgiveness

Leader: The hope of the world, which came to light with the birth of Jesus, does not consist of abstractions and intellectual propositions, but arises from the fact that we are loved. It is the altogether astounding assertion of the Christian faith that God loves us enough to become one of us—to make that love as visceral as food and shelter, as broad as the earth we tread, as encompassing as the air we breathe. Just as God knows and chooses to share our dependency upon these requisites of physical life, so God knows our need for spiritual reconciliation, and implants in our history the transcendent healing of Jesus the Christ.

People: Hearing this word, we cry together, "Thanks be to God!" Amen.

Call for the Offering

Is there any better time than Christmas to remind ourselves that Christian generosity originates in God's mercy, not with our goodness? The very birth that we celebrate is a gift of love on a scale that defies description and makes meager any act of human generosity. But be of good cheer: God is concerned not with the limit of our charity but with the fullness of our hearts. Only let your giving be prompted by the same depth of love that roused God to make of Christ a gift to the world and our giving will be blessed beyond description. It is, after all, part of the promise of Christmas.

Prayer of Dedication

Generous God, if we could carry everything that we own to this table in one act of selfless extravagance, we still would not requite the love that you lavish on us in the birth of Jesus. Accept this day's offering, then, as evidence of our good intention; and bid your Holy Spirit instruct us how to make real our pledge to spend our whole selves in your service, whom to serve is the best and finest expenditure of all.

Prayer of Thanksgiving

Our hearts overflow with gratitude, generous God, for gifts that tumble in upon us in such profusion that we cannot keep track: for the birth celebration of one who comes to save us; for the determination of his parents who would not be denied by an unprepared world; for the magic of angel songs that cleaved the night and jolted untutored shepherds into clarions of cosmic news; for fundamental Love that refuses to abandon your people to a frightful world; for the promise of life that challenges the finality of death; for joy in community and kindred that is now ours to enjoy because of this birth; for the transformation that now overtakes us and makes us agents of your mercy; for blessings not counted because we lose sight of them in our excitement. For all these, and for secret blessings known only to you, we yield our gratitude and praise.

Last Sunday of Christmastide
—

Invocation

Redeeming God, as you made your presence known to us in the birth of Jesus, make known to us your presence here among us, who gather in his name and at his call. Since we can discharge our summons to be the church of Christ only as you empower us, grant us the mediation of your Spirit to energize us and weld us together to fulfill our commission. Then may we be found good and faithful servants, at whose witness others, as yet untouched, come vividly to discern your presence in the newborn child, Emmanuel, God-with-us.

Call to Praise (from Micah 5:2–4)

Leader: But you, O Bethlehem of Ephrathah, who are one of the little clans of Judah,

People:	From you shall come forth for me one who is to rule in Israel,
Leader:	Whose origin is from old,
People:	From ancient days.
Leader:	Therefore they will be given up until the time when she who is in labor has brought forth;
People:	When the rest of this one's kindred shall return to the people of Israel.
Leader:	And my servant who is to rule shall stand and feed my flock in the strength of God.
People:	And they shall live secure, for this one shall be great to the ends of the earth
Unison:	And shall be the messenger of peace.

Prayer of Praise

All-mighty God, whose will is love, whose love is all-encompassing: we stand in wonder at the shining realization that it is us whom you love. Being perfect in yourself, you require no other. Yet you call us out of nothingness and declare that you need us. Had you chosen to do so, you could have created us senseless puppets; yet you stand us on earth in perfect freedom, asking only that we use it as your friends. You have at your command every mechanism of power, yet seek to secure our loyalty in a child, a gospel of love, a call to shalom. It is too wonderful for us to grasp and, with the host of heaven, we are reduced to crying: "Glory to God in the highest, and on earth, peace among God's whole human family!"

Call to Reconciliation

During Christmastide, we celebrate the shining demonstration of divine mercy that is the infant Jesus. But even as we welcome the light, it turns to illumine our unworthiness to receive it. This is not a cruel trick on God's part, by which we are forced in one moment both to acknowledge the gift and to disown it. It is evidence, rather, of the goodness of God that commands our devotion as it comes to us in Christ. Our confession is less an acknowledgment of our fault than a proclamation of God's majestic goodness, which seeks to embrace and redeem a sinful world. Join me now, as we acknowledge the helplessness to which God responds in compassionate affirmation.

Prayer of Confession

Help us, God of mercy, for you alone can save us: from the selfishness that closes our hands against the needs of the poor; the mean-spiritedness that causes us to see others of your children as less worthy to enjoy the fruits of life than we; the chauvinism by which we shun the needy because they are not of our social class; the narrowness of vision that blinds us to your ultimate victory, making us reluctant servants and timid stewards; the fear that inhibits your divine grace that would, if only we let it, reach through us to secure for others the *shalom* of God. Forgive and reconcile us, for the sake of the child whose birth we would not diminish by our insufficiency, but would publish abroad, to bring hope to a pain-filled world.

Declaration of Forgiveness

Leader: In this we have cause for joy that equals the wonder of this day: that God never desires our condemnation, but our renewal, seeking to enlist us in the ranks of those whose zeal is as unqualified as is the exuberance of the Christmas angels who shouted the shepherds awake and proclaimed the acceptable day of the Sovereign. In the name of God, I declare that our sins are, indeed, forgiven.

People: Hearing this word, we cry together, "Thanks be to God!" Amen.

Call for the Offering

Christians are never justified in following the counsel of those who deem themselves worldly-wise—who ask, "How little I can get away with. What is the least I can pay?" as if they were buying a car or a bag of groceries. Christians are companions of God, whose concern is for all creation and whose historic acts on behalf of weary humanity stun the imagination. Ought we not to imitate our God? The question is not how little, but how much: how much will I do, how much will I give, how much will I commit, to reconcile the world. And when, better than now?

Prayer of Dedication

Moved by your love that is poured out for us in the gift of Jesus, O God, we now bring our own gifts: to ensure that his birth is proclaimed to all we might reach, his story shared with all who will listen, his love mediated to those most needful of its mercy. By these gifts let your word be conveyed, your purposes be served, your will be done.

Prayer of Thanksgiving

We thank you, our God, for the remarkable account of Christmas: that your Word, come in a child's flesh, is prompted by your love for us, not our readiness to receive the Christchild; that you have called to your purpose, through time, a people possessed of the vision to see in this event a story worthy of hearing and worthy of telling; that because of them, we who are later born are also privileged to encircle the manger; that your love, born of our sister Mary, will not and cannot be confined to a stable, but bursts out a flood tide of redemptive grace to wash over humanity. Thank you, God, for the event. Thank you for the story. Thank you for the stewardship of the community of this faith. Let us so grasp these essentials that, in us, story may again become event, an incarnate blessing cascading like angel song on the people of our town, our nation, our world.

3

Epiphany and Season Following

Our word "Epiphany" derives from the Greek *epiphaneia,* "appearance," from *epiphainein,* meaning "to [become] manifest." In early liturgy, the event was often referred to in the plural—feast of the Epiphanies—commemorating multiple events in which Christ's divine nature became evident, e.g., the birth and the baptism of Jesus, the itinerant Star of Bethlehem and arrival of the Magi, the miracle at the wedding at Cana, the feeding of the five thousand. In the fourth century, leaders in the Greek church referred to it as the Theophany, or Day of Lights, i.e., the illumination of Jesus, or the light that shone in Jordan. In the Western church, it became the Festival of the Three Kings, or simply Twelfth Day, a reference to the fact that January 6 falls twelve days after Christmas. It also provided the framework for Shakespeare's *Twelfth Night* and for the popular Christmas song "The Twelve Days of Christmas."

Epiphany was one of the earliest festivals to become established in the Christian church. It was first mentioned by Clement of Alexandria in 194 C.E. and later in a homily by Hippolytus, who died around 235. By 300 C.E. it was widely observed and was cited around 304 C.E. in the Acts of Philip the Martyr, bishop of Heraclea in Thraceby, as "the holy day of the Epiphany."

As late as 386 C.E., Epiphany and Easter were the two great feasts observed by the church at Antioch. Chrysostom refers to the feast of the epiphanies (plural), implying the dual commemoration of both Jesus' baptism and second coming. Included in the commemoration was the blessing of springs and rivers, from which water was drawn and stored for use during the ensuing year in lustrations and baptisms. There is little doubt that Jesus' baptism was the central motif, a fact that points to the then-unsettled debate concerning when in his life Jesus became manifest, i.e., was understood to be the Christ. Both Chrysostom and Jerome argued that this did not happen at Jesus' birth but at his baptism (this ongoing debate is further outlined in the introduction to the preceding section on Christmas).

While Eastern churches continued to see the baptism of Jesus as the central motif and to view Epiphany as the season of choice for being baptized, Western practice obscured that connection, emphasizing instead the visit of the Magi, also called the wise men or three kings. The number three is not scripturally supported. Matthew provides no count (see 2:1). The number seems to be assumed, by tradition, from the listing of gold, frankincense, and myrrh as the proffered gifts. Still, there is no evidence that these constituted three discrete gifts. One is suspicious of the influence of numerology in the selection of the number. The number 3, as is well documented, is significant in a number of biblical stories, not to mention the doctrine of the Trinity.

Central to the contemporary view of Epiphany, however, is the significance underlying the Magi's story, not its detail—a point often lost, I think, in our observance of the day (or our nonobservance! One suspects that many churches slide right by Epiphany with hardly a nod). Jesus was a Jew and, in the faith of the early church, the promised *Jewish* Messiah of God. Among Jewish Christians (and *all* Christians were Jews at the outset) it was assumed that Jesus was concerned only with Israel. The Gospels say as much. Matthew reports (10:5–6) that before sending the disciples out the first time, Jesus instructed them to avoid Gentiles and Samaritans, going only to the lost sheep of the house of Israel. Mark's Jesus, with atypical bruskness, rejects the Syrophoenician woman's plea for her daughter by saying it would not be proper to throw the children's bread to dogs (7:27). Yet Jesus' identity as the *Jewish* Messiah would not hold. Time and again non-Jews, even demoniacs (e.g., Mark 5:5:6), are reported to have recognized him, that is, apprehended his unique nature.

This is the significance of the story of the Magi: Gentiles from a distant land, with no reason to know—certainly no *Jewish* information—came wandering out of the night to acknowledge, with gifts and homage, the kingly character of the infant Jesus. They aptly symbolize the central theme of Epiphany as observed in the West: the manifestation of Christ to the Gentiles, i.e., the recognition, by Gentiles, of Jesus' messianic nature. The theme is nowhere so movingly phrased as in the *Nunc Dimittis,* the benediction of Simeon on first witnessing the infant Jesus in the temple: "my eyes have seen your salvation, which you have prepared *in the presence of all peoples, a light for revelation to the Gentiles,* and for glory to your people Israel" (Luke 2:30–32, emphasis added). By these and related stories, the New Testament evangelists made the revolutionary claim that the fulfillment of God's ancient promise effected not only Israel's redemption but the redemption of humanity. Jesus becomes manifest, visible, his identity apparent, to the whole world.

Because the length of Epiphany is determined by the dating of Easter, it is subject to considerable variability, complicating the task of preparing liturgical material. To write for the longest possible period results in preparing material that will be used, at best, once or twice a decade. At the same time, eight-week sequences will arise and some pastors will not care to duplicate selections. For this reason, sufficient material is provided below for an Epiphany season of five Sundays. Where the season exceeds five Sundays, alternate material may be selected from the section on the season of Pentecost, without running out of material, because the two seasons balance each other: for each Sunday included in Epiphanytide, one is subtracted from Pentecost season, and vice versa. The author recommends only that, during years when Epiphanytide is longer, the material written explicitly for the season be used first and material from Pentecost later, immediately before pre-Lent. In this way, representation of the central themes of Epiphany will not be needlessly diluted.

Prayers and Liturgical Readings

First Sunday of Epiphany

—

Invocation

Light of the nations, who came to us in the person of a child in a manger and bids us join the holy family, open now our eyes to see, as did the Magi, the ascending of the holy star; that we, like them, may be aroused to get up and search out the child and bring our gifts. Then we will bow before this child to worship and go our way again, knowing that we have here looked into the face of God.

Call to Praise (from Isaiah 60:1–3, 6)

Leader:	Arise, shine; for your light has come,
People:	And the glory of God has risen upon you.
Leader:	For shadows shall cover the earth,
People:	And thick gloom the peoples;
Leader:	But the Light of Heaven will rise upon you,
People:	God's glory will appear over you.
Leader:	Nations shall come to your light,
People:	And monarchs to the brightness of your dawn.
Leader:	They shall bring gold and frankincense,
People:	And shall proclaim the praise of the Sovereign.

Prayer of Praise

Epiphany bursts upon us, O God, and wakes us with the brilliance of the sun of righteousness risen with healing in its wings. We heard the angel song and joined with them our voices, praising God in the highest and bidding that earth may indeed know peace among the whole human family. With the Magi, we lay gifts beside the infant savior, knowing that their value is established not by our giving but by his receiving. With Mary and Joseph, we wonder at the infant entrusted to our care, to keep and ponder in our hearts until he grows to direct and redeem our lives. Praise, O God, for the wonder of Emmanuel, the word made flesh, by whom we come to know who we are and whose we are.

Call to Reconciliation

In the Gospel According to Matthew 2:1–12, we read the story of the wise ones who came from the East to Jerusalem, looking for the child who had been born sovereign of the Jews, the ascension of whose star they had witnessed. In church tradition, these visitors are also called the Magi—a term connoting priestly standing—or kings, indicative of royalty. Whether we call them wise, or reverend, or royal, one thing is clear: in the presence of Jesus, they knelt—an acknowledgment that they were in the presence of one worthy of adoration. By joining in confession, we also acknowledge the holiness of the one into whose presence we come, who deserves our humility and tribute.

Prayer of Confession

Epiphany bursts upon us, God of our wake-up call, and catches us sleeping. The shepherds, angel driven, have knelt by the manger in muffled wonder while we were distracted by the social clamor of seasonal activities at the inn. Camel-borne for untold days, the Magi, bearing gifts, seek only the privilege of giving them, then return home deeming themselves rewarded while we fret over how much we have spent or how little we received. Mary and Joseph, unbidden parents of Word made flesh, ponder God-with-us while we shove the decorations back into the attic as though we cannot wait for trauma and trouble to reclaim our days. Forgive, sacred Redeemer, not that we violate Christmas, but that we trivialize and ignore it. And even as we drag our feet, do not, we pray, withdraw the gift; for even in our blind silliness, there is that in us that knows how desperately we need it.

Declaration of Forgiveness

Leader: So powerful is the love of God that the mere birth of a child rattled the throne of the ruling monarchy, and sowed the seed of a triumphal sovereignty that eventually would make pathetic the power of the Roman empire. So spacious a love can easily overcome the evils and failures with which we struggle. Receive forgiveness from the only one able to give it and rejoice in our redemption.

People: Hearing this word of grace, we say together, thanks be to God!

Call for the Offering

At the end of a journey of unknown distance and duration, the Magi came into the presence of the infant Jesus and knelt, because they believed themselves to be in the presence of royalty. When we come into the presence of Jesus, we ought also to kneel—not because we are in the presence of royalty but of divinity. When the Magi came to Jesus and knelt before his royalty, they brought gifts, symbolic of their veneration—what was owed to one of noble standing. When we come to

Jesus, we ought also to bring gifts, symbolizing our devotion—what is owed to one who is holy. Bring now your gifts to our sovereign, and holy, child.

Prayer of Dedication

We bring here, parent God, our gifts to lay before your gift: our pledge of nurture for your child; our commitment of resources to sustain the ministry that is never ours, always his; our sacrifices to be joined with his own, whose birth brings hope to our world; that your full purpose in making incarnate your word in human life may be widely shared, clearly spoken, triumphantly heard, through all the earth.

Prayer of Thanksgiving

Out of the night they came, you who command the heavens, following a star whose origin they did not know, whose destination they could not see. Yet they came, true to the light given them, disobedient to false commands. Out of the night they came, into the light of holy mystery, your reclamation in child's clothing, hope too young to speak, power too fresh to heal. Yet they did not turn away, but left their gifts, trusting in a life yet to be lived. Out of the night of our uncertainty we come, O God, Magi in our time, to the child's light: not always sure why we come, struggling against the seductive lies of those who would misuse us for evil intent, trusting in the promise that through this child, we too will come to know. Thank you, God of holy design, for their coming; for their steadfastness that would not yield to uncertainty; for their grace in the face of corrupt intent. Thank you for the image of their star, risen anew for us and our time. Thank you for story and promise, conviction and hope, that give life meaning, reveal your intent, and reclaim the world.

Second Sunday of Epiphany

—

Invocation

God of our deliverance, who in Christ came to a world that did not know you and a people who did not recognize you: penetrate now our lives as you invaded theirs, an Epiphany of Word made flesh; and as we see and recognize your love in Christ for our here and now, our time and place, infect us too with grace and truth. Then bring us, with the

Magi, to our knees, knowing that no gift that is ours to give is near so precious as the gift before whom we bow.

Call to Praise (from Matthew 2:1–10)

Leader: After Jesus was born, Magi came from the East asking, "Where is the child who has been born King of the Jews?

People: For we have seen the star at its rising, and have come to pay homage."

Leader: Then turn you to Bethlehem, for so it has been written by the prophet:

People: "And you, Bethlehem, in the land of Judah, are by no means least among the rulers of Judah; for from you shall come a ruler who is to shepherd my people Israel."

Leader: They set out, and there, ahead of them, went the star they had seen at its rising, until it stopped over the place where the child was.

People: When they saw that the star had stopped, they were overwhelmed with joy.

Unison: Sharing their elation, we also rejoice before God, and lay before the child the gift of our adoration.

Prayer of Praise

The mystery that induced the star-marked Magi to go wandering in quest of a child not of their own tribe and clan now tugs at our souls, beckoning God, and bids us, like them, quit all and search. The authority of the child's weakness that brought them, finding him, to adoring knees, bids us bend our pride and kneel in awe before the mystery of sacred helplessness. The purpose that pronounced their mission completed now raises us, like them, to our feet, where we stand to praise you for mystery experienced and weakness empowered. And now we return to our own country, here to praise the majesty of godhead made infant flesh, by which we are healed, by which we become servants in the service of humanity, for the child's sake. Praise the God of this new light!

Call to Reconciliation

Can we look at the star that led the Magi to Jesus and not sense the majesty of the One who commissioned its passage? Can we consider the journey those wise ones undertook and not recognize that there is—always—much more here than we have yet perceived or imagined? Can we look at the Christchild, God-with-us in utter simplicity, and not be overcome with humility? Come, let us yield to the mystery and wonder of the God-child moment, confessing those things that prevent us from fully receiving it and asking God to remove them from us. Let us confess our sin.

Prayer of Confession

Into the deep night of our world, merciful God, the Christchild comes, a shining dawn of graciousness and mercy whose very presence accuses us and illumines our secret and hidden shadows. O these are things at which we do not want to look, much less did we mean to own them: our inconstancy in faith and smallness of generosity, our withholding—in the face of evident need—that which could give life to another. How dismal we are, that we clutch possessively the very gifts that could, in one instant, give hope to others and salvation to us. Forgive, patient Majesty, whose desire for our renewal is made so evident among us in the infant Christ.

Declaration of Forgiveness

Leader: Among the best known and most reassuring of passages in the entire heritage of Christian scripture is this: "For God so loved the world that God gave God's only Child, that whoever believes in that Child should not perish but have eternal life. For God sent that Child into the world, not to condemn the world, but that through the Child the world might be saved" (John 3:16–17). In that reassurance, let us take hope!

People: Hearing this word of grace, we say together, thanks be to God!

Call for the Offering

The Gospel writer Matthew informs us that Magi, originating in a distant country, showed up early in Jesus' life and, on the evidence of astrological observations, presented the child with gifts rich in both symbolism and material value. And they didn't yet really know who he was. We do know. More, we know what Jesus has given us. This being the case, what gifts ought we to lay before the Child of God? Let each of us answer that question within ourself, then give it substance in this morning's offering.

Prayer of Dedication

Decree, our God, that we who worship in this place may present not only these material gifts but our whole selves, as living gifts, holy and acceptable to you; that we may become fit dwelling places for the Christchild, in the light of whose epiphany our day is brightened and made clear. So may others, seeing the light of our kindness, turn again and give you praise and thanksgiving.

Prayer of Thanksgiving

Words seem inadequate to convey how much we mean to express of thankfulness, O gracious Spirit. Our vocabulary is too meager, our grasp even of our own language insufficient to capture all for which we are grateful. So teach us, by the light of the child Jesus, to see in simple words and simple acts the vehicles of gratitude. Open our spirits to pour out, in speechless ecstacy, the burden of our indebtedness. Then we will worry no longer whether our words are sufficient, because we will become living bundles of thankfulness, whose every thought will be an expression of wonder, every act a dance of praise, every word a hymn of celebration to our sovereign who is now, indeed, God-with-us.

Third Sunday of Epiphany
—

Invocation

We are challenged by the example of the Magi, O God, to lay aside the preoccupations of the day to stalk a star that proclaims a savior's birth. Grant us the vision to see what they saw, so we can cut loose from the secure familiarities that make us timid and journey to lay before the child our gifts—not the commodities of the marketplace, but lives devoted to his service. Thus do we mean to glorify you and acknowledge the authority of Christ in the world.

Call to Praise

Leader: It is the time of Epiphany, when Gentile strangers from distant lands came searching for a child;

People:　And finding the baby with its mother, presented precious gifts they carried with them, declaring they had found a newborn monarch.

Leader:　It is the time of awareness, when it dawns on us that one we thought a child of the Jews is a child for the whole human family;

People:　Now we see, as God declared generations before, that all humanity is empowered to become a holy nation, the people of God.

Leader:　Let us enact the wonder of mystery unveiled,

People:　Praising the God who publishes salvation in swaddling clothes.

Prayer of Praise

Creator Spirit, true sun of the world, ever rising and never setting, whose light nourishes the whole Earth so that the creation sings for joy: when we sleep, the voices of other people cry your praise; and when they sleep, we echo the song they began. As we rest and play, their labor serves your glory; and when they take their leisure, our labor proclaims the grace of useful work. Let it ever be so, O Holy One, that amid the rhythm of waking and sleeping, of working and playing, your name will never be without witnesses among the families of humanity who look and see and proclaim your sacred majesty.

Call to Reconciliation

Our dawning awareness of the global significance of Jesus, which we dramatize in the events of Epiphany season, places us under a call to humility. We like to imagine that if we had lived at the time of his birth, we would have recognized Jesus for who he was and led the shepherds and the Magi in homage. We flatter ourselves. Jesus himself admonished us that if we fail to see him in the folk who are daily our neighbors, we would not recognize him, even if he sat down beside us in this room. In honest moments, we know this to be the case; and in the act of confession, we have opportunity to acknowledge it before God, in the hope of being made more fully, more sensibly, aware. Join me, then, in holy restitution.

Prayer of Confession

O God of pure intent, the sweet innocence of your child indicts us who tolerate greed and selfishness, while declaring them necessary evils of business and commerce. The simple affirmation of this tiny savior challenges us, who condone the councils of social and political cynicism that abandon to their despair the children of need. The promise of healing that shines about our infant redeemer's face impeaches our failure to grapple with the ignorance and want that shackle the nations. Forgive, redeemer God, and teach us again that it is our calling to give, not to receive; to save, not to be preserved; to spend our lives, not withhold them; that all that we are, and have, and do may serve your glory.

Declaration of Forgiveness

Leader: For all who are able to admit their own failings and are ready to accept God's intervention of mercy, there is at this time of year a symbol of exceptional wonder: for who can look into the face of the infant Jesus and not receive reassurance? If by the love of this child God can assail even the gates of hell, then nothing that we are, or have been, is beyond the reach of God's reconciling mercy.

People: Hearing this word of grace, we say together, thanks be to God!

Call for the Offering

When we bring our offerings to support the works of mercy that are the special task of the church, we show that we, like the Magi, recognize who it is that sits on Mary's lap. We invite you now to clothe that recognition in flesh, just as in Jesus God clothes the redeeming Word in flesh. And as the gift comes alive in us, it may through our generosity come alive in others, giving them, also, both reason and opportunity to praise God.

Prayer of Dedication

Here are our gifts, great Giver of life, and here are our lives. We lay both before you, knowing that they are already yours to receive or to give, as you will; but knowing, as well, that you wait for them to be given freely, as you have given yourself freely to us, earning, thereby, the thankful gift of both our goods and our lives, through Jesus Christ our Savior.

**Prayer of Thanksgiving (in observance of the
Week of Prayer for Christian Unity)**

God of all joy, we thank you that in the epiphany of Jesus Christ you show us the way to true life and receive as your children those who seek peace and righteousness, by whatever name we are called, in whatever language we speak. We thank you that your promise of eternal life is made to the humble, the merciful, the pure in heart, without concern for the manner of our worship or the niceness of our liturgies. We rejoice in the richness and diversity of peoples and societies and denominations that acknowledge the sovereignty of Christ. And we thank you, most of all, that we are honored to be numbered among them.

Fourth Sunday of Epiphany

Invocation

Reveal yourself to us, eternal Spirit; be visible to us as tangibly as we are visible to one another. For if you are not here, our gathering is without meaning; and if you are here and we do not recognize you, our gathering is in vain. So teach us to recognize you, that we may more ably recognize one another. Then the epiphany of Christ will be manifest in us, engaging us in true worship, as befits the community that is called by his name.

Call to Praise

Leader: Now is the season of light, when heaven's shining proclaims Messiah's birth.

People: Now is the season of hope, when a star's rising proclaims a promise fulfilled.

Leader: Now dawns for all the world the rising sun of righteousness.

People: Now spreads abroad the growing light of holy intent.

Leader: Now is manifest the divine substance in human flesh;

People: Now visible the purpose of God in the unfolding of our history.

Leader: We see, and seeing, know.

People: We hear, and hearing, understand.

Unison: Now join we voices of proclamation: the one who comes among us is the Christ of God, the giver of peace, the author of our redemption. Thanks be to God!

Prayer of Praise

Praise God, who was from ancient times, whose promise to Abraham and Sarah took substance in Israel's history. Praise God, who was in the time of turning, when the promise who is Christ extended the call to reconciliation until it embraces the whole people of Earth. Praise God, who is present in our time, seeking to redeem our labor, urging upon us the mantle of ambassadors for Christ. Praise God, who will be present in the time of fulfillment when, once more, the morning stars shall sing together and all the heavenly host shout for joy. Praise God in all times. Praise God in all seasons. Praise the Sovereign of Hosts!

Call to Reconciliation

Epiphany teaches us, in symbolic terms, that we are strangers to Jesus, who was, after all, born a Jew and reared under the Mosaic law, a child of the ancient Hebrew covenant. Epiphany also proclaims, however, that even as we stand outside that historic fellowship, God draws us through Christ into the circle of covenant relationship, adopting us as daughters and sons. Imperfectly prepared to hear this news, we are, if we be honest, stung by its pronouncement. After all, we know we have not earned such an honor. But in the symbolic act of confession, in admitting that we are undeserving, the way is opened for us to receive the most astounding news of all: we are pursued not because we are worthy, but because God's reach will not be bridled. Raise your voice in common confession, and let us pretend to restrain God no longer.

Prayer of Confession

The realization of Christ shines ever brighter in the world, O Great First Light, but our vision is hindered by blinders of reluctance. All about us, acts of self-giving inspire and amaze, but we hesitate, fearful that giving love may require too great a gift of self. At our doorstep, souls who do not know your Christ move by, hungering for what they cannot name, while we concern ourselves with whether or not they would fit in. You call us to signify divine compassion in the world, but we withdraw within the circles of our presumed security and abandon Jesus without a moment's thought. Be merciful, defining Creator, who alone can name—and dissolve—our sin. Grant us fortitude, courageous Jesus, who alone knows, because you lived it, the way and need of our flesh. Invigorate us, Holy Spirit, who alone can animate us to engage the tasks of our calling, and complete the work of God.

Declaration of Forgiveness

Leader: In his second letter to the Christians at Corinth (5:16–21), the apostle Paul expressed, in vivid language, the conviction that God was in Christ with the intention of being reconciled with the world, no longer holding against us the misdeeds of humanity. They are forgiven. The old order is gone, God's new order has already begun. And we, who recognize God's intent in Christ, are now given a new charge: we are entrusted to spread abroad the news of our own reconciliation and God's eagerness to grant it to others.

People: Hearing this word of grace, we say together, thanks be to God!

Call for the Offering

For most of us, the reconciling love of God did not first come as a direct revelation, as if God picked up the phone and dialed our number. It came through another human being who, in some special way, touched our life—a parent, teacher, or friend. For most of us, too, it came accompanied by some extra measure of joy and realization, a deeper sense of the meaning of life. The task before us, as practitioners of Christian stewardship, is to determine how we shall, in that same way, embody God's call to someone else. Clearly, many of us cannot go ourselves; but we can, through the offering, make it possible for someone else to go. Bring your gifts now and imagine that in doing so, you help to buy a ticket for the redeeming love of God to travel to where someone most needs to experience it.

Prayer of Dedication

The Magi brought tributes to lay before our infant savior, O God, acknowledging in him your promise for the redemption of the world. Now we bring our gifts, but lay them at the foot of the cross, acknowledging that the hope of the world may not rest secure in a manger, but must risk itself in mature acts of mercy that alone can overcome the world's pain. Help us, saving Deity, neither to fear the self-giving nor doubt the vision of your ultimate victory.

Prayer of Thanksgiving

Who shall teach us, Generous Provider, to name your goodness? For we know it in ourselves more surely than any other can define it for us. And who, more than we, may number your blessings? For we have benefits beyond counting. Surveyed against the mass of humanity, our scarcity is abundance, our poverty limitless wealth. So we, of all people, are bound to thank you: for the innumerable blessings of our days; for not only showering us with prosperity but inviting us to make it useful in the service of humanity, and thus to acquire unspeakable riches of the spirit. So thanks be to God who, in Jesus, is an epiphany to us, a revelation before the face of the whole human family; who, in giving to us, teaches us to become gifts; who, in blessing us, prepares us to become a blessing. Amen, God; so may it be!

Fifth Sunday of Epiphany

—

Invocation

Speak to us again, merciful God, through the tiny but growing child of Bethlehem and Nazareth, that our wonder at the mystery of Christ may not fade with the passage of days, but increase in proportion to his mounting wisdom and stature. So we will be prepared not only to rejoice at his birth, but to embrace his teaching, endure his betrayal, and participate in his death and resurrection.

Call to Praise (from Mark 1:9–15)

Leader: In those days Jesus came from Nazareth of Galilee and was baptized by John in the Jordan.

People: As he came up out of the water, he saw heaven torn apart and the Spirit, dove-like, descend on him.

Leader: A voice spoke from heaven: "You are my child, the beloved; with you I am well pleased."

People: The Spirit drove him into the wilderness, for forty days with wild beasts, tempted by Satan, served by angels.

Leader:	Then came Jesus back to Galilee, proclaiming the good news of God.
People:	Then came Jesus saying, "The time is fulfilled, and the Reign of God has come near. Repent, and believe the good news!"
Unison:	We will, and believing, give glory to God!

Prayer of Praise

Hail to you, God our Creator, cloaked in radiance, sharer of light, by whose grace we have vision to see and know the way. Hail to you, God the Sacred Spirit, wellspring of wisdom and giver of knowledge, by whose mediation we are able to discern the true from the trivial and devote ourselves to things ageless and redeeming. Hail to you, God and true child of humanity, first among the redeemed, architect of reconciliation by which we become one with you and with one another. In adoration we cry your name, sing your praise, share your presentness in our lives. Praise the triune God!

Call to Reconciliation

Epiphany season was adopted by the church to identify and celebrate the dawning recognition that Jesus was not simply a Jewish reformer but the bearer of a new covenant between God and the world beyond Israel. Confronting that mystery also confronts us, however, with our reluctance to recognize it, and our resistance to receive it ourselves. Yet it also demonstrates that God possesses the means to free us to see and to embrace it. Join me, then, in making such confession, so that together we may know the God who comes in Christ.

Prayer of Confession

The light of your revelation grows among us, God of radiance, a gleaming blossom in the chill of our February, its mystery more palpable than our own flesh. But we remain bundled in our coldness, huddled against the brevity of arctic days, and forgetful of your sovereignty over our seasons and our fears. Forgive us, Parenting Deity, who loosed the fire of your child into the winter of ancient Israel, kindled the spark that would enflame the springtime of your love and set ablaze the heart of humanity. By your light, overcome our dusky gloom; by your love, erase the habits of our uncaring; by your Word now manifest in our flesh, teach us the thrill of obedience and the joy of compassion. Then shall your love germinate and bloom in us and we in the world in which you intend our participation.

Declaration of Forgiveness

Leader: The flip side of confession is profession: by declaring ourselves in need of God's mercy, we affirm our confidence in God's mercy. This is the other gift of Epiphany—that we know in our own lives, our personal histories, the affirming intervention of divine love that heals our infirmities and pardons our faults. In brief, we are incorporated into the good news that God was in Christ, and become, ourselves, part of the hope of the world.

People: Hearing this word of grace, we say together, thanks be to God!

Call for the Offering

In Matthew's account of the Sermon on the Mount, Jesus challenges his listeners (5:14–26) in symbols that speak to us especially well during the season of Epiphany: "You are the light of the world. A city set on a hill cannot be hid. Nor do men light a lamp and put it under a basket,but on a stand where it can give light to the whole house. Let your light so shine before humanity, therefore, that others see your good work, and seeing it, give glory to God." During the season of Epiphany, we celebrate the realization growing among the nations that Christ is the advancing light. It is within our power to assist in that process, by fueling the light of the gospel. I invite you, friends, to make your gifts as ones who know how to shine before humanity.

Prayer of Dedication

Let these gifts become a part of your Epiphany to the world, God of the incarnate Word. Let their employment in acts of mercy manifest Christ's presence among those whose need for relief, and whose need of his presence, is greatest. Then will grace truly be born in us, who by this giving mean both to thank and serve you.

Prayer of Thanksgiving

In mystery and silence, in ways seen and unperceived, in unexpected encounter when we are least prepared to greet you, Holy Being, you are present in our days, bringing new life out of destruction, hope out of despair, growth out of tribulation. From this we learn to be thankful that you do not leave us as we are at any moment in time, but labor tirelessly to make us whole. We are grateful for your unseen hand in the unfolding of our histories; the attention of your Spirit's gentle guidance; the joy of knowing that we are your people and may yet grow to be so more fully. We thank you, Holy Presentness, that by your ongoing participation in our life both individual and corporate, we become vehicles by which others may be called to hope and reconciliation. Fulfill in us now the intent of your will.

Pre-Lent and Transfiguration

Ninth, Eighth and Seventh Sundays before Easter
Liturgical Color—Ninth and Eighth Sundays before Easter: Green
Liturgical Color—Transfiguration: White

Pre-Lent is the period of three weeks between the conclusion of Epiphany season and Ash Wednesday, which marks the start of Lent. While historically observed only in the liturgical denominations (Roman Catholic, Episcopal, and Lutheran), it is included here for those who might choose to take active note of it. In church tradition, these three Sundays were called the "Gesima" season, from their Latinate numerical references: *Septuagesima, Sexagesima, and Quinquagesima*. While not precisely accurate, the terms imply 70, 60, and 50, respectively, and designate the number of days, loosely counted, until Easter. For purposes of this book, the names are mainly of traditional value and will not be given further emphasis.

The final Sunday before Lent is designated Transfiguration Sunday and deserves more detailed attention.

It is curious that Transfiguration receives such scant attention—if any at all—among nonliturgical Protestant churches. The event has something for everyone: theological richness, an aura of mystery, the glorification of the person of Jesus, even a nod at dispensationalism! Among denominations that pass over the Pre-Lent observance, emphasizing the Epiphany theme right up to the start of Lent, Transfiguration is a logical capstone for the former and preview for the latter. It portrays a "manifestation" of Christ's divine and messianic nature that will be unequalled until the resurrection—which it also prefigures, by granting us a glimpse of the splendor of the risen Christ even as we acknowledge, by means of Lent, that crucifixion is the prerequisite to glorification.

Three elements structure the moment: First, Jesus is transformed by a remarkable radiance of face and garments. Mark's description is especially driving: "his clothes became dazzling white, such as no one on earth could bleach them" (9:3). Second, two persons of central importance to Hebraic history appear with Jesus: Moses, the prototype of Messiah (Deuteronomy 18:15) and giver of the law, who himself was transfigured; and Elijah, whose return would precede and portend "the great and terrible day of God" (Malachi 4:5). Finally, a voice from heaven, in a reprise of Jesus' baptism, proclaims, "This is my beloved child; to this one you shall listen." It is a phrase leaving no doubt that Jesus is cloaked with divine sanction.

For the disciples privileged to be present (Peter, James, and John) the Transfiguration was the very epitome of what we are wont to call a "mountaintop experience"—a brief moment when everything comes together with life-amending transcendence. Nothing before is quite able to prepare us for this moment; nothing that follows will elude its indelible mark.

In an exquisite poetic notation, Eunice Tietjens captured the Transfiguration's formative impact on everything succeeding it:

> But I shall go down from this airy space, this swift,
>   white peace, this stinging exultation,
> And time will close about me, and my soul stir to the
>   rhythm of the daily round,
> Yet, having known, life will not press so close, and always
>   I shall feel time ravel thin about me;
> For once I stood
> In the white windy presence of eternity.
>   —from *Profiles from China* (1917)

Transfiguration provides opportunity for us to gather the luminous hope that can carry us through the dismal events that lie immediately ahead—betrayal, corrupted justice, crucifixion. The heady wonder of Transfiguration braces us for the deprivation of Lent.

Prayers and Liturgical Readings

Ninth Sunday before Easter

—

Invocation

You Holy One of history, whom we your children call by many names and by no name; whose majesty is so robed by compassion as to allow itself now, around the world, to appear a myriad of discrete images in a host of individual minds, permitting us to trust who we may not see: to us who are multitude, speak now your uniting word. Bless our gathering and our parting, our hopes and our ambitions, our intentions and how we carry them out; and in all things may your will be done, your purpose served, your truth prevail, through Jesus Christ our Savior.

Call to Praise (from Psalm 67:3–7)

Leader: Let the peoples praise you, O God;

People: Let all the peoples praise you!

Leader: Let the nations be glad and sing for joy,

People: For you judge the peoples with equity and guide the nations of earth.

Leader: Let the peoples praise you, O God;

People: Let all the peoples praise you!

Leader: The earth has yielded its increase; God, our God, has blessed us.

People: God has blessed us; let the ends of earth tremble in awe!

Prayer of Praise

The star-spangled heavens of winter's night; the bluster and blow of arctic storm; the sparkle of birds sunlit against the sky and scurry of small animals snow-borne from food-store to borrow, bring music to our winter musings and proclaim the glory of our God. So too, the chill of outdoor sport and the warmth of hearth and bed cause wonder and praise at the goodness of life. Praise, then, O God, for seasonal variety, for rhythms of rest and renewal, for beauty and wonder. And praise, too, for eyes to see and ears to hear, for minds to perceive and spirits to rejoice. Heaven and earth indeed proclaim your glory, O God; to which we add the chorus of our voices in the resounding Amen!

Call to Reconciliation (from Psalm 51:15–17)

In the hymnbook of the ancient Hebrews, at Psalm 51, the psalmist writes, "O God, open my lips, and my mouth will declare your praise. For you have no delight in sacrifice; if I were to give a burnt offering, you would not be pleased. The sacrifice acceptable to God is a broken spirit; a broken and contrite heart, O God, you will not despise." Hearing the psalmist's declaration, let us—with broken spirits and contrite hearts—join in unison confession.

Prayer of Confession

Majestic Creator, your call to righteousness shatters the facade of our self-satisfaction, as your holiness exposes our half-truths and facile commitments. Hold up before us now the true measure of virtue, that we, being refined by your discipline, may admit our shortcomings and have the courage to face our selves. Sicken us at the thought of pretense. Help us to throw aside the affectation that masquerades as virtue and reclothe us in the seamless garment of truth. Let selfishness be overpowered by love, and personal privilege by justice. Then will your rule come in us, and through us reach to all who are touched by our lives.

Declaration of Forgiveness (from Psalm 40:1–3)

Again, in Psalm 40, the psalmist takes up the theme of redemption. Listen: "I waited patiently for God, who inclined to me and heard my cry, who drew me up from the desolate pit, out of the miry bog, and set my feet upon a rock, making my steps secure. God put a new song in my mouth, a song of praise to our creator. Many will see and fear, and put their trust in the Lord."

Call for the Offering

Several thousand years ago the Hebrews heard this commandment from God: "Each of you shall give as you are able, according to the blessing of God which has been given you" (Deuteronomy 16:17). Serving the God whom the Hebrews served, we ought also to see ourselves bound by the same obligation. Bring your gifts, then, according to the blessing with which God has blessed you.

Prayer of Dedication

Bless our gifts, O God, according to the spirit of their giving; and, according to the power of your wisdom, put them to work for the support and fulfillment of your purpose, which works among us even when we fail to see it; for the ultimate triumph of which we wait, working as partners with Christ, at whose call we offer both these gifts and our prayer.

Prayer of Thanksgiving

Eternal God, who calls us to be among your covenant people: thank you for sharing your creative power with us—that we can imagine things that are not and bring them into being. When we consider our qualifications to be entrusted with so awesome a gift, we are overwhelmed; for the creative power you grant us carries with it the power of destruction: our desire threatens to outpace restraint, our ambition to exceed wisdom. Thanks, then, you trusting divinity, for your love that dares to risk the future to our hands, anticipates our participation in holiness even when we do not merit it, and continues to call us to be a holy nation, your partners in destiny. Thank you for keeping faith with us; and grant us the constancy to keep faith with you.

Eighth Sunday before Easter

Invocation

Eternal God, you who command the power to fling the galaxies across the void of an expanding universe, yet greet us where we least expect to confront you—in a bush aflame, a still small voice, the birth of a child: deliver us now from any doubt that hinders us from believing we shall meet you in this company of our fellowship. Teach us humility, that in greeting one another, we may expect to be greeted by you; that in speaking to one another, we may expect to hear your word of life and affirmation; that in sharing the bonds of community, we will share with you the full measure of abundant life—on which we pray now your blessing.

Call to Praise

Leader: Let the people praise you, O God. Let all the people praise you.

People: For in praising you, we acknowledge the source of our being and of the truth we bear.

Leader: Let the people praise you, O God. Let all the people praise you.

People: For in praising you, we acknowledge the root of our faith and the awesome power of thought and imagination, of consciousness and conscience, that marks us—of all creatures of earth—with the stamp of your image.

Leader: Let the people praise you, O God, let all the people praise you.

People: For in praising you, we are constrained to acknowledge those things beyond our individual selves that contribute to our life in community.

Unison: So may we rightfully yield to you our fitting debt of gratitude.

Prayer of Praise

The stars in their courses and planets in their orbits praise you, O God. The rhythms of seasons—of birth and death, hibernation and migration, earth-wrapped bulbs waiting the bidding power of the ascending Sun—herald the mystery of your design. Let not our voices alone be silent. Let not our lives alone be absent in pursuing your intent; but let the hue and call of our songful prayer complete the harmony of adulation due our Creator, who bends to share with us the consciousness of design, the mystery of being, the wonder of praise.

Call to Reconciliation

In the opening verses of Psalm 36 we find these words—an appropriate call to confession: "Transgression speaks deep within the hearts of the wicked; there is no fear of God before their eyes. For in their own vision, they flatter themselves into believing that their iniquity will not be identified and despised. The words of their mouths are mischief and deceit; they have ceased to act wisely or to do good." The children of

God are called to abandon this self-deceiving conduct and to turn to the way of God, the first step of which is to acknowledge our need to do so. To that end, let us join in our unison prayer of confession.

Prayer of Confession

God of life, who calls us into the ways that lead to life: we confess the frequency with which we choose the path that leads to death. God of light, who surrounds and fills us with insight and understanding: we confess how often we choose to journey in ignorance so that we may continue to have our own way. God of holiness, who declares that no other gods shall be put in your place: we confess the idolatries of power and wealth to which we readily turn, in the vain belief that they will give our lives meaning. God of love, who calls us to lives of redemptive loving: we confess our devotion to our petty hatreds and global distrust. Forgive us these our sins, holy God, and turn us again to the way that leads to life, to right loyalties, to true love; for the sake of Jesus Christ, who modeled all these things for us and before us.

Declaration of Forgiveness

Later in Psalm 36 we read these reassuring words: "How precious is your steadfast love, O God! All people may take refuge in the shadow of your wings. They feast on the abundance of your house, and you give them drink from the river of your delights. For with you is the fountain of life; in your light do we see light." Let us carry this promise of God's compassionate mercy and forgiveness with us and share it abroad with all of God's people.

Call for the Offering

In the book of Tobit 4:7, Tobit, believing that he is dying, gives his son some last advice. The words are an appropriate call for our offering. "Give alms from your possessions. . . and do not let your eyes begrudge the gift when you make it. Do not turn your face away from anyone who is poor, and the face of God will not be turned away from you." Turn now toward those who need our help and know that God turns toward us.

Prayer of Dedication

O God, who has given of your bounty to us all: accept this offering of your people and so follow it by your blessing that some need may be satisfied, some hurt relieved, some justice realized, through Jesus Christ our Savior.

Prayer of Thanksgiving

You Holy One who inhabit eternity, yet place us in a universe bounded by time and space; whose vision discerns not only what has been but comprehends what yet may be: remove the bonds that inhibit the full flow of our thankfulness. Lacking the power fully to discern your goal, we cannot wholly envision your triumph. So our thankfulness is reserved, our gratitude conditional. Grant us the apostle's enduring patience to face trial with unremitting hope and the prophet's serene confidence to point to your ultimate victory. Then, the fetters of fear removed and faith reconfirmed, we will shout full-throated our thanksgiving for the grace that redeems our time and history, through the intervening love of Jesus Christ our Savior.

Transfiguration Sunday
—

Invocation

As Jesus' transfiguration enlarged the apostles' sense of your attendance upon their time and place, O God, enlarge our awareness of your presence in our own histories, that the twin visions of Moses and Elijah, of law and prophecy, may beget in us their larger grasp of globe-girdling *shalom,* your intended time of universal peace and justice, by which the eyes of every people will be opened to see your saving grace and all flesh stand redeemed.

Call to Praise (based on 2 Peter 1:16–18)

Leader: We did not follow cleverly devised myths when we made known the power and coming of Jesus;

People: For we were eyewitnesses of his majesty.

Leader: For he received honor and glory from God when that voice was conveyed to him by the majestic glory:

People: "This is my Son, my beloved, with whom I am well pleased."

Leader: We ourselves heard this voice come from heaven, while with him on the holy mountain.

People: This is a frightful moment, too radiant with holiness for mortal endurance.

Leader: Do not be afraid: for this shining Christ is God's luminous mercy come among us, fitting us also to live in the light, so that we, like him, may serve God.

People: Then it is good we are here. We will subdue our fear, listen, and cry praise to the Holy One who is transfigured in our sight!

Prayer of Praise

O Holy One, who fills our world with transforming brilliance, that all who choose might escape the shadows and go in the light: we praise you for the gospel of your love; for your word of salvation for all people; for the revelation of your glory to the nations. We bless you for the faithful of every age who were witnesses to this truth; for the labors of all who, at personal risk, challenged prevailing beliefs and called the nations to account; for the stimulus toward renewal that moves within the church of Jesus Christ, reforming our vision and amplifying our understanding. Hasten the time of fulfillment, when the kingdoms of this earth shall indeed become the dominion of God; and all humanity, by whatever name or tongue, will stand redeemed and praise you with one voice.

Call to Reconciliation

Wherever we look in the biblical record, whether in Deuteronomic law, prophetic pronouncement or apostolic teaching, and especially in the words of Jesus, we are told that only those who come in humility may stand in the presence of God or receive the transfiguring light that molds us into vessels suitable for God's purpose. Let us now, therefore, set aside our pride, divest ourselves of every shred of arrogance, and make our confession in honest humility; then turn again to hear the assurance of God.

Prayer of Confession

Like James and John, O Transforming Presence, we misinterpret the signs before us, even when we stand on the mountaintop. Like Peter, idly chattering at the emergence of miracle, we distract ourselves with details and fail to see the larger wonder before us. Beholding our Savior transfigured, shining with holy purpose, it takes the very voice of God to silence us and command our attention. So we fall down before you, declaring our blindness to holy things, our obsession with particulars, our failure to apprehend your presence in the faces and events that inhabit our days. Forgive us, majestic Maker, who through the shining Christ seeks to redeem us, teach us the purpose of being, and incorporate us into your sacred history, by which the nations are summoned and all life made glorious.

Declaration of Forgiveness

Matthew's account of the Transfiguration teaches a subtle lesson concerning the assurance that is ours because of Jesus. When the irrepressible Peter, with characteristic exuberance and bad timing, begins to talk to Jesus, God's voice silences him. The disciples are terrified and fall to the ground—as well they might. "But," records Matthew, "Jesus came and touched them, saying, 'Get up, and do not be afraid'" (17:4–7). So it is with us: when we fall in fear before God's majesty on account of our sin, Jesus comes and touches us, lifting us to our feet and promising, "you have nothing to fear." Thanks be to God.

Call for the Offering

Through Moses, God gave the law to the people of Israel to be the sign and seal of covenant relationship. Through the prophets, God impressed upon the world the searing, but liberating, burden of moral righteousness. These are forms of light, meant to guide and instruct us. As Christians, we are privileged to receive the light of the presence and word of Jesus. These are God's gifts to us. How shall we respond? Let each of us consider this question as we envision ourselves standing among the disciples, witnessing the transfiguration of Christ and asking: God, what gift can I bring?

Prayer of Dedication
All gifts over which we exercise control are but a weak imitation of the perfect gift of your love for us, O God; yet you receive and affirm them as if they were the world's riches—as in truth they may become with your blessing. Receive them, then, not in the feebleness of our giving, but the vigor of your receiving. Then shall they be gifts indeed!

Thanksgiving
Almighty and gracious God, we thank you for the transforming light of a very special day, for the vision it reveals and the fresh sense of purpose it bestows on us who are the church of Jesus Christ. Thank you for work we are given to do and for strength and skill to do it. Thank you for your truth, which conveys your will, and lights our path to pursue it. Thank you for your Spirit that moves among us, energizing us to complete the tasks of servanthood, even when our resources are at their lowest ebb. Thank you that in your generosity, you continue to supply these things when we do not deserve them, or when we accept but do not use them. Your way is wonderful beyond explaining, Forbearing Monarch; and for that we are most thankful of all: that because it is your way, we need not try to explain it, but may be content to rejoice in it.

Ash Wednesday

Forty-sixth Day before Easter
Liturgical Color: Purple

The reader may be confused by the period designation cited above. Everyone knows that Lent runs for forty days. What often is overlooked, however, is that Sundays are excluded from the count of days because Sunday—the first day of the week—is a celebration of our Savior's resurrection, i.e., a "little Easter," not strictly a time of penitential preparation for the crucifixion. We properly speak, therefore, of Sundays *during* Lent rather than Sundays *of* Lent—a distinction unique to this season of the church year. So even though liturgical material for the Sundays during Lent bears the unmistakable stamp of penitence and soberness, the days themselves are not included.

In any event, Ash Wednesday formally introduces the season of Lent, from which its observance is historically inseparable. The season—and therefore Ash Wednesday—has had an on-again/off-again quality for communions born of the Reformation. One frequently encounters people raised in the Free church tradition, and even the Reformed, who are somewhat baffled by their first encounter with Ash Wednesday and have only a passing acquaintance with Lent itself. Suffice it to state here that the purpose of Ash Wednesday in the Western tradition is, as the popular phrase has it, to "jump-start" Lent—to move us dramatically and definitively into a season unique in the church year for its severity of purpose.

In the case of Ash Wednesday, it seemed appropriate to provide a model liturgy in its entirety, rather than a set of prayers and liturgical readings suitable for Sunday worship, for two reasons. First, as noted above, Christian Sunday worship possesses a unique stamp. In my judgment, we miss opportunities to enrich liturgy and give it dramatic impact if we simply move the "usual" Sunday format to a weekday. This is especially true of the great Lenten observances that fall during the week—Ash Wednesday, Maundy Thursday, and Good Friday, and Saturday's Great Vigil of Easter. These days constitute the few weekdays often given clear-cut liturgical significance throughout the Western church. As such, they merit unique treatment.

Second, because of the aforementioned uncertainty occasioned by the Reformation, some few congregations—even to this day—have little experience of Ash Wednesday and few resources upon which to draw that uniquely lend themselves to "non-Sunday" worship.

Congregations with a developing interest in fully observing the church year may therefore find this a useful place to begin; and those who already mark the day may benefit by a new addition to their liturgical options. The model liturgy below emphasizes the distinctly confessional character of Ash Wednesday. It is self-consciously penitential and reflective, the better to establish the unique quality of Lent and to launch the people of God along the path that leads inevitably to the cross—the church's essential way-station without which we are unable either to comprehend or to celebrate the empty tomb.

An Ash Wednesday Liturgy

For the Congregants

On entering the church, please take the slip of paper provided, and list briefly those things in your life on which you most desire God's healing intervention, or which you want most to change during this Lenten season. Place the paper in the offering plate at the appropriate time.

Option 1. The papers will be burned, symbolizing our intent to sacrifice to God's sovereignty the concerns written on them. [If there is to be a distribution of ashes, add] The resulting ashes will be distributed during our concluding act of worship.

Option 2. These offerings will be placed on the table, symbolizing our intent to submit them to God's sovereignty and to seek God's help in resolving them during Lent.

Focus on Lent [1]

Greeting

Leader: In the name of the Father, and of the Son, and of the Holy Spirit. *(Or: In the name of our Creating, Redeeming, and Sanctifying God.)*

People: Amen.

Leader: The grace of Jesus Christ and the love of God and the fellowship of the Holy Spirit be with you all.

People: And also with you.

Liturgical Proclamation (adapted from the Letter to the Hebrews)

Leader: Long ago, God spoke to our ancestors in many and various ways by the prophets;

Right: But in these last days he has spoken to us by Jesus the Christ,

Left: Whom God appointed heir of all things, and through whom the worlds were created.

Leader: Therefore we must pay greater attention to what we have heard, so that we do not drift away from it.

Right: For if the message declared through angels is valid, and every transgression receives a just penalty;

Left: How can we escape if we neglect so great a salvation?

Unison: Let us offer acceptable worship to god, with reverence and awe, for our God is a consuming fire.

A hymn. *

Call to Reconciliation (adapted from Hebrews 4)

Take care, brothers and sisters, that none of you may have an evil, unbelieving heart that turns away from the living God. For we become partners of Christ, if only we hold our first confidence firm to the end. Indeed, the word of God is living and active, sharper than any two-edged sword, piercing until it divides soul from spirit, joint from marrow; it is able to judge the thoughts and intentions of the heart. And before God no creature is hidden, but all are naked and laid bare to the

*All who are able are invited to stand.

eyes of the one to whom we must render an account. Since, then, we have a great high priest who has passed through the heavens, Jesus, the very child of God, let us hold fast to our confession. For we do not have a high priest who is unable to sympathize with our weakness, but we have one who in every way has been tested, as we are, yet without sin. Let us therefore approach the throne of grace with boldness, so that we may receive mercy and find grace to help in time of need.

Prayer of Confession

Leader: In the silence of our hearts, O God, we confront the knowledge of what accuses us. Easily we convince those nearest us that our conscience is clear. With difficulty, but by the careful screening of our thoughts, we are able to persuade even ourselves. But we cannot deceive you, for your eye sees to the innermost core of our being; and with firm insistence, you call us to the task of honest self-assessment. God, have mercy.

People: God, have mercy.

Leader: Unveiled by the probing of your vision, we have nothing further to gain by hiding from ourselves; and as our defenses fall away, we lose both the capacity, and the need, to hide from others. So in this company of friends and peers we cry our shame and seek your forgiveness. Christ, have mercy.

People: Christ, have mercy.

Leader: Now cleanse and purify us, our God, not only of our sin, but of our guilt and our fear of discovery; that with the whole company of your people, we may acknowledge our forgiveness and proclaim to the world the reconciling love of God. Holy Spirit, have mercy.

People: Holy Spirit, have mercy.

Leader: May almighty God have mercy on us, forgive all our sins, and bring us to everlasting life.

People: Amen.

The Offering of Our Sacrifices[2]

Scripture Lessons[3]

A reading from the Hebrew Scriptures.

Following the reading:

Reader: This is the word of God.

People: Thanks be to God.

Special music or an appropriate unison reading from the Psalms.

Reading from the Early Church Letters (the Epistles)

Following the reading:

Reader: This is the word of God.

People: Thanks be to God.

Reading from the Gospels*

Before the reading:

Reader: Please rise, and remain standing for the reading of the Gospel. God be with you.

People: And also with you.

Reader: A reading from the Holy Gospel According to [author].

People: Glory to you, O God.

Following the reading:

Reader: This is the Gospel of our Savior.

People: Praise to you, Christ Jesus.

Sermon or Reflection

A Litany for Ash Wednesday

Leader: O God of history, who created us and calls us apart to be the Church of Jesus Christ, we witness again the return of the season of Lent.

People: Empower us now faithfully to follow the footsteps of Jesus, as he sets his face steadfastly toward Jerusalem and the cross.

**All who are able are invited to stand.*

Leader: For the unfathomable love that you extend to us in taking our flesh, bearing yourself the pain and frustration, the anxiety and ambiguity of life,

People: We praise you, Incarnate Word.

Leader: For your death on the cross, by which you did not withhold even your own life as the price of reconciliation with your broken world,

People: We thank you, loving Redeemer.

Leader: That you alone, of all the powers in heaven or on earth, are sovereign of creation, justly entitled to our undivided loyalty and our unconditional obedience,

People: We proclaim, O God of majesty.

Leader: That our loyalties are divided, our obedience conditional, our labor in pursuit of our calling halfhearted,

People: We confess, O God our Judge.

Leader: Then call us to action, great Author of history,

People: As you are active on behalf of your creation, seeking in holy love to save us from aimlessness and sin.

Leader: Let us use this Lenten season wisely,

People: Seeing that you put before us the ways of life and death, urging us to choose life, that we may live.

Unison: May we, at the end of these forty days, come to the foot of the cross prepared to receive the unspeakable gift of sacrifice that shatters the power of death, not by our merit, but by your grace and might, through the intervention of Christ Jesus, in whom we live, through whom we pray.

The Prayer of Our Savior

Distribution of the Ashes[4]

Hymn*

Benediction (from Hebrews 13:20–21)
Now may the God of peace, who brought back from the dead our Savior Jesus, the great shepherd of the sheep; by the blood of the eternal

*All who are able are invited to stand.

covenant make us complete in everything good, so that we may do God's will, working among us that which is pleasing in God's sight; through Jesus Christ, to whom be the glory for ever and ever.

Notes

1. It may be desirable for the minister to provide a brief introduction reminding the congregation of the nature and character of Lent and how it will be observed during this and subsequent services.

2. Let ushers pass through the congregation, collecting the slips of paper on which have been recorded the people's individual hopes and expectations for Lent and bring them to the table in offering. If option 1 is used, a suitable container for burning the papers must be provided and the papers set afire, taking due care for safety (a large stainless steel bowl with a protective lining of aluminum foil works well, placed on a metal stand beside the table, and feeding the papers into the flame a few at a time). If there is to be a distribution of ashes at the conclusion of the service, the burned papers will cool sufficiently through the remainder of the service to be used. However, paper ashes do not work well for the traditional "imposition of ashes," i.e., marking of foreheads with the sign of the cross. They work best if mixed with some palm ashes. In liturgical church tradition, palms are burned following the Palm Sunday service each year and the ashes stored for use on the following year's Ash Wednesday. You may choose to begin this custom in your own congregation. Otherwise, you should be able to secure a small quantity from a neighboring Roman Catholic, Episcopal, or Lutheran pastor. Mixed with the burned papers, two or three tablespoons will suffice for a congregation of one to two hundred people.

3. For those interested: Ash Wednesday may seem an appropriate time to revitalize our sense of mystery or awe that transforms a text (the writings of the ancient Hebrews and early Christians) to scripture— the Holy Bible. This may be achieved, in part, by the use of dramatic devices that set the reading of Scripture apart from other readings and announcements and emphasize its central place in Christian life. The approach suggested here is one traditional way for doing so. Your congregation might choose to develop its own approach.

4. The traditional method for distributing, or "imposing," the ashes is to invite all those wishing to receive them to the front of the room, in single file, where one or more people may be stationed to receive them. If seating is arranged in such a way as to make it helpful, traffic instructions might be given to reduce confusion. In some cases, each person approaching is asked, "Will you repent and believe in the gospel?" After receiving an affirmative reply, the person ministering, using the thumb, marks the congregant's forehead with ashes in the form of the cross, saying, "Remember that you are dust, and to dust you shall return." In other cases, the question is omitted and the second statement alone is used while marking the forehead. The distribution of ashes is neither a sacrament nor an ordinance in any communion of the Western church. It is a tradition, in some cases a well-established and revered one, but, still, basically a dramatic device the church utilizes the better for Christians to understand themselves and their calling. Anyone, therefore, may serve as "minister." While some congregations may prefer that those doing so have recognized standing as pastor, elder, deacon, or the like, this is not necessary. Each congregation is free to decide, in employing the symbol, who might best embody their intentions.

6

Lent

The word "Lent" is derived from the Old English word *Lencten,* meaning spring, which in turn derives from the Old High German *lenzin* or *lengizen,* referring to the lengthening of days. The season we call spring, in fact, was originally called Lent. But since the Christian fast was observed during the early months of the year, Lent gradually adhered strictly to church practice and spring (from *springan,* to leap or move rapidly—a reference to the freshness of life) came to designate the season.

The evolution of Lent is complex, comprising a rich mix of piety, doctrine, and politics. In the time of Irenaeus, around 200 C.E., the fast was very short but very severe and might entail a total fast for forty hours, from Good Friday afternoon to Easter morning. By the mid-third century in Alexandria, it was customary to fast through most of Holy Week. The first mention of a forty-day Lenten observance, or *Quadragesima,* came from the Council of Nicaea in 325 C.E., by which time emphasis had shifted to preparation for baptism, absolution of penitents, and spiritual retreats. Fasting continued to play a part, but was not rigorously enforced. In the Western church, for a period of time, this observance lasted thirty-six days (not including Sundays), because thirty-six, being one-tenth of a year, was considered a "perfect number." This custom was amended, however, as inconsistent with Jesus' forty-day fast in the wilderness and eventually was settled as a true *Quadragesima.*

The choice of forty is richly grounded in biblical tradition and adds metaphorical power to the season of Lent. In an essay on the significance of numbers in the Bible, Maureen A. Tiley notes that Scripture contains 120 references to the number 40: "As the product of 4 times

10, it took on the qualities of stability (represented by four—the legs of a table, the corners of the earth) prolonged and fulfilled (represented by ten, a complete number)." (See "Typological Numbers: Taking a Count of the Bible," *Bible Review* 8, no. 3 [June 1992].)

Among the better-known events numbered at forty: the days of Noah's deluge (Genesis 7:12, 17); the days Moses spent on Mount Horeb (Exodus 24:18); the years of Israel's sojourn in the wilderness (Numbers 14:33–34); the days of Elijah's journey to the cave of the "still, small voice" (1 Kings 19:8); and, of course, Jesus' forty-day wilderness sojourn.

From the start in the early church, Lent seems to have carried special significance for new converts to Christianity. Since baptism was most commonly performed on Easter, Lent early served as a period of preparation for this signal rite of passage. The entire effort dramatized the seriousness of the decision and pressed upon the novice Christian the weight of commitment required. In periods when public confession of Christian faith was tantamount to a death sentence, baptism was not a step to be taken lightly. As the season was extended, it also appears to have broadened its embrace until it became a period of penitential waiting for the whole body of the faithful, as the church prepared itself for the awe-full events of Good Friday and Easter.

Lent provides the pastor an opportunity to restructure the liturgy to lend dramatic impact to this most introspective of worship seasons. In some traditions, the Gloria and the Doxology—two items of exuberant joyfulness—are omitted from the liturgy between Ash Wednesday and Easter, accentuating the season's character as a period of penitence and sober self-evaluation. Their return to the liturgy on Easter further dramatizes the contrast between the church's pre- and post-resurrection moods.

Prayers and Liturgical Readings

First Sunday during Lent

Invocation
More sober are we now, holy and sovereign God, than at any other time of the year; for now comes the season of our self-examination and we

need deep encouragement. Do not abandon us here, therefore, but by your authority as Judge of the world lay your cleansing hand upon us, that our passage through these forty days may purge us, even as it glorifies you.

Call to Praise (from Lamentations 3:40–41 and Micah 6:6, 8)

Leader: Let us test and examine our ways,
People: And return to God our Maker.
Leader: Let us lift up our hearts to our Creator,
People: We will raise our hands to God in heaven.
Leader: With what shall we come before the Author of Being,
People: And bow before our Sovereign on high?
Leader: God has shown us what is good: and what is required of us?
People: To do justice, and to love kindness, and to go humbly with God.

Prayer of Praise

As the seasons turn again to Lent, our God, we turn again to reflect on the mystery of our calling. Who is this man proclaimed Savior by so many who never saw him? How can we deal logically with a stranger who came to us unbidden, sealed with his own blood the declaration that to lay down one's life is the greatest expression of love, and still inspire others to lay down their own lives beside his? What impossible goodness is this, to take upon himself the sorrow of the world, yet pause at the end to ask forgiveness for the sorrow-givers? Then praise, our God, for the mysteries, and exultation for this time of reflection, wherein we may, with sober penitence, find the purpose of our days.

Call to Reconciliation

While there is no season during which we are justified in pretending to be above fault, or during which we need not admit our shortcomings, it is especially appropriate that we swallow our pride and acknowledge our sin during Lent. This is, after all, the season during which we reenact the sacrifice that Jesus made precisely to free us from the illusion of self-sufficiency, an illusion that, in the end, will always fail us. Knowing this, let us unite our voices in common confession.

Prayer of Confession (based on Lamentations 1:12–14, 20)

Is it of no concern to you who pass by? Look and see if there is any sorrow like our sorrow, which was inflicted on us by God on the day of fierce anger. From on high the Holy One sent fire that drove deep into our bones and spread a net to trip our feet and turn us back; we are left stunned, faint all the day long. Our transgressions have been bound into a yoke; by the divine hand they are fastened together, weighing us down and sapping our strength. See, righteous God, how distressed we are; our stomachs churn, our hearts are wrung within us, because we have been very rebellious. God, have mercy; purge our sin, restore our souls, and make us whole.

Declaration of Forgiveness

Leader: Were it not for God's compassion, the acts of repentance and confession would have no value. It is precisely because of God's tangible mercy, evident nowhere so vividly as in Jesus' passion and death, that we are able to summon the courage to acknowledge our fault and ask forgiveness. To do so under any other conditions would be to take a risk of incomprehensible gravity. But the very pain that Jesus endured reveals to us a God who suffers not only for us, but with us. There is no more eloquent affirmation. Our sins are forgiven. Give God thanks.

People: We affirm this sacred declaration by adding our unison amen.

Call for the Offering

A little-known passage from the book of Proverbs commands our attention when we consider our call to stewardship. Chapter 19, verse 17, states that when we are kind to the poor, we make a loan to God, who will repay us for our actions. We invite you now to present your offering, understanding that you do not give it away but lend it to God; and that as human need is met and suffering alleviated, you will be repaid your kindness with compounded interest.

Prayer of Dedication

We bring our gifts, tender Father God, not because they will secure your forgiveness for the ills of our lives, but because we are forgiven.

We bring our gifts, stricken brother Jesus, not because they will secure our place in the circle of your family, but because we are your family. We bring these gifts, all-seeing Mother Spirit, not because we know what they need to accomplish, but because you do. Receive them and receive us who bring them, not because they or we are worthy, but because of your unparalleled love.

Prayer of Thanksgiving

Words of appreciation spring easily to our lips, O God, when our hearts are joyful, life is going our way, the sun is shining, and our achievements are rewarded. Gratitude comes hard when life seems unfair, we are down and depressed, our sky is overcast, and our efforts go unrewarded. Wean us from this dependency on the satisfaction of personal cravings, you who met the reviling mob by laying aside life itself as gift sufficient to our need. Loose in us the joy that deals generously with the triumphs of others, regards the splendor of small things, and is grateful simply to share in the sacred trust of life. So we will learn to thank you on good days and bad, during sunshine and gloom, in elegance or simplicity, a people who know they neither deserve nor have earned some reward; but are liberated by Christ to celebrate all life, all resources, all kinships, as gifts of your unfailing grace.

Second Sunday during Lent
⎯

Invocation

Surround us, ever-present and loyal Deity, with a growing sense of the constancy of your Word, just as Jesus—tempted by evil in the wilderness—leaned on the Word and was delivered. Remind us here that even when all we depend upon abandons us, the Word remains and that we ourselves, by its undergirding, may be victors. So shall we, approaching the cross, see ever more evidently the constancy of your Word made flesh, who lived and died and rose again, the imperishable victor.

Call to Praise (from Amos 5:14–15, 24)

Leader: Seek good, and not evil, that you may live;
People: And so the God of hosts will be with us, just as we have said.
Leader: Hate evil, and love good, and establish justice in the gate;

People: It may be that the God of hosts will be gracious to us.

Leader: But we must let justice roll down like waters,

People: And righteousness like an everflowing stream.

Leader: So will we offer true praise to God,

People: Who alone is worthy of our adoration.

Prayer of Praise

Who has a story that compares to ours? Is there another creator willing to be emptied for the life of the created? Has another god elected to abandon the serenity of heaven to take up residence with the likes of us? Has ever deity taught that there is no greater love than to lay down one's life for one's friends—and then gone out and done it? Has any other lover broken the bonds of time and death so that loved ones might live freed from their tyranny and gain the promise of eternal life? Only you, Holy One who is, and was, and is to be. Wherefore we cannot add to your story, but by praising and glorifying your name we may become a part of it. So say we all, Amen!

Call to Reconciliation

In the seventh chapter of Micah (verse 9), the prophet speaks of sin and forgiveness, addressing first the moral corruption of Israel, then the compassion of God. It is a passage of singular eloquence, in which we are struck not by Micah's groveling, but by the strength and dignity of his resolve to accept divine anger. Attend to the word of God, the first taken from verse 9: "I will bear the indignation of God against whom I have sinned, until God pleads my cause and executes judgement against me. God will bring me forth to the light. I shall behold God's deliverance." Join me now as we adopt together the spirit of Micah's confession.

Prayer of Confession (based on Romans 7:15–25)

In the depths of our souls, Holy God, we search for light but find only shadow. With the apostle Paul we cry, in frustration, that while we can will what is right, we cannot always do it. We fail to do the good we mean to do and commit the wrong we mean to avoid. Who, indeed, can deliver us from these bodies over which death so easily exerts its reign? Intervene then, merciful Magistrate, in the lives and affairs of us who desire to live according to your purpose but are helpless to do so except your Holy Spirit intercede to teach and guide us. Let your light shine into our gloom, your cleansing judgment purge us, your forgiveness heal and restore us, that we may be as loving and serving as you desire us to be: with all our heart and mind and soul and strength.

Declaration of Forgiveness (based on Micah 7:18-19

Leader: In verses 18 and 19, the concluding lines of his prophecy, Micah speaks assuringly of the faithfulness of God: "Who is a God like you, pardoning iniquity and passing over the transgression of the remnant of your possession? You do not retain anger forever, because you delight in showing mercy. you will again have compassion on us and tread our iniquities underfoot. You will cast all our sins into the depths of the sea."

People: We affirm this sacred declaration by adding our unison Amen.

Call for the Offering

Measured against the standards of the world, we are among the most privileged people who have ever lived, at this or any other time. And this is true even for those of us who, because of the untold wealth of our society, think of ourselves as possessing only modest resources. We can claim to be deprived only against the backdrop of the overabundance of our nation. We need also to remind ourselves, from time to time, that God has something more in mind for us to do with these privileges than hoard them for the satisfaction of personal cravings. Let concern for the whole family of humanity now summon our generosity and guide our hands in the morning offering.

Prayer of Dedication

We hear, Compassionate One, the wailing of hungry children. We hear the silence of lives whose only defining quality is emptiness. We hear the cries of wrenching pain. We hear the mute petitions of those whose prison of ignorance awaits the liberating key of knowledge. We hear the muffled pleas of prisoners of conscience whose only crime is a refusal to accede to tyranny. Into this gaping hole of human need we pour our offering which, were it all there is, would accomplish little; but we do so with confidence, because we are secure in the affirmation of your love that makes miracles of small gifts, and by tokens of earnestness transform the world.

Prayer of Thanksgiving

Surrounded by vice, O God, we are summoned to virtue. Tempted by opportunity for easy gratification, we are commanded to practice restraint and strive for the high ground. Were we left to our own resources, which of us could hope to survive? Our best effort seems never of itself to be good enough, no matter how righteously we will ourselves to live. With gratitude, therefore, we acknowledge that we are not left alone but receive from you all that is needful, if we but yield to your direction. Then thanks, you holy Majesty, for the light of your law; thanks for the chastising trump of the prophet's cry; and thanks, most of all, for your spirit's yearning within and among us, lighting our path and directing our way, through Christ our Redeemer, who wills always our confirmation as citizens of God's domain and who lay down his life to secure it.

Third Sunday during Lent
—

Invocation

From all that preoccupies us, God both judging and forebearing, we draw apart to submit to our Lenten self-appraisal: to reflect on the mystery of the events that unfold before us, plumb our souls' deeps in search of all that enables us to receive them, and name and expel all that hinders us. Will you, merciful One, assume command of our time and our labor, that this hour of worship and reflection may be more yours than ours, and we be more your people than our own.

Call to Praise (from Isaiah 55:6–7)

Leader: We will seek you, O God, while you may be found,
People: We will call on you while you are near.
Leader: We will forsake the ways of wickedness,
People: And abandon unrighteous thoughts.
Leader: We will return to your presence, so that mercy may be granted us,

People: To you who are our God and will abundantly pardon.
Leader: Then will we know divine mercy,
People: And sing your praises, Most Holy One.

Prayer of Praise (in observance of Race Relations Sunday/Black History Month)

We speak your praise, O God of the nations, whose creation is rich beyond our imagining; who calls into being the families of life and gives to each a splendor uniquely its own; who invites us to wonder at the wealth of earth that washes over us in myriad waves of sight and sound; who proclaims, by the act of creating, the mystery of worth, challenging and chastising us for our narrowness of vision; who proclaims in love the unity of the human family, taking us by surprise with sisters and brothers wondrously diverse and beyond counting. Your creation is truly beautiful, O Lavish Spirit, and wonder-filled the life you give us to share together.

Call to Reconciliation

A central ingredient of the season of Lent is the recognition that we are unworthy of the love that God showers on us, and least of all worthy to be the recipients of that love as it pours down from the cross. Of all the seasons of the year, therefore, we ought during this one to attend most closely to the office of confession, lest we find ourselves standing at the cross ill-prepared to be there. Let us raise our voices to God in common confession.

Prayer of Confession (in observance of Race Relations Sunday/Black History Month)

We know, O God of justice, what you require of us in relation to our sisters and brothers of every race. With heavy hearts, we confess our failure to abide by your precepts. We do not work with diligence to end racism in our town. How then can we demand it of our nation or criticize the conduct of foreign governments, or decry the injustice of separatism, the abuse of empire, the travesty of genocide? Deliver us from the hypocrisy that allows us to see ourselves the example for others, when history demands that we should fall on our knees and confess our shame. Forgive us, too, merciful Judge, that because we claim to speak for you, others—seeing our faults—mistrust your justice that was promised in law and prophecy and embodied in Jesus Christ, in whose name we pray.

Declaration of Forgiveness

Leader: In the first letter of John 2:1–2 this reassurance is offered to the early church: "My little children, I am writing these things to you so that you may not sin. But if anyone does sin, we have an advocate with God, Jesus Christ the righteous; and he is the atoning sacrifice for our sins, and not for ours only but also for the sins of the whole world." Even now, in this season when our failures and inadequacies most preoccupy us, we are reminded forcefully of the expansive mercy of God.

People: We affirm this sacred declaration by adding our unison Amen.

Call for the Offering

We are no more justified in concluding that poverty is a consequence of sloth than we are in concluding that an old woman trapped in the terror of violent social upheaval is paying the penalty for an inadequate lifestyle. From a scriptural perspective, social suffering is an indictment of the failure of human beings to fashion and maintain the kind of societies that capture the intention and participation of God. We may not be able to solve all the problems or heal all the pain, but we can help to underwrite the building of genuine community by the exercise of genuine generosity. The offering is one avenue for doing so, in the support of which we are now invited to participate.

Prayer of Dedication

Unlike your love for us, God of consummate affection, or your compassion for your creation, or your zeal for justice, the gifts we bring are driven by finite motives: given openly, but with doubt; earnestly, but fenced about by personal agendas; compassionately, but with our guard up, lest we give more than we mean. Thank you for accepting our gifts in spite of our doubt, our reservations, our guardedness. Take them and spend them as prodigally as your Son spent his love on us. Then we will take pleasure in our giving, as we rejoice in him.

Prayer of Thanksgiving (in observance of Race Relations Sunday/Black History Month

Creator of wondrous diversity: we yield our gratitude for the richness of life; for diversity of color no less stunning in human skin than fall leaves and spring wildflowers; for multitudes of language by which peoples voice their ideas and ideals, hopes and histories, failures and faith; for multiform cultures, these cradles of art and civilization, of customs and values, that challenge our minds, arouse our emotions, and brighten our souls. What splendor is here; what riches surround us; what opportunity engages us. Let us then seize the moment that is ours, O Ground of our being, our lives a celebration of your creativity, our gratitude a witness to your mercy, our actions an embodiment of your affection for all your peoples.

Fourth Sunday during Lent
—

Invocation

Caught between the cradle and the cross, O God, we grapple with the events of your history and struggle to know our place within its surge and flow. For there is here both meaning and mystery, constraining us to comprehend what we can and trust to you for the rest. Only let us know now that you are with us in this sacred enterprise, to guide and mentor our labor, so we miss not your final goal.

Call to Praise (from Psalm 34:1–3)

Leader: We will bless our Sovereign at all times;
People: God's praise will continually fill our mouths.
Leader: Our souls make their boast in God;
People: Let those who are afflicted hear and rejoice.
Leader: O magnify with me the One Who Is;
People: Let us exalt God's name together!

Prayer of Praise

From the ways of self-deception and self-indulgence, O God of the narrow way, we turn aside for an hour to herald your majesty, the mere presence of which judges us and finds us wanting. How shall we not despair, to confess—as we must—the pain that we cause by our failure to live as members of the household of the redeemed? Yet here is mystery, Holy Judge: that as we stand to acknowledge our shame, your forbearance reaches out to embrace us. Then praise for your healing compassion, that restores our commitment to decency in the face of corruption and champions rectitude against the challenge of avarice. We will praise you, Creator Spirit, before one another, our town, and the whole world!

Call to Reconciliation

In Psalm 1, in singularly uncompromising language, the psalmist rehearses a central tenet of biblical faith: that God's call is to righteousness. Listen! "Happy are those who do not follow the advice of the wicked, or take the paths that sinners tread, or sit in the seat of scoffers; but their delight is in God's law, on which they meditate day and night. The wicked are not so, but are like chaff that the wind drives away. Therefore the wicked will not stand in the judgment, nor sinners find a place in the congregation of the righteous; for God watches over the ways of the righteous, but the way of the wicked will perish." Let us, by our confession, seek a place in the congregation of the righteous, that God may watch over us, also.

Prayer of Confession

Even during Lent, God of holiness, it is difficult to admit the wrong that afflicts us. From our earliest days we have been taught to think of ourselves and of what we do as good. Nor does our training make it easy to say otherwise. The lesser promptings of our natures teach us to feign ignorance, to deny responsibility, to protest innocence. When openly accused, we erupt in angry self-defense. Yet our lies are with us. Our own consciences accuse us. Like Peter, we have betrayed. With James and John, we yield to sleep when the Savior needs our wakefulness. Like Sapphira and Ananias, we withhold and make false claims that serve our greed. Oh, the blight of our souls is bitter. Take away our pretense, give us honest hearts, and heal what warps and breaks us, if not for our sakes, for the sake of Christ.

Declaration of Forgiveness (from Psalm 34:4–6, 18, 22)

Leader: I sought my God, who answered me and delivered me from all my fears. Look to God and be radiant; so your faces need never know shame. This poor soul cried, and my Maker heard me and saved me from all my troubles. God is near to the brokenhearted, saving those whose spirits are crushed and redeeming the servant's life. None who take refuge in God will be condemned.

People: We affirm this sacred declaration by adding our unison Amen.

Call for the Offering

We Christians are often so preoccupied with striving for goodness that we forget how ready God is to accept mixed motives. If the incarnation means anything, it means that God knows, from first-hand experience, how easily the human will is pulled in two directions at once; how, in seeking good, we inadvertently do harm; or—more mysteriously— how we may do good even though moved by less than generous intentions. In this spirit, I invite you to bring your offering, knowing that while our motives and actions may be imperfect, God can make the results sublime.

Prayer of Dedication

We are grateful, God, that you know our anxieties and struggles and accept our mixed motives, so that even we who give uncertainly may give with consciences unafraid; and by our gifts, nourish your ministry of word, sacrament, and mercy to a hungering world.

Prayer of Thanksgiving

Who shall teach us, God of grace, to name your goodness? For we know it in ourselves more surely than any other can declare it to us. And who, more than we, can enumerate your blessings? For we have benefits beyond counting. Surveyed against the mass of humanity, our scarcity is abundance, our poverty unlimited wealth. So we, of all people, are bound to thank you for the unspeakable blessings of our lives; who showers us not only with prosperity, but invites us to make it useful in the service of humanity, thereby to acquire unspeakable riches of the spirit as well. Then thanks be to God in our Savior Jesus Christ, who in giving teaches us to be givers; who in blessing us prepares us to become a blessing. Amen, O God: so may it be!

Fifth Sunday during Lent

Invocation

Now come the frightful days of passion, our God, when the Word made flesh turns steadfastly toward Jerusalem, knowing well its complex history as both the core of Israel's ardor and the death trap of prophets. We wish not to look on these things, less so the more terrible ones to follow, until your child's flesh is broken on the tree and grace has gone out of the world. Steady us on our journey, O God of dreadful mercy, and reassure us once again that there lies before him—and us—both conclusion and renewal.

Call to Praise (from Psalm 30:4–5)

Leader: Sing praises to our Redeemer, you faithful ones,

People: And give thanks to God's holy name.

Leader: Whose anger is but for a moment,

People: But whose favor is for a lifetime.

Leader: Weeping may linger for the night,

People: But joy comes with the morning.

Leader: God will turn our mourning into dancing,

People: So that our souls will sing for joy and never be silent!

Prayer of Praise

We cry your praise, our God, who calls us through this Lenten journey to stand wondering at the foot of the cross, where Jesus acts out his own teaching: that no greater love can be shown than to give one's life for a friend. Knowing we have not fulfilled the obligation of true friends, how can we even begin to think ourselves worthy of his death? What a wonder is here, O Source of redeeming grace: that the one of whose death we are not worthy, by dying, delivers us from death and makes us worthy of the gift of life. Praise God for incomprehensible mystery! Praise God for unspeakable love! Praise God for the gift of life out of death!

Call to Reconciliation

In this passage from the Letter of James 4:7–10, we find our call to confession: "Submit yourselves . . . to God. Draw near to God and God will draw near to you. Cleanse your hands, you sinners, and purify your hearts, you double-minded. Lament and mourn and weep. Let your laughter be turned into mourning and your joy into dejection. Humble yourselves before God, and God will exalt you." Mindful of James's admonition, let us give voice to our humility and penitence.

Prayer of Confession (based on the prophecy of Amos)

Eternal God, who turned aside Amos from following the flock and drove him to the high place at Bethel, there to sound the trumpet voice of judgment: we hear, as did ancient Israel, the cry of God that bares our pretense, blights our smugness, and names our transgressions, not alone in our cities, but in our sanctuaries. As we worship you now, let your word ring round our ears again, proclaiming to our own time the intended day of the Sovereign's teeming justice and abundant mercy. Then may our worship be true and our service pure.

Declaration of Forgiveness (based on Romans 8:1–4)

Leader: By these words from his letter to the Romans, the apostle Paul reassures us: "There is therefore now no condemnation for those who are in Christ Jesus. For the law of the Spirit of life in Christ Jesus has set you free from the law of sin and death. For God has done what the law . . . could not do: sending his own son in the likeness of sinful flesh . . . , he condemned sin . . . so that the just requirement of the law might be fulfilled in us, who walk not according to the flesh, but according to the Spirit."

People: We affirm this sacred declaration by adding our unison Amen.

Call for the Offering

Jesus reminds us (Luke 6:43–45) that as one can tell the character of the tree by the fruit it bears, one can judge the character of persons by the quality of their actions. We do well to remind ourselves that as God judges us by the quality of our mercy, others will judge God by the quality of our generosity. I encourage you to be of that understanding as you bring your offering.

Prayer of Dedication

Into the chasm of human need, gracious Divinity, we broadcast the substance of our concern, represented by these gifts and all that we mean by giving them. We do not know the scope of all they may accomplish, but you do. We do not feel the suffering they may alleviate, but you do. We cannot measure the true dimensions of their power, but you can. So we entrust them to your wisdom, confident that whatever good they may do will be insured by your mercy that surpasses our understanding.

Prayer of Thanksgiving

We turn in thanksgiving to you, Author of our history, as your commanding child, charged with the energy of divine mission, turns his face steadfastly toward Jerusalem, there to assault the practitioners of thievery, the strongholds of privilege, the archives of self-righteousness, and sweep them aside in one holy gesture of restoration. Withal, he will lose his life. But how thankful we are for his coming to tutor us that compassion, not power, will triumph; that justice forges the consequences of history; that sacrifice will break the back of the oppressor. Then tributes and triumphals, you amazing divinity, who imposes glory on the chaos of evil, and ordains victory out of the jaws of death.

Palm/Passion Sunday

Last Sunday preceding Easter
Liturgical Color: Purple or Red

In the framework of Lent and Easter, Palm Sunday comes as a jarring contradiction. Having spent five weeks in a confessional mood, it is disconcerting just seven days before the death of Jesus to suddenly shift to triumphal celebration, knowing full well that in a few days we will need to shift right back again. Many church folk seem unsure how to approach the day; and some appear downright embarrassed, as if to ask, "What are we *doing?*" The contradiction is more apparent than real, actually, and it exists for two reasons. First, Palm Sunday is contradictory by theological intention. But second, it is doubly contradictory for our generation because we have inherited a long-standing confusion about its language.

The first contradiction is generally recognized. Jesus came to Jerusalem to assert his presumed "royal" nature. This theme is a central motif throughout the Passion narrative. But Jesus' definition of what constitutes royalty differed fundamentally from that of the society he sought to address. At their Passover observance, or Last Supper, Jesus cautioned the disciples about the popularly held view (Luke 22:25–27) and asserts that he—the acknowledged "king"—is in fact among them as a servant. Luke quotes Jesus as referring to "benefactors" (v. 25), a title conferred on hellenistic kings, as an illustration of the contrast. On reviewing the accusations against Jesus, Pilate asks, "Are you the King of the Jews?" (Matthew 27:11; Mark 15:2; Luke 23:3; John 18:33). The theme turns derisive as Pilate's soldiers robe Jesus in royal purple, fabricate a crown of thorns, and bow in mock obeisance; and in the contemptuous chants of the crowd when he is led out for crucifixion. The supreme touch of irony is saved for last, however, and takes the form of the taunting sign hung on Jesus' cross. From a sociopolitical point of view—a "worldly" view—it is a clear case of failed rebellion. Jesus and his followers were stupid or, worse, suffering from delusions. They challenged the established powers and lost. Case closed.

Not so fast, urge the Gospels. John's account (18:36–38), while the most embellished, does us the service of spelling out the implications. Pressed by Pilate as to why he does not mount a more vigorous defense against the charges of the mob, Jesus responds with revealing precision: "My realm is not of this world; *if it were, my servants would fight*" (emphasis added). Pilate tries again: "So you are a king?" Again Jesus shifts the ground of the discourse: "For this I was born . . . to bear witness to the truth. Everyone who is of the truth hears my voice." Ever the philosophical sycophant—not to mention frustrated judge—Pilate teases, "What is truth?"

The point is clear: Jesus' orientation is to a transcendence that neither Pilate nor the mob is able to grasp. He rode into Jerusalem on a donkey because it was more important to adhere to the ancient messianic prophecies (Isaiah 62:10–11; Zechariah 9:9) than to excite the prejudices of a society blinded by the force of arms. The entire moment was intended to distinguish between the historic methods of God and the prevailing worldview of brute force as the ground of authority.

But something equally profound is at work here, which, I believe, leaves us slightly abashed by Palm Sunday even after we have redefined messianic sovereignty, namely: our failure to realize that the event was "triumphal" only in the theatrical sense, never in substance. I am deeply indebted for this realization to Marvin H. Pope, Louis M. Rabinowitz Emeritus Professor of Semitic Languages and Literature at Yale University and a member of the Old Testament Committee for both the Revised Standard and New Revised Standard Versions of the Bible. Pope clears away the contradiction created by our perception of Palm Sunday as a victory procession that concluded in abject political defeat. (See Pope's "Hosanna—What It Really Means," *Bible Review* 4, no. 2 [April 1988].)

The problem, Pope demonstrates, is one of language. The central word of Jesus' entry into Jerusalem was "hosanna," a term that we equate with "alleluia" and use as an acclamation or greeting. Pope challenges this assumption by noting first that "hosanna," a Hebrew word, appears in the New Testament, a text the earliest surviving manuscripts

of which are in Greek. Why, Pope asks, didn't the Gospel writers translate it, like everything else they both wrote and quoted, into Greek. The
reason, he believes, is because they did not understand the word either.
"Hosanna" is composed of two Hebrew elements, *hosha* and *na,* the
meanings of which are very clear. *Hosha* means "save," and *na* means
"please." Pope provides a rich body of background too detailed to
describe here; the reader is encouraged to refer to the article. For purposes of this introduction it is sufficient to quote Pope's precise transla-
tion of the cry of the Palm Sunday crowd (Matthew 21:9) as: "Help [or
save], please, O Son of David. Blessed in the name of God is he who
comes. Help [or save], please, O Most High."

Pope's insight peels away from Palm Sunday some of the accretions
that became attached to it because of this semantic confusion. If we
imagine the Palm Sunday crowd pleading, "Save, please, O Son of
David," the triumphal entry fits logically into the Passion narrative and
makes coherent the passage from the descent of the Mount of Olives to
Golgotha.

I provide this background in part to apprise the reader that the Palm
Sunday material following has been influenced by Pope's interpretation
and therefore departs to some degree from many of the traditional set-
tings. I have done so, however, in the firm belief that it better captures
the true character of that remarkable day and therefore better serves
the liturgical needs of the community of faith.

The earliest account of a Palm Sunday liturgy was that of a Spanish
lady, written during the fourth century and included in a detailed
account of Holy Week ceremonies in Jerusalem. In the West, however,
the palm festival apparently was not introduced until some time later.
Pope Leo I, who died in 460 C.E., observed *Dominica passionis,* or Passion Sunday, the tone of which was not one of rejoicing but of mourning. The first mention of the blessing of palms does not appear until the
sixth century. During the Middle Ages, the observance became increasingly popular.

In a strange twist of liturgical history, however, the palm motif was
abolished during the Reformation of the sixteenth century, and the
mood of the "Sunday next before Easter," as it was then styled, once
again appears to have centered on the humiliation and passion of Jesus.
Clearly, however, the suppression of the *Dominica palmarum* was unsuc-

cessful, as evidenced by its current observance throughout much of the church—further evidence that what people treasure has greater influence on the form of our liturgies, finally, than what religious hierarchies dictate.

Prayers and Liturgical Readings

Invocation

Now begins to break upon our ears the distant triumph song. Now we hear the muffled shouts of apostolic excitement and the rustle of approaching palms. Now the rising swirl of dust announces the emerging procession. Prepare us, God, to receive your coming triumphal Child, astride a humble beast—this contradictory vision, this metaphor of paradox—by which meekness and humility begin the work of dismantling pretentious power and the true quality of majesty is revealed.

Call to Praise

Leader: They brought the colt to Jesus, and after throwing their garments on its back, they set Jesus upon it. As he rode along, people spread their clothing on the road. As he was approaching at the descent of the Mount of Olives, the whole multitude of disciples began to rejoice and praise God joyfully with a loud voice for all the mighty works they had seen, saying,

People: "Hosanna, Son of David. Blessed in the name of God is he who comes. Help, please, O Most High."

Leader: Let us who also are disciples gather by the roadside and join our voices with the others of the crowd.

People: We will lift our voices in praise and supplication.

Prayer of Praise

What a wonder is this, that the holy Sovereign, child of the Almighty, straddles a donkey, toes dragging in the dust, and rides into the nation's capital, while his hardly noble followers and the ungenteel riffraff carry on and wave tree branches in the air and drop their clothing on the street for the dumb beast to trod into the dirt. What amazement is here, that anyone should take seriously this processional comedy, this public embarrassment, when there is important business to attend to. Yet we must know: why do they turn aside and shout? Why do some eyes shine with joy and others brim with tears? What do they want? What does he bring? Teach us, God of paradox, of their yearning that parallels our own. Waken us to the promise of their—and our—deliverance. Then open our reticent mouths in shouts and fill our hands with palms to wave at the mystery of his sacrifice and our enrichment. Take our coats, and our cloaks as well, to pave the highway of the Savior's coming. And the praise and glory be yours.

Call to Reconciliation

If we propose to join the disciples as they mark Jesus' entry into Jerusalem, we ought also to have the humility to join them in admitting that, ere the week is over, we too will fall away and abandon Jesus to face alone his torment and passion. Be reminded that none of them, nor any of us, stood finally at his side; and raise your voice with mine in confession of our failing.

Prayer of Confession

In humility, Sovereign Jesus, you rode into Jerusalem astride a donkey, giving flesh to prophecies the city had ignored and vindicating the prophets who were scorned in the speaking of them. In humility we greet you, whose coming commends us even as we are unable to commend ourselves. For we are unworthy, yet you declare us worthy; we are undeserving, yet you validate us; we corrupt ourselves, yet you conspire to make us incorruptible. Then ride on, unpretentious Majesty, to your death, by which we die; and your resurrection, by which we rise triumphant. And with your apostles, we will trumpet both your power and our need, crying: Help, God! Blessed indeed in the name of God is the One who comes!

Declaration of Forgiveness

The evangelist Matthew provides a lengthy record of Jesus' teaching after his entry into Jerusalem that first Palm Sunday, including the parable of the marriage feast. It is not the kind of story we normally choose as evidence of God's forgiveness. But listen again. When the usual guests fail to respond, the king orders his servants into the streets, instructing them to "invite to the marriage feast as many as you find." Then Jesus concludes the parable with these wonderfully encouraging words: "And those servants went out into the streets and gathered all whom they found, both bad and good; so the wedding hall was filled with guests." There is a place for us all, dear friends, both the good and the bad, at God's banquet table.

Call for the Offering

If we listen carefully to what Jesus teaches, we will understand that the measure of giving is never determined by the size of the gift but by the generosity of the giver. Shortly after entering Jerusalem, Jesus spent much of his time in the temple. One day, sitting with his disciples across from the temple treasury (Mark 12:41–44), he taught them—and us—a vital lesson. Observing a poor woman dropping two copper coins into the temple treasury, he commended her highly, while declaring that the far larger contributions of her wealthy neighbors were pale shadows cast by the light of her spiritual extravagance. Let each of us, then, with prayerful reflection, offer to God whatever gift we believe will earn the commendation of Christ.

Prayer of Dedication

We join the disciples, O God, to trumpet our hosannas to Jesus as he rides in unpretentious triumph into Jerusalem. But if we express ourselves only in words, we make no greater witness than the stones that Jesus said would cry out in place of the crowd, if it were silenced. So by these gifts we mean to say more, to supply flesh to our ardor, praying that they will shout your triumph in places where our voices cannot reach, by extending down some new street, through some new household, across some new town, the redeeming love of Christ.

Thanksgiving

Only amazement will satisfy this day, you God of endless surprises, who sent our redeemer ambling into the seat of political and economic power on the back of a small beast, there to proclaim that such power is a fleeting commodity, while humility and compassion secure the victory. We thank you for the lesson of Christ's glory who—though one with you—took the form of a servant and joined himself with us in human suffering and death. Then receive our acclamation, even as the hosannas ebb and fade and we, like those other disciples who surrounded him that day, show our true selves by abandoning him to his hour of torment and desolation. For only then, terrible God, can we grasp in full gratitude the infinity of your compassion and the scope of our restitution. And thanks be to God!

Maundy Thursday

Thursday before Easter Sunday
Liturgical Color: Purple

"Maundy" is derived from the Latin *mandatum,* meaning "command." The term springs from Jesus' words on the occasion of the Last Supper. The imperative is less clear in the synoptics, in which Matthew and Luke stray only in minimal detail from Mark's model: the bread, Jesus said, was his body; the cup of wine, his blood poured out for many. His followers were instructed to remember and repeat this event as a memorial. Out of this tradition grew the sacrament of the eucharist, variously titled the Last Supper, the Lord's Supper, or Holy Communion. Clearly it was a seminal moment in the doctrinal development of the early church.

John's account, unique in this as in many other phases of the Gospel narrative, makes no mention of the elements we now associate with the "last supper." John's Jesus first washes the feet of his disciples (an event absent from the other accounts) to hammer home the concept of servanthood as the genre of their calling. From there, however, John's Jesus engages in an extended, reflective sermon, in which a "new command," a fresh mandate, is clearly delineated. It is the requirement that the disciples love one another. "I give you a new commandment, that you love one another. Just as I have loved you, you should love one another. By this everyone will know that you are my disciples, if you have love for one another" (John 13:34–35).

Whether we choose to try to reconcile such differences in the accounts is rendered inconsequential in light of the clear intention of Jesus' words: his purpose is not to start a new liturgical tradition, but to establish a new covenant, a covenant that, in time, will frame the relationship between God and the entire world. The framing of such a covenant is a logical leap from the Hebraic grounding of Christian faith: in Genesis 12, God promises to make of Abram and Sarai a great nation, in consequence of which "all the families of the earth shall be blessed." The evidence of that covenant was to be the circumcision of Abraham (his new, covenantal name) and all their male progeny (Genesis 17), distinguishing them as over against all other families of humanity. The second chapter of this covenantal history occurred when God made a covenant with Israel at Sinai, for which the abiding evidence was the Law, by which Israel's moral character and spiritual responsibility are defined. Recall that this covenant was cut as the climatic event of the Exodus, Israel's liberation from human bondage, to the end that the nation be free to fulfill its sacred task as God's chosen people. And the signal event that prefigured the Exodus was Passover, a shared meal of explicit content that was to be rehearsed each year, as long as Israel has breath and wherever in the whole world Jews gather.

The crucifixion of Jesus, for which the signal prefiguring event was the Last Supper, places the Christian experience firmly in the line of this covenantal history. The crucifixion seals the covenant between God and the non-Jewish world. In brief, the promise to Abraham is fulfilled: because of ancient Israel's faithfulness, all nations of the world now may count themselves blessed. As Jews are called to live under the Law, which gives shape and direction to their life in community, Christians are called to live under grace, the liberating knowledge that God's self-giving love in Jesus Christ reaches out to embrace us in life, and beyond life. Now even death is denied the last word.

This liturgy of Maundy Thursday is designed to remind us of these central themes; to reenact with dramatic impact the final events of Jesus' life, bring them forcefully into the consciousness of the congregation, and remind us that we are branded by God's forgiving love.

The term *tenebrae* itself is a Latin term meaning darkness or shadows, and was adopted into Roman Catholic tradition in the early sixteenth century to depict the gloom that obscured the world because of the betrayal and crucifixion of Christ. The term applies equally to the garden where Jesus repaired with his disciples following the Passover celebration and the aftermath of the crucifixion, when the Gospels record that darkness descended for a period of three hours.

One element of the liturgy below is strange to many Protestant congregations—the ceremonial washing of feet. Drawn from John's account of the Last Supper, as noted above, the custom has long standing in the Roman Catholic and liturgical Protestant communions. The custom, significantly, requires greater humility on the part of the participating laity than of the pastor. Even the disciples found it so (read again the Johannine account): given human temperament, it is easier to be the washer than the washee! But it is theologically a profound gesture: God can serve us only if we allow ourselves to be served, to sit back and let it happen! I include it in this liturgy because it logically belongs here and because, once experienced, a congregation will apprehend, as it never has before, the meaning of grace.

The Maundy Thursday liturgy is most effective when begun at dusk, so that the darkness encircling the congregation at the end of the service is broken only by the light of a single "Christ candle." The timing is appropriate not only to the dinner hour of the Last Supper but to Jesus' later travail in the garden, prior to his betrayal. It is recommended that, as the event concludes, the congregation depart with only the Christ candle to light their way, except as concern for safety dictates. It is especially dramatic if the congregation honors the admonition to leave in complete silence and to maintain that silence as long as possible. During such a moment, the liturgy moves out of the sanctuary with the scattering congregation and takes command of the night. Few experiences, in my judgment, better set the stage for Good Friday.

A word about setting: the sanctuary should be set for the celebration of the eucharist or communion according to the custom of the parish. Somewhere prominently positioned on or around the table should be thirteen candles. Symbolism is enhanced if the candle representing Christ is slightly larger than the others. These candles should be lit at the start of the service and extinguished serially during the concluding portion of the liturgy, to represent the "falling away" of the disciples, until only the Christ Candle remains. The lectern or pulpit may be used for the Scripture readings following the eucharist, or a special reading stand may be added. If those reading are also to extinguish the candles, be sure to provide a pathway from lectern to candles and back that can be negotiated safely when only one or two candles are left. Sufficient light will also be necessary to read but should not shine into the eyes of congregants. Those who are irritated make poor candidates for spiritual engagement!

A Liturgy for Maundy Thursday

Invocation

Never is your holiness so evident, God of wonder, than when it bows to all that is unholy. Never is your mercy so profound as when it submits to all that is merciless. Never is your love so freighted with mystery as when it resigns itself to enmity's loathing. Nor never do your holiness, your mercy, and your love possess us so irresistibly as when they are sacrificed for us in the coming obedience unto death. Now show us your son's passion and suffering and prepare us to receive them in all their power, that in our rush to the tomb, we do not overlook the realities that brought him there.

Foot Washing

In some congregations, twelve representative members of the congregation are seated in the front of the room, while the pastor, representing Jesus, washes their feet by dipping them in a basin of water and drying them with a towel. Alternatively, any who wish to participate may gather in the front, where each in turn washes the feet of the next person until the circle has been completed. In either case, the person washing and the one whose feet are washed may rise afterward and extend signs of peace to each other.

Call to Praise

Leader: On this holy and dread night, the Child of God gathers his friends one last time.

People: We, too, are friends of Jesus. We will join the gathering also, to remember the history of Israel's liberation.

Leader: What a touch of irony is this: even as we remember, Jesus' own liberty is taken away.

People: It must not be. We will stand side-by-side to protect our friend.

Leader: No children, we must not, for we cannot. What Jesus does now, he alone can do and can do only as he is alone.

People: Then what is there left for us to do?

Leader: We can raise hearts and minds and voices in solemn praise of Christ's royal sacrifice.

People: Then let us do it, for the sake of God's glory and our own
          need.

A hymn of praise.

Prayer of Praise

We shudder with dread, holy God, to witness our Savior's love betrayed
by human lust and blind ambition. Now wait the graveclothes to shroud
your majesty, the crowds to shout approval of your death, the cross to
receive your flesh and we your mercy. In this, most of all, we praise
you: that your sacred life is judged fit price to secure our redemption,
and we—who are so ready to impose pain—are deemed worthy to
receive your pain as a gift. As you lay aside your power, we will praise
you. As you empty yourself to save us, we will adore you. At your dying,
we will weep for you and our tears will cry your glory. Now take your
cross, mighty Child of God, this bloody instrument of oppression that
means to break you, and transform it into the symbol by which all in the
world that is evil and corrupt are brought to task and their power shattered.

Call to Reconciliation

If we compare the inexpressible love of God in Christ that led to the cli-
mactic historic moment we are here to reenact with the quality of
mercy that we typically display toward others, we begin to fathom the
difference between God's holiness and our humanity. This, in turn,
brings us to our knees in humility, and in our humility, to confession. It
is not that we are always to be preoccupied with our sin. (Even Peter,
who is about to deny Jesus, will shortly learn the astonishing scope of
divine tolerance.) But it is to acknowledge, by naming our imperfec-
tions, that God alone is holy. It is a notion understood by people of faith
far into our human past, and, for that reason, we draw on their words—
from Psalm 25—for our antiphonal confession. Let us pray.

Prayer of Confession (based on Psalm 25:4–10)

Leader: Make us to know your ways, O God; teach us your paths.
Right: Lead us in your truth and teach us,
Left: For you are the God of our salvation;

Unison: For you we wait all day long.

Leader: Be mindful of your mercy and of your steadfast love, for they have been from of old.

Right: Do not remember the sins of our youth or our transgressions;

Left: Instead, remember us according to your steadfast love,

Unison: For your goodness' sake, O God.

Leader: Good and upright is our God;

Right: Wherefore sinners are instructed in virtue.

Left: God leads the humble in what is right,

Unison: And instructs the obedient in the holy way.

Leader: All the paths of God are steadfast love and faithfulness.

Right: God's friendship is for those who live in holy awe,

Left: For those who keep the divine covenant and decrees.

Unison: For your name's sake, O God, pardon our guilt, for it is great.

Declaration of Forgiveness

Leader: John the Evangelist reports (17:20–21, 24) that Jesus concluded the Last Supper with a lengthy prayer for his disciples, including this heartening passage: "I ask not only on behalf of these, but also on behalf of those who will believe in me through their word, that they may all be one. I desire that those also, whom you have given me, may be with me . . . to see my glory, which you have given me because you loved me before the foundation of the world." Those others to whom Jesus refers, friends, include you and me, who believe in Christ through the apostle's words, who Christ asks to have present with him in glory. All this, just hours before his betrayal! Hear, friends, and know the awesome compassion of our God.

People: We hear, and hearing add our voices to the hymn of thanksgiving of all who have known and will yet know Christ as Savior and Ruler.

A hymn of Thanksgiving.

Call for the Offering

If we come to witness the passion of Christ, let us expect to be changed. If we follow to the garden, let us anticipate that our eyes will be opened to the violence of humanity. If we presume to stand at the foot of the cross, let us expect to learn the meaning of sacrifice as God conceives it and bids us live it. For as long as we do not, life—in this place—goes unredeemed and Christ is still nailed to the cross. Where we embrace these things, then redemption is here among us and the very gates of hell cannot prevail against us. Let our offering reveal our expectations.

During the Dedication, let the bread and wine of the eucharist be carried through the congregation and placed on the table, in preparation for the celebration of the Last Supper.

Prayer of Dedication

We bring to your table, Christ Jesus, the gifts of our hands, by which we bear witness to both your grace in our lives and our intention to make that grace evident in the lives of those who may be touched by your love working through us. We bring also these gifts of bread and wine, born of the earth of which we ourselves are constituted and made ready for us by the labor of human hands. In these gifts the stuff of earth now flames with the grace of heaven, and we know in our own flesh the spirit of the living God.

Celebration of communion according to the tradition of the congregation.

Prayer of Thanksgiving

With grateful hearts, merciful God, we witness the arrival of Jesus in Jerusalem, not because he bears the marks of grandeur, but because he comes to save us. For we know, as his disciples could not, that his journey was not over when he gained the city to sit with them to break bread. Now he must descend its avenues of betrayal and injustice and exit again its gates, where the gentle beast that bore him is replaced by the beam of a cross. So we thank you for the crucifixion we are about to witness, not that it was unique, but that it was so very common; that as

Christ accepted birth in a stable, he now embraces death at the public execution of criminals; that all of life, from its meanest to its most sublime, might finally know the determination of its God.

The Office of Tenebrae

After each reading, two candles, representing some of the disciples, will be extinguished, followed by a moment of silent meditation. At the conclusion of the service, only the Christ candle will remain.

> Psalm 55:1–8, 16–19
> Lamentations 3:1–9, 16–24
> Psalm 88:1–12
> Luke 22:39–53
> Psalm 143:1–8
> Hebrews 4:12–5:5

Leader: Almighty God, look with mercy upon the whole family of humanity, for whom our Savior Jesus Christ accepted betrayal, deliverance into the hands of sinners, and death on the cross; whose suffering reveals to us the depth of heaven's love; who now lives and reigns with you and our Mother Spirit, one God, forever.

People: Amen.

The Prayer of Jesus (whispered in unison)

Following the prayer, let the congregation depart in complete silence, maintaining silence for as long as possible.

Good Friday

Friday preceding Easter Sunday
Liturgical Color: Black

By scholarly consensus "Good Friday" is considered a corruption of "God's Friday," the day observed as the anniversary of the crucifixion of Jesus. Called by more names than any other event in the church year (four in Greek, six or seven in Latin), its origin yet remains obscure. It may have originated by chance with Jewish Christians, habituated to an annual celebration of *pesach,* the Passover, on the fourteenth of the Jewish month of Nisan, with the fifteenth to the twenty-first observed as "days of unleavened bread." Among the Gentile churches, on the other hand, there appears at the outset to have been no yearly cycle of festivals at all. These events were adopted into the church through time, as they served particular liturgical and doctrinal needs. (See the introductions to Christmas and Easter.)

From its origin, Good Friday was observed as the most rigorous of fasts. After the fourth century, even the eucharist was prohibited and, in Spain, churches were closed as a sign of mourning! Through most early liturgies, with influences continued into the present (for example, reflections on the "seven last words" of Jesus) every effort was made to deepen the impression of profound and universal grief. Good Friday and Holy Saturday (the day following) are the only days when black serves as a liturgical color, with one exception: if the Easter Vigil is observed, the appropriate color is white.

In many communions, it is customary to simplify the liturgy for Good Friday. Those with an interest in the drama of worship will immediately recognize here an opportunity to use such a change was a dramatic device, the more profoundly to engage congregants in the solemn quality of the day and it substance. Because of this history, I have again provided a complete liturgy (with some modeling after traditional forms) rather than prayers and responses appropriate to a full service of worship.

This liturgy has greatest impact if conducted in a sanctuary stripped of all color and of all symbols customarily present, with the exception of a cross standing alone on the communion table. Leaving candles unlit or removing them altogether further enhances the uncustomary somberness of the room. Subdued lighting, sufficient only to allow the congregation to read its part, deepens the solemn tone of betrayal and sorrow. A brief can also be made for conducting the service without music of any kind. We Americans have an inordinate fear of silence. For many of us, the constant presence of sound—one wants to say noise—seems to be all that stands between us and emotional consternation! Too often, I suspect, the incidental music of services is really a cover that both hides the sounds of activity during worship and diverts us from the holy labor of turning inward to confront ourselves as we prepare to be confronted by God.

It seems unlikely that there was music on Golgotha; and we step closer to these dreadful events, perhaps, if we receive them with something approximating the day's true atmosphere. Furthermore, setting these conditions for Good Friday doubles the dramatic impact of Holy Week's climax, because of the contrasting explosion of color and brilliance that attends Easter Sunday. If worship is drama, then this is among the best theater we can generate to help our people feel the concluding events of Christ's life, as well as recite them.

A Good Friday Liturgy

A reading of Isaiah 53:1–9, concluding with:

Leader: This is the word of God.
People: Thanks be to God.

Call to the People (from Lamentations 1:12; Romans 5:6–8)

Leader: Is it nothing to you, all you who pass by?
People: Look and see if there is any sorrow like his sorrow.
Leader: Rarely will anyone die for a righteous person—though perhaps for a good person someone might actually dare to die.

People: But God's love for us is proven in that, while we were still
            sinners, Christ died for us.

Unison: Behold the Lamb of God, who takes away the sins of the
            world!

The Reproaches

Leader: Oh my people, how have I hurt you and in what way have I
            offended you? Testify now against me. In gentleness and sym-
            pathy I entered the world, to bear what you have borne and
            to share the melancholy mortality of all living things; but you
            erected a cross and bid me hang upon it.

People: O God, holy in majesty, have mercy on us.

Leader: I called you to me, taught you the ways that lead to eternal
            life, healed and nurtured you, and promised to remain with
            you always; but you subjected me to a travesty of justice and
            sentenced me to die.

People: O God, holy in majesty, have mercy on us.

Leader: I set you apart to be a holy people, to bring hope and light to
            the world, and promised you the abiding presence of the
            Holy Spirit; but you deny me still and bow before the idola-
            tries of greed and power.

People: O God, holy in majesty, have mercy on us.

Leader: I continue to visit you daily, harking to the voices of pain that
            cry out for justice and mercy and recalling in you the sacred
            power of love; but daily you ignore the suffering and leave
            me hanging still upon the cross.

People: O God, holy in majesty, have mercy on us.

Leader: And still I call to you, bending to you as a mother to its child,
            beckoning toward a future where life knows no boundary
            and death holds no sway; but your desire is for the things that
            cannot save, while the way that leads to life lies empty.

People: O God, holy in majesty, have mercy on us.

Call to Reconciliation

Hanging on the cross, scorned by his accusers, ridiculed by the criminal
at his side, Jesus still reached out in compassion. In the presence of such
charity, only the callous would turn away. If we are, as we claim, Christ's

sisters and brothers, let us approach him now and seek forgiveness for all wherein we have contributed to the evil that hung him there. Let us pray.

Prayer of Confession

Hear, dying Sovereign, how with a single voice we lament your dying, and name the sorrow we endure because of our sin. Yet in ways private and corporate, visible and secret, we nourish the evil we claim to deplore and kill the virtue we profess to admire. We list the things that inhibit greater self-sacrifice, denying that they are mostly of our own creation. With embarrassment, we admit that the shadows around us are our own invention, but cling to them because they are more comfortable than the light. Take hold of us, Jesus, even at your dying, and be that example of forgiveness that so compels our remorse that we may never again build crosses, deny justice, withhold mercy.

Declaration of Forgiveness (Isaiah 53:11b–12)

Leader: "The righteous one, my servant, shall make many righteous, and shall bear their iniquities. Therefore I will allot him a portion with the great, because he poured out himself to death, and was numbered with the transgressors; yet he bore the sin of many, and made intercession for those same transgressors." Bear this mystery, friends: the Christ who now hangs on the cross before us, even as he dies, prays for our redemption.

People: What wonder is here? Thanks be to God!

The Accounts of the Crucifixion

These passages contain the traditional "seven words" of Christ on the cross. A moment of silence will follow each, to allow for personal reflection and meditation. Please rise for each reading and be seated following for the meditation. Each reading will be preceded by:

Leader: God be with you.
People: And also with you.
Leader: A reading from the Holy Gospel According to [author].
People: Glory to you, O God.

Each reading will be followed with:

Leader: This is the Gospel of our Savior.
People: Praise to you, O Christ.

Matthew 27:24–26, 32–50
Luke 23:32–49
John 19:17–30

Litany for Good Friday

Leader: Our Savior enters now the valley of the shadow of death, where all the powers of evil wait in savage glee.
People: Gracious God, have mercy on your holy Child, who dies for love of us.
Leader: Our Savior submits now to the worst that all the powers of earth and Hell can array against this brightest of the heirs of heaven.
People: Gracious God, have mercy on your holy child, who dies to save us.
Leader: Our Savior yields now to the powers of evil: love yields to hate, light yields to shadow, life yields to death.
People: Gracious God, have mercy on your holy child as the love, light, and life go out.
Leader: We pray for all in the world whose lives know the trauma of the fear of death as a daily companion, in all its terrible manifestations
People: Have mercy on them, redeeming Spirit.
Leader: We pray for all in the world who scoff at this cross, not yet realizing their own loss, but who may yet turn again and be reconciled.
People: Have mercy on them, redeeming Spirit.
Leader: We pray for ourselves, who though we stand at the foot of this cross, have yet to grasp the full miracle of its sacred forfeiture.
People: Have mercy on us, redeeming Spirit.
Leader: In this hour of fear, O God, grant us faith:

People: That we may continue to trust your unfailing grace and presence, even when defeat and despair appear to triumph.

Leader: In this hour of dread, O God, grant us hope:

People: That we may realize all that has already been accomplished,
receiving in it an earnest of what will yet be achieved.

Leader: In this hour of despair, O God, grant us love:

People: That though Christ's spirit takes flight, his compassion lives
on in us who, even in death, are called by his name.

Unison: In obedience to his necessity, we surrender again to you this
word made flesh that you willed to dwell with us, full of
grace and truth; and as the silence envelopes him and us, we
will wait in patience for your Word again to address us.

Veiling the Cross

Let one or two of the congregation approach the table, take a black veil
folded there, and carefully drape it over the cross. The veil may be left in
place throughout the weekend—especially if the church is to be open
for private prayer and meditation—until preparations are begun for
Easter worship.

Strepitus

The Strepitus is created by the slamming shut of Bibles and hymnals,
and symbolizes the sounds accompanying the death of Jesus: the earthquake and the closing of the tomb. On the signal of the leader, the congregation is invited to join in by forcefully closing hymnals and, following the Benediction, to leave the church in complete silence.

Moment of silent meditation.

Benediction

Leader: Now the passion of Christ is ended. Now he is taken from
the cross and laid in the tomb. Now we are in the world
alone. Go in silence, and in fear and trembling wait upon the
will of our God, in the sure hope that we will not be left
comfortless and that God will yet have the final word.

People: Amen. So let it be!

Easter and Eastertide

Easter Sunday and Six Sundays Following
Liturgical Color: White

One suspects that if Christians in the United States knew the origin of the word "Easter," the reasons behind the manner of its observance in our society would become instantly clearer—and embarrassing. Like our names for the days of the week, "Easter" survives from Teutonic legend. The English term is derived from the Old English *Eostre,* the name of a goddess whose festival, *Eostron,* was celebrated at the vernal equinox and from which modern biology and medicine derive the term "estrus," the period of fecundity. Little wonder that its most common form of observance is by recourse to that ancient fertility symbol, the egg, delivered by that notoriously prolific breeder, the rabbit!

The name for the event in European languages more closely relates it to its historical and theological roots in Israel and derives universally from the event's proximity to the season of Passover—in Hebrew, *pesach.* From this came the Latin *pascha* and its English derivative "paschal." Thus we find *pasqua* (Italy), *pascua* (Spain), *paaske* (Denmark), *paasch* (Holland), and *pasg* (Wales). Only in English (and thus the United States), by some quirk of irony, did the pagan original remain the name of choice for this most central of all events in the life of Christ and therefore of the church.

There is no evidence either in the New Testament or in the Apostolic writings of the observance of Easter in the early church. This is consistent with the general absence of any notion of the sanctity of special times among early Christians. Commenting on 1 Corinthians 5:7, for example, St. Chrysostom observed, "The whole of time is a festival unto Christians because of the excellency of the good things which have been given." Such festivals as early Christians observed were Jewish holdovers, commemorated not for their significance in Hebraic history but for their presumed foreshadowing of Jesus. Thus pesach was observed, not to commemorate the overflight of the angel of death prior to the Exodus liberation, but to proclaim Jesus as the true Paschal lamb and first fruit from the dead, an observance that evolved into Easter.

This foundation in Hebrew history early resulted in a bitter debate in the church, however. Jewish Christians held that the fast of the Pascal lamb must end on the first day of Jewish Passover (the fourteenth day of the lunar month of Nisan, at evening), with the resurrection feast following immediately, regardless of the day of the week on which it happened to fall. Gentile Christians, unhampered by the finer points of the Jewish calendar, reversed the process. Identifying the first day of the week as the day of resurrection, they commemorated the crucifixion on the Friday preceding, without regard to the date of the month it fell on. Strong-handed attempts were made to resolve the controversy. In 197 C.E., Victor of Rome excommunicated Christians who insisted on the 14 Nisan date. Settlement of the issue once and for all was among several reasons Constantine summoned the Council of Nicaea in 325 C.E. But the problem was not entirely solved even then. There remained the lack of a definitive rule by which the paschal moon was to be fixed. The solution, simply stated, was that Easter is observed on the first Sunday after the full moon following the vernal equinox. Even this abstruse solution did not solve the problem, because of variations caused by longitude and the employment of different calendars, a confusion reconciled finally by the adoption of the Gregorian calendar in 1582—and even then England and Ireland held out until 1752! The Eastern, or Orthodox, churches still follow the pre-Gregorian formula, resulting to this day in different dates of observance.

Because Easter is dated partly from the lunar cycle and not solely the solar calendar, we refer to the date of Easter as "variable." The ripple effect of the dating of Easter impacts on the church calendar in both directions, including the entire period from the conclusion of Epiphany to the date of Pentecost.

As with Christmas, the Easter season, or Eastertide, is in some communions honored mainly in the breach. This is especially likely in nonliturgical churches, that is, those whose liturgies do not conform to a clearly delineated church-year calendar. In consequence, we often devote a preponderance of energy to preparation and little to follow-through. How many congregations, for instance, consume Advent not in genuine preparation for Christmas but in premature celebration of it, and by December 26 cannot wait to pack the last decoration into the closet and deposit the wreathes in the back alley with the rest of the trash?

Eastertide is an opportunity to explore—and celebrate—the full implications of the momentous event that alone in Christendom out-ranks Christmas as *the* central and sacred event. We do well to explore in some depth what it means to live as children of resurrection, heirs of the grace of life that is redeemed, as persons who are reconciled.

It is worth reminding ourselves, yet again, that Christianity is a post-resurrection faith and that it was as much so for the apostles as for us. Consider: Paul's letters are the oldest, purely Christian writings we possess; yet he never met the physical Jesus; and by the time his conversion experience knocked him flat on the road to Damascus, Christianity had already taken sufficient root that there was an embryonic church worthy of his zealous persecutory efforts. Mark's version of the Gospel—the oldest attempt to record the story of Jesus systematically—is dated around the mid-point of the first century, almost a quarter century after the Easter experience. In brief, it was only by post-resurrection hindsight that the apostles finally began themselves to realize the full implications of the Christ event. We need ourselves to cover that same ground, to retrace their spiritual pilgrimage.

The liturgical material below was written with this in mind. Much of it highlights the resurrection theme as the predominant concern of the church from Easter day until Pentecost. A few exceptions are provided for. It is perhaps no accident that the development of Mother's Day and its placement in the middle of Eastertide occurred at a point in history when most American Protestants paid scant heed to the church year. But there it is, though now variously labeled the Festival of the Christian Home. Whatever we call it, some congregations will want prayer and response material that takes this quintessentially American observance into account.

The second event to which some attention ought to be given is Ascension, which commemorates Jesus' final parting from his disciples with the promise that he will send them the Holy Spirit (a promise we see fulfilled at Pentecost). Since Ascension falls on Thursday before the final Sunday of Eastertide, it goes largely unnoticed among congregations outside the liturgical traditions. Certainly, few mark it by a service of worship. It seems to me, however, that an image of such importance in the Christian experience deserves at least passing attention. For that reason, several of the pieces that follow were composed specifically for use on the Sunday before Ascension.

Finally, one prayer was prepared for use around Earth Day, which is fixed on April 22. Some congregations may not care to take notice of such an event in worship. But for those who believe it is appropriate to do so, this piece can be used on those years when April 22 falls on a Sunday, or on the Sunday preceding that date.

Prayers and Liturgical Readings

Easter Sunday
—

Invocation

Greet us now, risen Christ, with the same cry your people heard on the first morning of your resurrected life. For at your "Hail!" we, too, are amazed and come to lay hold of your feet to worship you. Then, having heard for ourselves the dread-full sounds of your awakening and witnessed the mystery of your empty tomb, send us back, charged to tell our sisters and brothers of your love that death could not kill, your word that the power of hell itself could not erase. And by us may others see, and know, that you live indeed!

Call to Praise

Leader: People, why have you come here?

People: We have come to care for the body of Jesus, who was crucified. We come to prepare him for burial, as our law requires.

Leader: He is not here. He was raised, as he told you.

People: Do you ask us to believe that Jesus, whom we saw dead, lives?

Leader: Come see for yourselves. Here is the shroud that covered him; there, the place where he lay.

People: We see. His place really is empty. We hardly know what to say.

| Leader: | Rejoice with me in this great blessing, give praise to God; then go and tell everyone what you have seen here. |
| People: | We will join you, singing God's amazing glory, who alone could work such a thing. |

Prayer of Praise

What words can we use, risen and resurrecting Messiah, to represent the elation of heart, excitement of mind, brimming-overness of spirit that grips us on this most excellent of days, when death's presumed and presumptuous grip is shattered and your soaring spirit-flesh raises its shout of triumph and carries all life's liberation before it. The dawn of eternity lightens our morning, and we see revealed the promise of our inclusion at the reunion feast of the children of God. With trumpets and triumphals, with voices abandoned to praise, we echo back the victory song: "Where, O death, is your victory; where, O death, is your sting? Thanks be to God, who gives us this victory through our Savior Jesus Christ!"

Call to Reconciliation

Since the very dawning of the Christian church, the resurrection story has proven difficult for some, unbelievable for others. Even committed Christians wrestle with honest doubt in the face of reports of events that defy everything we objectively know about human mortality. There is more at stake here, however, than mere assent to the Gospel account. Even as we witness the power of resurrection in myriad people and events, extending from Christ's time to ours, and feel the stirring of new life as it invades the dead places of our souls, we face a new hurdle: our own reluctance to receive it. Let us now raise a common voice to God and ask help for our reluctance and hope for our healing.

Prayer of Confession

O Most Holy God: the events of Easter trumpet the resurrection of Christ and proclaim that death's power over life is bankrupt, calling us to live as those who need fear death no longer. Yet, like the women at the tomb, we are silent, fearing what people may think of us; like the apostles, we dismiss as idle talk the startling news of Christ's liberation; like Thomas, we doubt; and doubting, remain in our fear and indecision.

Withal, we fail to live like those for whom Christ died and rose again. God of our faith, we believe; help our unbelief. Then, as you did for the disciples before us, open our eyes to recognize him who even now moves among us in newness of life. So we will feel the power of resurrection let loose among us and go from this place with courage, rejoicing to do the work of our risen Savior.

Declaration of Forgiveness

Leader: None of those who ran to the tomb that first Easter morning was prepared for what greeted them when they arrived. So it should come as no surprise to us that we are ourselves ill-prepared. On the other hand, each of those folk found a risen Christ who was prepared—to replace hopelessness with reassurance, dread with confidence, death with life. Then thanks be to God, who by grace unbounded gives us a share in the victory of Christ Jesus our Savior.

People: In awe and wonder, we greet the risen Christ; with praise and thanksgiving, we receive the gift of our own resurrection. Alleluia!

Call for the Offering

The drama of Easter constrains us to consider what it means to live as resurrected people. No longer ought we to behave as if tomorrow holds more misgiving than hope; no longer need we be anxious for our own welfare; Christ has assured it beyond the capacity of any power, in life or in death, to destroy it. And so, in spite of ourselves, we are freed from worrying further about what our peers declare essential, to think instead about what Christ declares essential—the pouring out of our tangible love in the name of mercy. This offering is just that: both tangible and merciful. Celebrate Christ's liberation, and your own, in your gift.

Prayer of Dedication

God of light triumphant, we bring our gifts to this table and lay them here, compelled by the mystery of Christ to conduct ourselves as children of the resurrection. Transform this product of mere custom into a miracle of mercy, and by it bring hope to a suffering world in which too many still wait, in pain and despair, to hear the story of a cross overcome, a stone rolled away, a tomb unattended. We pray in the name, and by the mercy, of our again and still living Sovereign, Jesus Christ.

Thanksgiving

All that we most dread, and all for which we most yearn, hang fast upon this day's news, O Ancient of Days, monarch of life and death and resurrection and life eternal. The mortality that dogs our steps, the losses that haunt our generations, the shadows that loom before our way, are rolled away with the stone, and our lives and relationships stand rescued at the tomb's open door. Now we see, if dimly, the garden where the redeemed of God gather and hear, if softly, the songs of joy and chatter of reunion, signified in the garden of Jesus' resurrection triumph. Thank you, God, for this story. Thank you for this promise. Thank you for this jubilation!

First Sunday after Easter
—

Invocation

Resurrecting Power, grant to each of us here present, individually and as a company of your people, a vision of your intention for the Easters of our lives. If you will do this, we will experience for ourselves the astonishment of the women who approached the tomb and found it empty. Startle us, too, with the presence of the risen Christ in the garden of our days, and we, too, will fall on our knees and worship in awe and amazement.

Call to Praise

Leader: A hundred generations have come and gone since Jesus' friends visited the tomb and found it empty.

People: Yet the mystery remains fresh, the wonder like new.

Leader: A week has passed since we ourselves celebrated anew our savior's rising.

People: We have not forgotten, nor can we forget.

Leader: For we do not know how soon we may know in our selves the promise of resurrection.

People: It will come. In God's time it will come.

Leader: Then we shall leave it in God's hands,

People: But not silently. We will punctuate our waiting with song and petition and acts of praise. Glory be to our sovereign God!

Prayer of Praise

The cry that Christ is risen rings in our minds and hearts, our God, as the renewal of life about us strikes our eyes and ears at each new dawning. With the ascending sun, we rise to praise you. The stirring of the breeze, burdened with the aroma of spring flowers and damp earth, makes us mindful of your mercy. In the transparent twilight, when the air resounds with the calls and trills of small things newly liberated from prisons of ice and mud, we recall your love that serves us in ways beyond knowing. As our souls are open to the emergence of spring's fullness, open our spirits to the mounting surge of resurrection's power among us who witness, with hymns of praise, the sun of righteousness rising, with healing in its wings. Then may our lives, not just our words, converge to praise you who are the source and ground of our being.

Call to Reconciliation

Even as we witness the power of the resurrected Christ in the lives of the early church; even as we witness its power in the people and events of our own time; even as new life invades our souls, we confront again the ancient hurdle: our hesitation to receive it in our selves. To live under the power of resurrection places demands on us that we are not always prepared to meet. As long as we live "in the body," to use Paul's phrase, the struggle within us, between the good that we crave and the evil we abhor, goes on. At the very door of the empty tomb, we need again to raise our voices to God, to seek help for our reluctance and hope for our healing.

Prayer of Confession

The events of Good Friday and Easter astonish and confound us, holy God, because they make plain your willful presence in events that intend death or life for your whole creation. How slow we are to learn from them! Misjudging their power, we seek plausible explanations, hoping to domesticate them and render them manageable. Abashed by a wonder we are loath to own, we overlay our celebration with dignity, lest we embarrass ourselves by publicly testifying to miracle. Forgive the reluctance, patient God, that absents us from the empty tomb and the shouts of alleluia. Then make of our days a succession of Easters, by which the stones are rolled back from those other tombs of fear and ignorance and division and want, that all humanity may revel in the promise of life without ending.

Declaration of Forgiveness

Leader: The entire drama of Jesus' death and resurrection lays to rest, once and for all, the power of sin to govern our lives and compel our deaths—not physically, for we remain as mortal as ever we were. The resurrection has not changed that. What has changed is the central quality of life: we are no longer people defined solely by physical limitations, but people liberated by spiritual renewal. As Christ died and was raised, so by forgiveness we die to mortality and are raised in the power of Christ's spirit.

People: Hearing this word of joy, we say together, Thanks be to God!

Call for the Offering

Those who encountered the risen Savior found themselves possessed by an enthusiasm the energy of which they could not easily define, much less explain away. Little wonder that one of the signs of Christian faith among those early "followers of the way" was a liberality that seemed limitless. What they received, they early discovered, could not be repaid even by giving away everything they possessed, including life itself. In like manner, we voice the alleluias in our hearts by giving from what we are given, simply for the love of Christ. Bring your gifts and give praise to God.

Prayer of Dedication

We come, risen Savior, as did the women to the tomb on the first Easter, our gifts possessing limited physical value but earnest intentions. Surprise us now, as you surprised them that wondrous dawn, by transforming us from persons bearing gifts to serve the dead into persons who are gifts to the living; and may you be given the praise and the honor.

Thanksgiving

Source of life and empowerment: we thank you that you do not abandon us to the living death that confronts us in our despair, but lift us above the power of the grave in company with the risen Christ. We thank you, too, that we are liberated with him to newness of life; to know in ourselves, in those we love, and in all creation, the transcendent power of resurrection. Let it come alive in us this day and every day, holy Spring of grace, welling up in us for the release of your people and the glory of your name.

Second Sunday after Easter

—

Invocation

We gather, risen Christ, to celebrate your restoration, daring to believe in the power of life over death, of good over evil, of unity over division, of reconciliation over brokenness. Ignite in us the flame of resurrection, incorporating us individually and collectively into the living body of Christ and making of us agents of reconciliation among our own people and all the peoples of earth.

Call to Praise (from Romans 6:9–11)

Leader: We know that Christ, being raised from the dead, will never die again;

People: Death no longer has dominion over humankind.

Leader: The death Christ died was died to sin, once for all;

People: But the life Christ lives is lived for God.

Leader: We also must consider ourselves dead to sin and alive to God in Christ Jesus.

People: So we will, and praise the Source of generosity for this gift of infinite kindness!

Prayer of Praise

The air of waning winter begets the smell of spring, great Keeper of the changing seasons; and while the doors of your winter storehouses are not yet fully secured, our spirits sense within us the rising promise of emerging leaping joyful wakening life. So we cry your praise for cosmic rhythms and abundant promises that remind us: we are children of vitality, created for life, not death. So may our lives, congruent with our calling, praise you; and by our faithfulness may the world know us, and you affirm us, as children of the living God.

Call to Reconciliation

Think of that person you know or have known whom you are willing, after the most careful scrutiny, to call "good." Such a person will likely be kind, self-giving, thoughtful, and deeply spiritual. Chances are that person will also be among the least self-centered, most humble people you know, unwilling to own any other claim than that this way of life is what is expected of us. Now think of yourself. Are you prepared to lay claim to an equal goodness? Even Jesus chided a man (Mark 10:17–18) for calling him good, asking, "Why do you call me good? No one is good but God alone." How then shall we not bow before our good God, to avow our negligence and our need? Please join me in common confession.

Prayer of Confession

Bear witness, Great Star of resurrection power, to the shadows that our unredeemed behavior casts across the light of your Son's triumph. In poverty of spirit, we sell ourselves to whoever makes the most extravagant promises and feel betrayed when they do not deliver. Ignoring the proclamations of Creation's Author, who bids us sacrifice all to pursue the revealing light of life, we devote our energies to the acquisition of things, which surround and fetter us until we can neither see the way nor follow. By the door of the empty tomb, merciful Redeemer, focus our minds on emptiness, until it fully dawns on us that no thing can finally hold those who belong to Christ, who shattered death's fastness and bolted to the light, bidding us follow and live. Forgiven then, we will live and love in his name.

Declaration of Forgiveness

Leader: While Jesus (Mark 10:17–18) refused even to let himself be labeled good, he never rejected others who conceded their fault and asked for his intercession. We are among those others. We come here, as to the door of the empty tomb, to wonder at the restorative power of the life and the love of

Christ, who acquiesced in the death that a frightened and faithless humanity imposed, then rose up to destroy it, so that it might not destroy us.

People: Then let us declare to one another and to all who are within hearing: we are forgiven! Alleluia! Thanks be to God!!

Call for the Offering

This is the season of Christ's resurrection. It is also the season during which—in terms of symbolic history—we Christians realize who Jesus really was. For the first time, all the evidence, the whole story, is available to us. With that realization comes a second: the realization of just who it is that Christ calls us to be—persons from whom a death sentence has been lifted, able for the first time to model for all around us the promise of victorious life. We are invited now to act out that assurance: not to give hesitantly, as if fenced about by anxiety, hoarding against an uncertain future; but with joyful release, as ones who trust in God's mercy to secure our lives, both temporal and eternal.

Prayer of Dedication

At the scarred feet of the risen Christ we kneel, O God, to place at your disposal some of the goods that you have placed at ours. Vouchsafe to us the joy of knowing that we here share Christ's healing power; but more, confer upon those who benefit by our tributes a share of the new life in Christ that is prepared for us all in his resurrection.

Thanksgiving

God of mercy and mystery: with wonder we hear again that Christ is risen and acknowledge our wonder at all that this news signifies: that if death could not block the power of your love in Christ, it cannot turn aside your love for us. If death no longer can threaten what is truly important, we may embrace life with fearless abandon. If the cross be emptied of its power, we can hoist our own and help others lift theirs, the while trumpeting the impotence of all such instruments of desecration and violence. For this, high Redeemer, we pour out our thanks and rehearse with your people the ancient proclamation: by the wisdom of this foolishness we are redeemed; by the strength of this weakness we are saved. Amen! Thanks be to God!

Third Sunday after Easter

—

Invocation

Source of all true joy, brightness of the season of our celebration: bless us now with a vision of our risen Savior, this luminous center of peace that passes understanding; this gift that the world can neither give nor take away; this ground of purity who makes radiant the work that we do in your name. Make now of our liturgy an act of praise and thanksgiving that reflects back to you the boundless love delivered to us in Christ Jesus our Savior.

Call to Praise (from Romans 8:9–11, 14, 17)

Leader: Anyone who does not have the Spirit of Christ does not belong to Christ.

People: But if Christ is in us, although our bodies are dead because of sin, our spirits are alive because of righteousness.

Leader: If the Spirit of God who raised Jesus from the dead dwells in us, we will also, through her, be given life in our mortal bodies.

People: For all who live by the Spirit of God are children of God;

Leader: And if children, then heirs, heirs of God and co-heirs with Christ,

People: Provided we suffer with him in order that we may also be glorified with him.

Unison: Let now that Spirit of Holiness, who gave Christ back to us, loose our tongues in praise and thanksgiving.

Prayer of Praise

In such a time, you who hold the seasons in thrall, how shall we not praise you? In the ascending sun that warms the earth, the vanguard thunder that heralds the storm, the softening earth from which new life pushes skyward, we witness the wisdom of your design and the unfailing mercy that it yields to all that lives. Praise, nature's Monarch, for the warbling song of birds. Praise for new growth with its promise of continuing plenty. Praise for aching muscles and stretching limbs, as we shake off the confinement of winter and play again in the ascending air. Most of all, praise for faithfulness toward all you have made and declared good, which you carry with consummate tenderness, nowhere so graphically displayed as in the stunning drama of heaven's child, whose death and resurrection heralds our own and invests in us your purpose for time and being. Praise to you, Author of life both temporal and eternal.

Call to Reconciliation

Which of us, by careful enumeration, can compile a list of our own goodness, kindness, and generosity so compelling that we would dare to stand before heaven's throne and argue the case for our own righteousness? But if *we* lack this confidence, what hope is there for us? Who will argue our case? The remarkable affirmation of Scripture is this: that the very Holiness before whom we are summoned will both argue the case in our behalf and dispose of the judgment against us. It is a remarkable claim, but one with a price: that we willingly confess our need for such intercession, by honest and unaffected contrition. Let us pray together.

Prayer of Confession

Healer of broken hearts, we bow in awe before you, because we are too ashamed to stand. Endowed with capabilities that stagger the imagination, we apply them to prodigal pursuits and grasp at things beyond our understanding. Confronted by your divinity and our humanity, we still play at being God but succeed only in becoming petty idols. Shown opportunities to extend compassion, we anxiously cross to the other side and rush on. Invited to share resources with your people in want, we grasp to acquire more, building lavish wealth for ourselves by stealing bread from children. In all, we drain Christ's crucifixion of its power and his resurrection of its glory. God help us and lift us to the newness of mercy and compassion that are worthy of the disciples of a risen Christ.

Declaration of Forgiveness

Leader: In his letter to the church at Ephesus (2:4–6), the apostle Paul wrote these words of reassurance: "God, who is rich in mercy, out of the great love with which we were loved, even when we were dead through our sins, made us alive together with Christ, and raised us up with him, and sat us down in heavenly places." Receive the forgiveness of God in Jesus Christ, our resurrected Savior.

People: Hearing these words of joy, we say in unison, Thanks be to God!

Call for the Offering

Eastertide is the season of the church year when we are invited both to witness and proclaim that death and hell themselves are not sufficient to challenge the authority of Christ. That authority becomes evident among us whenever caring Christians engage in acts of love and compassion that imitate Christ's own acts of mercy and healing. The offering is our ongoing opportunity to demonstrate the legitimacy of our claim to this belief. Give now, from the warmth of your hearts and watch Christ come alive among us and among those we touch.

Prayer of Dedication

The barren cross beckons us, God of the empty tomb, to remember the riches that Christ laid aside for us, and calls us to bring our own gifts. Let Christ's sacrifice bear fruit in us, and beyond us, to the benefit of others for whom the Savior also died and rose again.

Thanksgiving

Yours is the authority, Holy Sovereign, that burst the bonds of death, liberating the child of heaven and humanity to stand again upon earth and point the way to heaven. Ours is the thanksgiving that we, empowered by these gifts, are able to face both life and death, freed from anxiety about any harm they can do; able, even in the face of hell, to herald the love of Christ that reclaims us and stands us on our feet, inspirited witnesses to the majesty and compassion of God.

Fourth Sunday after Easter
─

Invocation

Just as the ascending light of spring warms earth and all its inhabitants, life-giving Spirit, so your rising child, heaven's promise of earth's redemption, sheds light and warmth on us who are called by his name and remade in his image. Shed that light so richly upon us now that we become the warmth of heaven stirring a winter-chilled world, embodiment of the rejuvenating spirit of the risen Christ.

Call to Praise

Leader: Come, children of Creation, and celebrate the wonder of spring.

People: Come, brothers and sisters of the human family, and rejoice at the renewal of life.

Leader: Come, people of God, and acclaim the resurrection of Christ.

People: Come, friends of Christ, and marvel at the empty tomb.

Leader: Come, you who are loved by God, and receive yourselves this gift of renewal.

People: Come, you who love God, and make your lives a witness to holy love.

Leader: Then will Christ be resurrected in us, redeeming life from death.

People: Then will we be resurrected in Christ, a blessing to the world.

Prayer of Praise (in observance of Earth Day)

How wonderful is the One who calls out of nothingness-chaos the splendor of our universe; of fertile earth attendant upon life-giving sun-star; of rhythmic turning seasons yielding fertility and rest; of life forms so intricately diverse that imagination staggers. How generous the One who gives us this universe as home, bestowing on us the resources of our necessity—yes—but trusting us also with the responsibility of limits; who bids us exercise, as no other can, authority over the stewardship of earth. How merciful the One who does not leave us alone in this awesome obligation, but in tender parenthood crouches to us in Word and Spirit, teaching us the meaning of love and constraint. Giver of life, may our words praise you ne'er so well as our lives, as we strive in obedience to embody your whole creation love.

Call to Reconciliation

Christ entered into the heart of despair, there to challenge and defeat the very powers of evil that sought the destruction of all life. But Christ could not have done so except by acknowledging their reality, calling them by name, and taking them under command. So the evils that continue to claw at us, purposing to topple and snare us, will not be defeated until we name them, admit the contribution that we ourselves make to their success, and submit them to Christ's authority. Come, friends, and confess together our sin, our sorrow, and our want of Christ's merciful intervention.

Prayer of Confession

The majesty of Easter is only weeks behind us, great Giver of life, but already we turn away from timeless things and resume our pursuit of what can only kill us. Resurrection's dawn fades into the business of the day, conducting us toward our evening reward of futility. Summoned to the task of modeling heaven's abundance in our own town and among our own people, we prefer to store up treasures on earth, an invitation to thieves to break in and steal and moth and rust to corrode. Spin us about yet one more time where we stand, tireless guardian of our souls, and point us to where the resurrection still burns and flames among us, a saving light even for the likes of us.

Declaration of Forgiveness

Leader: In the letter to the Colossians (2:13–15) we read this reassuring passage: "And when you were dead in trespasses and the uncircumcision of your flesh, God made you alive together with Christ, when all our trespasses were forgiven, and the record that stood against us, with its legal demands, was erased. God set it aside, nailing it to the cross, disarming the rulers and authorities, and making a public example of them by triumphing over them."

People: Hearing these words of joy, we say together, Thanks be to God!

Call for the Offering

A close reading of Scripture impresses upon us the simple fact that those in our tradition that we most admire, whom we most feel we should emulate, are people whose lives were placed entirely at the disposal of God. Such self-giving may take many forms. How we give is for each of us, individually, to determine. But as Christians, we have always this model before us: that Christ gave it all, the last shred of life, to benefit us. It is now our task to determine what we desire to give in return.

Prayer of Dedication

By bringing these gifts, O God, we mean to hurl against the prison of someone's pain the love of the resurrected Christ, whose compassion even death could not bind, whose love sets us free. As he awoke from death, awaken those who benefit by our gifts to a new confidence in the goodness of life and receive their praise, and ours, for your mercy.

Thanksgiving

At every step of our way, dear God, in gossip and story and media report, we are urged to dread the dangers and despairs that dog this odd commodity we call "modern life." How glad we are, then, for the old, old story of your love that triumphs over all that threatens to undo us, whether the complexity of life or the despair of death, and urges us to hope. In the music of Christ's resurrection we hear the prelude of our own triumphals and turn to sing your glory. The lives of your saints, both before our time and during it, stir in us the irresistible urge of life. Thank you, God, for evidence of these splendors that carry us beyond the power of abject resignation and rouse in us a hymn of hope, a psalm of joy, a symphony of thanksgiving!

Fifth Sunday after Easter

—

Note: Material for the fifth Sunday after Easter was prepared for use in celebration of Mother's Day or the Festival of the Christian Home. Where these observances fall in Eastertide will be determined by the calendar, which will in turn determine on what Sunday this material is appropriate.

Invocation

Great Original of our being and our generations, we first learned love at the hands of those who fed and clothed us, gave us homes and shaped us with discipline. From them, also, our spirits were nurtured and we learned of you. We come before you again, their God and ours, to celebrate their lives, their love, and their gifts. For their sakes, make evident among us your holy presence which alone is able both to bless and to complete our celebration.

Call to Praise

Leader: We come to celebrate the great Mother/Father Spirit, source of our being, whose love wills that each of us shall have a place;

People: The miracle of mothers, who shelter our flesh in their own, gathering and integrating our substance that we may live upon the earth;

Leader: Families of blood who give and share our names and provide us root and identity;

People: Families of spirit, who confirm us in holy faith and mediate the love that draws us into global human kinship.

Leader: Is not this One wise beyond mere human devising?

People: Is not our welfare more richly layered than we imagine, much less foresee?

Leader: Let us begin this day's praise, therefore, by embracing anew the holy command of God, given for our welfare:

People: We will honor our mothers and fathers, that our days may be long in the land that God gives to us.

Prayer of Praise

Praise, our God, for the blessing of mothers and fathers who bore us and first taught us the discipline of life. Praise for sisters and brothers who traveled with us the pathways of childhood's anxiety and hope, challenge and joy, discovering with us what it means to share. Praise for wider families and kinships, which define the place of our belonging and our sense of self. And praise, too, for those others who, though unrelated by blood, surround us with current and remembered affections: friends and associates, pastors and teachers, advisors and counselors who tangibly embody our greater family that is humanity. On this day, devoted to the celebration of family and home, we bring them all to mind and commend them to your mercy. So voicing our love for them, we speak your praise, who loves us all.

Call to Reconciliation

It is always appropriate for Christians to open themselves to be searched by the authority of holy judgment. But there are special occasions on which our spirits may benefit doubly from self-yielding. This is such a day. We not only celebrate the deep riches we possess because of our own mothers and the family nurture so much of which centers about them; we have also the opportunity to review the worthiness of our response to those influences. Have we honored them as God mandates? Let us open our deepest selves now to the God whom many of us received first in mother-love, confident that we will also receive a full measure of motherly compassion.

Prayer of Confession

Great Parent of mercy, who commanded the ancient Hebrews to honor mother and father that their days might be long in the land you would give them: Jesus made clear that this commandment of yours was binding on all humanity—including us. Yet on this day set apart to honor our mothers, we acknowledge our disobedience. It is not that we fail to love them; our hearts brim over with feeling when we recall their nurture and support. We would not willfully dishonor them. But we are given to forgetfulness. We move carelessly, and live impetuously. We value personal gratification above their sacrifice. In all these ways our love is compromised, our disobedience evident. Chasten us, You who alone know the full measure of our willfulness, and waken in us that sensitivity of mind and spirit that alone allows us to honor our obligation as children of obedience. Then truly honoring our mothers, we may truly honor you.

Declaration of Forgiveness

Leader: Jesus stunned his followers—and us—by suggesting they should think of God as abba, a word that Bible translators overdignify by rendering it "father." In the original, its meaning is closer to "daddy." God shares the hours of our days so closely as to be intimately engaged in the routine of life. Just as fairly, we may think of God's closeness as possessing the palpable warmth of a mother's tender embrace. Regardless of the metaphors we choose, the point is the same: God's love for us is constant and unqualified, God's forgiveness more enduring than we can even imagine.

People: Hearing these words of joy, we say together, Thanks be to God!

Call for the Offering

It is one of the sad realities of life that not everyone thinks of their parents as kind and loving or of their homes as centers of nurturing shelter. There is perhaps no greater betrayal than that felt by the child of uncaring parents or, worse, parents who, through abuse, cause indelible pain and despair. We do not raise this specter to cast a pall over this very special family day but to remind ourselves, who are a caring people, that some around us, perhaps among us, yearn for the gentle warmth and secure affirmation that has been ours, but that they have never known. Our offering is one way to provide, if only in token fashion, the assurance that love can be both genuine and enduring. Bring now your gifts, that some child's doubt may be transformed into faith and despair into hope.

Prayer of Dedication

Source of our being, great Mother of life, who wills the prosperity and peace of all to whom you have given life: receive these gifts as an earnest of our desire to make those blessings real. Let us be midwives at the birthing of peace for the whole world; for so your love desires.

Thanksgiving

All thanks to you, God of our mothers and fathers, for the beautiful relationships in which our lives are embedded: that we were cradled in love before ever we saw the light or breathed the air; that the arms that first held us, more than any save your own, willed our good and our thriving; that we received from them the nurture that undergirds health and the care that yields self-esteem. Thanks, too, that we received first, from those who love us best, the challenge that stimulates the mind's stretch; the moral sense that divines what ought to be in the context of what is; the self-discipline that channels creative energy; the social wakefulness that prepares us to serve the common weal. In all these, parenting Deity, we observe your hand that, loving us, teaches us how to love and how to live.

Sixth Sunday after Easter

—

Note: The material for the sixth Sunday after Easter was prepared specifically in celebration of the Ascension, which falls on the Thursday following.

Invocation

O Parent God, your child is leaving us: who came to live with us, whose life we have traced, whose lessons we have sought to learn, whose purity has singed the sin of our souls and focused the passion of our spirits. Again we plead: do not leave us alone in the world, but make evident to us your presence among us, without which we shall perish, with which we have hope of life.

Call to Praise

Leader: Gates, raise your arches,
People: Rise, you ancient doors,
Leader: Let the Monarch of glory in!
People: Who is the Monarch of glory?
Leader: Yahweh Sabaoth, the Holy One who Is,
People: This is the Monarch of glory!

Prayer of Praise

Now turns homeward the Sacred Child of Heaven, our brother for so brief a season, leaving us, dear God, to wonder at all on earth that was changed and need never be the same again: that we cowered before your radiance as a consuming fire, until your Child called you "daddy"; that we thought you far off, too distant to care, until our friend pointed to your mothering fingers smoothing our hair; we thought you stern and joyless, until our companion consorted with tots and bade us trust your governance as little children hugged firm in a grandparent's embrace. For all this, tender Sovereign, we adore you. For all this, Intimate Infinity, we extol you. For all this, Compelling Tolerance, we praise you. Receive again your own; and as humanity echoed angel glorias at his birthing, let heaven's choirs now add, at his returning, the great amen to our human anthem of praise.

Call to Reconciliation

Have you ever hurt someone you loved, perhaps without their ever knowing it, and either resisted the opportunity to ask their forgiveness or let it slip away? And then, when that person was taken from you, were stunned by the realization that the chance was now gone forever? In a figurative sense, that is where we stand at this season, when the church remembers the departure of the resurrected Christ from his disciples. Imagine we are there. Will you let him leave without taking advantage of the opportunity—perhaps now or never—to confess what lies most heavily on your heart and to ask his very special forgiveness? Then let us, with all our hearts, offer our confession.

Prayer of Confession (based on John 1:10–14)

Jesus has come and gone, and what have we to show for it? The Word came, who gave the world being, but the world did not comprehend. He came to his own people, but they did not accept him. God help us, *we* are Christ's people—the undiscerning, who fail to see the life that still comes to us, a light to all peoples. The Word takes flesh—*our* flesh—to fill us with grace and truth; but we see only the flesh's frailty, not the Word's invigorating virtue. Stop us in our tracks, you who fashion both Word and flesh. Persuade us anew that if we receive Christ, we will have the power to become children of God, born not of blood or the will of the flesh but of divine Spirit. Then Christ's leaving will not take your light wholly from the world; for it will shine on in us.

Declaration of Forgiveness

Leader: In his letter to the Romans (6:20–23), Paul takes note of the spiritual gift that comes to those who repent: "When you were slaves of sin, you were free from the control of righteousness. But what advantage did you gain? Nothing but what now makes you ashamed. The final destination of those things is death. But now, freed from the command of sin, and bound instead to the service of God, your gains are such as result in holiness, and the final destination of eternal life. For sin pays a wage, and the wage is death; but God gives freely, and the gift is eternal life, in union with Christ Jesus our Savior."

People: Hearing this reassurance, we thank and praise our generous God!

Call for the Offering

Imagine the disciples' feelings on Ascension day, as it dawned on them that Jesus really was leaving them, not to return until the appointed time that lies hidden in the mind of God. Is it not likely they started forward to keep him from going? Does any of us, losing a cherished friend, not feel our heart break? What do we generally do then, if not gather closer to those who also love, and are loved by, our absent friend? The offering is an opportunity to enact such a sentiment: by engaging in an act of generosity toward all whom Jesus loves, we honor the high regard in which we hold him. Give now as if giving to him—for indeed we are.

Prayer of Dedication

We give these gifts, God who is love, as we might give them to a precious friend leaving on a journey, as your holy Child leaves now to return home. Let them be evidence, at his parting, of our commitment to all for which he lived and died, a testimony before you of how deeply he moved us, how entirely our devotion has been won to the cause of justice, mercy, and peace.

Thanksgiving (based on Luke 4:18–19)

At this moment above all times, you Holy One who governs time end eternity, we are thankful for the life, death, and resurrection of Jesus Christ, heaven's child yet born of human flesh; dreamer with head in the cosmos and feet planted firmly upon our ground; clarion voice of good news for those ground down by physical and spiritual poverty; liberator of those held captive by oppression and those held captive by nothing more than their own fears; healer of every infirmity, whether of body or of spirit; dread of every oppressor, in life and beyond death; trumpet fanfare of the year of God's favor. To Christ, for Christ, and in Christ's name, we offer this prayer of gratitude and thanksgiving. Let it ascend with Christ to your throne of grace, our offering to make even more sweet the welcoming embrace of paradise.

Pentecost

Pentecost is the flip side of Babel. The ancient myth of Babel, which appears in Genesis 11, spoke eloquently to the Hebrews of an enduring truth: those who seek to play God will be confounded. Central to the myth is language and its ability to unite or divide us. In the Babel event, God uses language as a tool of estrangement. The moral: Where human communication is used in opposition to divine intent—where the function of language is corrupted and the words themselves, not just what they say, become a lie—language becomes destructive. We cannot even depend on it to perform so simple a task as coordinating our labor.

Pentecost conveys the countervailing power of God to transcend the limitations of strictly human communication. Where dependence upon our own feeble powers of speech so often yields misunderstanding, division, and frustration, the divine Spirit translates alienation into reconciliation, division into unity: "in our own languages we hear them speaking about God's deeds of power" (Acts 2:11). Again, the moral is obvious: where our communication is coherent with God's, we are able to overcome seemingly insurmountable obstacles and touch one another in love.

The timing of Pentecost is significant. It was not chosen accidentally. The early church was at pains to establish the legitimacy of its claims for Christ among people not readily prepared to affirm it. In the predominantly Jewish context of first century Israel, early Christians sought to establish that legitimacy by demonstrating the parallel between the experience of Israel at the first Pentecost and the church at the second.

Pentecost, a Latin word derived from the Greek *pente*, meaning "five," denotes the fiftieth day. Celebrated on the fiftieth day following the second day of Passover, Pentecost is also observed as the Feast of Weeks, *Shabuoth,* a festival at which the first fruits of the year's harvest are offered. In Jewish tradition, the date marks the receipt by Israel, through Moses, of God's gift of the law, said to have occurred fifty days after the Exodus—Judaism's seminal moment of liberation. It is not a casual notion. In Jewish theology, the law is the seal of Israel's covenantal relationship with God, that which stamps their union with both form and authenticity.

As the law is to Israel, the gift of the Holy Spirit is to the Christian church. Falling fifty days after *our* central, liberating moment—the resurrection of Christ—Pentecost fulfills Christ's promise to his disciples to send the Spirit, who would authenticate their relationship to God, who would be their ever-present guide to point the way and provide resources essential to stay on it, who would be the impetus that directed their conduct, making it possible for them to be children of love in all its manifold forms and implications. As the law is the road map that guides the Jews as they seek to remain faithful, through time, to the eternal covenant sealed at Sinai, the indwelling Spirit is God's compass to Christian people as they seek, through time, to remain faithful to the eternal covenant Christ sealed on the cross.

In brief, the Pentecost Christianity remembers and celebrates is to our pilgrimage what the first Pentecost is to Judaism—the moment in history when God affirmed and validated the covenant we are called to honor as people of faith.

Since it is dependent on Easter, the dating of Pentecost is equally variable and may fall over as wide a period. For the most part, it falls between mid-May and early June.

Prayers and Liturgical Readings

Invocation

Leader: Come now, divine rush of wind, and bluster and blow among us who gather here to wait the gift of the indwelling Spirit that Christ promises to those he calls to discipleship. As you descended to the flame-browed apostles of Pentecost, come to us, baptize our tongues with fire and equip us for lives of servanthood. Then send us out, Spirit-driven and passionate to live out, for the healing of a sick world, the gospel of Christ in whose name we pray; and let all the people of God cry,

Unison: Amen.

Call to Praise

Leader: Be wary, people of God, for this is a day of fire.

Right: The Spirit is here, a searing holiness among us.

Leader: It bids us, who know not the words, to speak.

Left: Then the words will no longer be ours, but those of One who commands us.

Leader: It compels us, who do not know the language, to hear.

Right: Then to us, newly enabled to listen, the hearing is a gift.

Leader: Be alert, people of God, for this is a day of mystery.

Left: The power of the Word is let loose among the likes of us.

Leader: This is not a time to be taken lightly.

People: No, but it is a time of light!

Leader: Then let us embrace the flame and pronounce the holy and compassionate word.

People: Let us recite the mighty acts of God; for the Spirit possesses us.

Unison: And behold: we possess the Spirit!

Prayer of Praise

Great Spirit of Power, mistress of the gifts of God, who endows us with life's breath, kindles love's flame, commends faith's conviction: hear our swelling praise on this day of your visitation. We praise you for the yearning that browses within us, seeking vent to express your glory; your intercession for us "with sighs too deep for words," that makes eloquent our muddled groaning; your rousing impulse that drives us out of our selves' preoccupation to be spent, in prodigal generosity, for others who will measure your love by our fire. Now settle your flame upon us, that your people may be a mighty witness, a community of languages retelling, for the whole world to hear, the mighty acts of God.

Call to Reconciliation

The name "Christian," you may know, was not the earliest title by which our forebears in the faith were called. They were first called, and first referred to themselves as, "followers of the way." The term pointed, obviously, to the way of Christ or, more correctly, to Christ as "the way"—the way of life and truth. If we are to follow Jesus as the way, we must be a people not only of love and compassion but of humility, a people who know that "there is none good but God." In our confession, we have opportunity to publish to ourselves and to all who observe us that what is good in us comes from God. As with all else that we have, our confession is a gift of the Spirit that kindles in us a Christlikeness, a readiness to receive, as individuals and as community, the discipline of our maker.

Prayer of Confession

The tasks to which you call us, Spirit Giver, are known to us; but our failure faithfully to engage them is evident. Like rain that is shed by our coats, your Spirit—in vain—seeks entry through the resistent clothing of our unwillingness. In humility we confess it: called to preach good news to the poor, we leave them in their grinding poverty; sent to announce recovery of sight to those who cannot see, we are content that we are not afflicted; charged to set the oppressed at liberty, we examine, and are satisfied, with the condition of their prisons; entrusted to proclaim the acceptable year of the Sovereign, we announce the acceptability of our own station, defined in terms of our own welfare. Merciful God, chasten our faithlessness. Send your Spirit's fire to dance among us and burn within us, trying our words and refining our intent. Then let us, like our forebears in the faith, yield to your sovereignty both the conviction of our minds and the allegiance of our lives.

Declaration of Forgiveness

On Pentecost day, as the apostle Peter explained for the amazed people gathered there the meaning of the events they witnessed, he quoted the prophet Joel (2:30–32) in words appropriate to this day of fire—words that give comfort to us when the Spirit moves among us: "I will show portents in the heavens and on the earth, blood and fire and columns of smoke. Day shall be turned to night, and the moon to blood, before the great and terrible day of God comes. Then everyone who calls on my name will be saved . . . as God has said."

Call for the Offering
We who have received the gift of the Spirit, of all people on God's earth, know the giddy joy of being benefactors of the generosity of another. But the Spirit does not leave us content in our elation. Having received in ourselves the mystery of divine compassion, we are fired to become gifts to others, in our vocations, our associations, our conduct. Let us again demonstrate the presence of Christ's Spirit among us, by pouring out our generosity on a world waiting eagerly, and hungrily, to hear, in their own tongues, the mighty acts of God.

Prayer of Dedication
As your Spirit's power has made zealous the devotion of your people throughout time, O God of fervent loving, set our gifts ablaze and let them be fuel for the fire of your compassion by kindling, throughout the whole earth, the flames of love and justice and peace.

Prayer of Thanksgiving
Out of this place of our sanctification, Holy One, into the breadth and wonder of this day of service, we take our leave. In here we have stood together, a like-minded company among whom we feel individually nurtured and secure; out there we must stand alone, witnesses to the courage of a self-giving Sovereign in a world of self-serving greed. Here we have been startled by mystery, struck dumb by the force of language as vehicle of purpose; out there our words' intention must translate into conduct's effect. In here we have felt the heat of your Spirit's companionship; out there we must make manifest the consequence of her embrace. We go with thanksgiving—for the sanctuary, the mystery, the power. We go in deep appreciation that, because you have visited us in here, we may dare to visit those others, out there. And because you go with us, we yield our hearts' gratitude, our minds' assent, our spirits' devotion.

Trinity Sunday

Sunday following Pentecost
Liturgical Color: Green

The church divides the year into two parts. The first half—from the start of Advent through the Ascension—traces and celebrates the key events in the life of Jesus. It constitutes the "festival year," during which occur Christianity's major "holy days." The second half, often referred to as "ordinary time," focuses on the life of the church in the world as the body of Christ: our life in community, our collective growth in faithfulness and individual growth in discipleship, our service to the community of humanity as ambassadors for Christ. This second part begins with Pentecost Sunday and continues until the last Sunday before Advent, when the cycle begins anew.

For many generations, the second of these periods was called Trinity Season or Trinitytide—the period following Trinity Sunday. It was a custom that made little sense. The seasons of the church year otherwise evoke key events in the life of Christ. It is incongruous then to name an entire season after a doctrine. In recent years, this incongruity has been corrected, returning emphasis to the fact that the season begins not with Trinity Sunday but with Pentecost the week before. It is an appropriate shift: the signal moment at which the apostles received Jesus' promised gift of the Spirit defines who we are as "church" and how we conduct our worship and our lives. The season that follows upon it appropriately bears the title Pentecost Season (see section 15).

Then what of Trinity Sunday? Its observance is symbolic of the early Christian community's new and expanded self-understanding, *as church,* that began to occur in the wake of Pentecost. As early Christians struggled to make sense, not only to the world but to themselves, of the Jesus experience and the ongoing influence of the Holy Spirit, the doctrine of the Trinity logically followed.

That the concept of the Trinity has been a difficult one goes without saying. It has been as much stumbling block as aid to faith. To some, it flies in the face not only of logic but of our Hebraic inheritance that valued, above all, the fundamental singularity of God. Radical monotheism is among Judaism's main gifts to world religious thought. "Hear, O Israel: our God is *one*." Christians cannot tamper with that revelation without severing the umbilical that ties us to our monotheistic root. A few respected scholars whose commitment to Christianity is not in question confess the delight they would feel if the doctrine had never been invented!

That the church has chosen to maintain it, in spite of the confusion and divisiveness the doctrine occasions, is evidence of mystery let loose among us. For Christians, the overriding question remains, "How can we speak of our historic encounter with God in a way that even begins to grasp the profundity of the experience without resorting to a metaphor?"

If I may be allowed a personal testimony: my grasp of this doctrine was aided by a bit of etymology. When late twentieth-century Christians (especially we of the persuasion *homo americanus)* speak of the "three persons of the Trinity," we unconsciously apply the most modern definition to a word that possesses a complex history: we presume that "person" intends what we mean it to intend when we employ it in speech or writing—i.e., an individual human being. When we visualize the Trinity, therefore, we visualize three separate entities, as if pointing to three, discrete human beings. But this perception is tenable only if we leave unchallenged its implicit distortion of the root word upon which the doctrine stands: *persona.*

The word is Latin, but sheds light on our dilemma only when considered in the context of the Greek stage. Two differences between ancient theater and the modern stage must be noted. First, ancient theatrical spaces were both large and open-air, making it difficult to see mood-revealing facial expressions. For this reason, masks were employed, accentuating the predominant mood of the character. Such masks were often equipped with a megaphonic mouth to focus the actor's voice and prevent sound from being dissipated behind the mask. This arrangement resulted in the name *persona,* from the Latin *per* (through) and *sonare* (to sound). The reader will recognize here the origin of the popular logo employed to decorate theaters or highlight high-school drama club posters, usually displaying two masks, one grinning, the other frowning or weeping.

Second, unlike modern theater, which generally stages one individual for each character portrayed, ancient drama often "starred" a single actor playing multiple parts. The "characters" of the drama were signified by different masks, which the actor held up severally to denote who was speaking at a given moment.

It was to this usage that the early church appealed to make concrete the Christian experience of God. The implication is quickly apparent: as the action proceeds, only one actor is engaged, but is perceived by the audience as mediated through the several *personae* that the actor employs. It was precisely the kind of metaphor the church sought: always we are engaged by the one and only true divinity but experienced through three *persona,* the three modes of the divine being that Christians have experienced. To employ the traditional trinitarian rubrics for a moment, we may note: God is Father, God is Son, God is Holy Spirit. Conversely, the Father is God, the Son is God, the Holy Spirit is God. But the Father is not the Son, the Son is not the Holy Spirit, the Holy Spirit is not the Father.

Precisely how these *persona* ought currently to be addressed is the topic of lively, at times quarrelsome, debate. It is an important issue and is discussed in the Introduction under the use of inclusive language, to which the reader is referred in lieu of additional remarks here.

Prayers and Liturgical Readings

Invocation

You who call the universe into being by speaking a word and carry the future of nations in sacred trust; who took upon yourself our mortal flesh and, laying it down, shattered the boundaries of mortality; who continues, generations unnumbered, to abide with us and labor through us, molding our gifts and redeeming our time: greet us again as we stand apart and call on your name, attend your word, seek your mercy, and receive our marching orders—you who alone holds sway to instruct us, heal us, and empower us.

Call to Praise (from Ephesians 1:3-14)

Leader: Blessed be the God and Parent of our Savior Jesus Christ, who has blessed us in Christ with every spiritual blessing in heavenly places;

People: Who destined us for adoption as children of God through Jesus Christ,

Leader: In whose blood we have redemption, the forgiveness of our trespasses,

People: According to the riches of grace that God lavishes on us.

Leader: With all wisdom and insight, the mystery of God's will has been made known to us,

People: So that we, who set our hope on Christ, might live to praise God's glory.

Leader: By whom we also, when we heard the word of truth and believed, were marked with the seal of the promised Holy Spirit.

People: Then we, who are God's own people, will praise our Sovereign's glory!

Prayer of Praise

We cry your praise, Creator of earth and life, Ruler of the universe, Author of all things that have been or yet will be. We cry your praise, O Christ of history, child of the holy and of humanity, bearer of healing news to all who are broken, food for a hungry world. We cry your praise, Holy Spirit who shelters and nurtures us in love, prods our consciences and energizes our spirits, and holds before us the way of life, lighting our way to pursue it. We cry your praise, one and triune Deity, in all the ways you meet us, and challenge us, and sustain us.

Call to Reconciliation

In ways beyond counting, God showers love on us. In Christian language we speak of God meeting us in three ways. The most traditional terms historically employed by the church are Father, Son, and Holy Spirit. But our language is rich with other terms we employ to address our triune deity—for example, as sovereign Creator, redeeming Judge, and nourishing Comforter. In all cases, however, we are called to acknowledge that when we use these terms, we address One who is consummately holy, righteous, and compassionate, into whose presence we may come—indeed, we should dare to step—only in humility. In humility, then, let us confess both the cause of our need and our confidence in divine charity.

Prayer of Confession

Timeless Sovereign, we measure ourselves before you and know we are wanting: where you call us to creativity, we are comfortable with leaving well enough alone; where you model exuberant generosity, we carefully keep our fingers together, the better to prevent too much from slipping away; where you propose that we be miracles to a world that knows too much suffering and too little hope, we stand on the sideline, life members in the association of bystanders. Forgive us, you Stimulus of imaginative wonder; forgive us, you Essence of self-giving; forgive us, you Keeper of commitment's promises, and provoke us to be instruments of recreation, reconciliation, reaffirmation—a genuine people of God.

Declaration of Forgiveness

The prophet Amos describes how a crushing punishment about to fall upon a deserving Israel was withdrawn by God because of the prophet's cry for mercy. A woman roundly accused of adultery, a capital offense under Hebraic law, was dismissed by Jesus with the simple admonition, "Go, and don't sin again." Paul admonished the Christians at Rome that the Holy Spirit was prepared to lead them to life, no matter how garish their past sin, if they would but receive her grace. Friends, if we repent, we are forgiven. Nothing more need be said.

Call for the Offering

When we consider the dimensions of generosity, we Christians stand between two extremes, each telling in its own way. At one pole stand the do-nothings, content to pursue personal pleasure and comfort, ignoring any pain by which they are not themselves inconvenienced. At the other pole are those truly remarkable people who, in commitment to God, have forsaken every personal comfort. Few of us feel called to follow the latter; and few (God be praised!) condone the former. In between is the broad path where the Holy Spirit of God meets us and bids us consider what, of all we have received, we are now prepared to devote to the ministry of Christ. Now is our moment to decide.

Prayer of Dedication

Moved by your urging, Sacred Spirit, we bring these gifts. To your enduring love, Christ Jesus, we commit them. As you intend, Great Originator of Life, let them be employed. They are yours, whom we proclaim our one and triune God—Creator, Judge, and Redeemer.

Thanksgiving

In more ways than we have yet imagined, supreme and eternal Deity, you have revealed yourself to this human family created in your image. In the brilliant explosion of light, the terrible splendor of wind and wave, the elegant complexity of life, the awesome power of human cognition, you reveal your intricate intentions. In your engagement with the human condition, adopting our form, embracing our limits, shouldering our mortality, we discern the presence of the holy in our histories, consecrating our flesh and birthing the hope of eternity. When a sanctifying presence moves among us, catching us unaware and startling us with how close we stand to mystery, we are overcome by the urgency of love and rejoice in the affirmation of worth. Thank you, you who alone are holy, for all that you are to us, all that you give to us, all that you require of us.

Sundays following Pentecost

Pentecost Season is far and away the longest block of the church year. The liturgical churches break the season down into four cycles that vary slightly according to the number of Sundays included during a given year. This practice has not generally been observed in the Reformed or Free churches, however, and I have chosen not to stress it here. The whole, in any case, bears a common thread of purpose: it is a time to do our homework concerning the nature and mission of the church and our obligations as Christians, individually and as communities.

The final Sunday of Pentecost season is assigned, in the liturgical traditions, to a celebration of the Reign of Christ—in the current sense that Christ is already Sovereign to those who confess him, and in the eschatological sense that Christ will come in glory at the end of time. It is a fitting theme with which to conclude the church year. To the extent that interest in historic liturgy continues to grow among Reformed and Free churches, as presently seems the case, this designation may be more frequently employed. I have not provided a separate set of prayers and responses, however, because it is unclear where, or how far, this trend will go. Those desiring to emphasize the Reign of Christ will find suitable material throughout the section.

Pentecost season may extend as long as twenty-eight Sundays, depending on the dating of Easter, though the count is more often fewer. I have provided material for twenty-five Sundays, reminding the reader that during years when the Pentecost season is exceptionally long, Epiphanytide will be correspondingly shorter. For those desiring to do so, prayers and responses not used during Epiphany may be employed here and vice versa.

Prayers and Liturgical Readings

Second Sunday after Pentecost

—

Invocation

In response to your call, Sovereign God, we come, because we need to hear your word, to be reminded that we are not alone, to feel again the shaping influence of this community that is the body of Christ, to focus our vision and inform our decisions, and because we require the power of your Holy Spirit to impel and sustain us in the task of discipleship. Bless our coming in, lend joy to our celebration, and commission our going out; that our coming, our presence, and our leaving equally may serve you.

Call to Praise (from 1 Chronicles 16:8–11)

Leader: We will give thanks to you, our God, and call on your name;

People: We will make known your deeds among the peoples!

Leader: We will sing praises to you,

People: And tell of all your wonderful works!

Leader: Glory to your holy name.

People: Let the hearts of all who seek you rejoice,

Leader: Seek your strength,

People: Continually seek your presence!

Prayer of Praise (from 1 Chronicles 16:28–34)

Ascribe to God, you families of the peoples, ascribe to God glory and strength. We assign to you, Bearer of majesty, the glory due your name; we bring an offering and come before you, to worship you in holy splendor. Let all the earth tremble before our God, who has firmly established the world so that it is not easily shaken. Let the heavens be glad and the earth rejoice, and let the word go up from among the nations, "God rules!" Let the sea roar, and all that fills it; let the field exult, and everything in it. Then the trees of the forest shall sing for joy before the One who comes to judge the earth. Exult the name of God, whose goodness and steadfast love endure for ever.

Call to Reconciliation

Where we are prepared to come before God in humility of spirit, acknowledging the weakness that hampers us and the sin that divides us, God is prepared with wonderful patience to forgive and renew us. Let us neither be indifferent to so tender a gift nor presume to be immune from its authority, but join in common confession before our merciful Judge.

Prayer of Confession

Who can stand in the presence of your holiness, O God; and which of us, after searching heart and mind, can compel your approval? Is there any justified in claiming to be good? Even Christ refused the title for himself, asserting that you alone are good. Against that measure, how shall we stand? We are convicted by our indifference to suffering, our laziness to extend mercy, our reluctance to share love. If there is any good in us, we refuse to claim it for ourselves but will wait for the confirmation that you alone can assign, which shows itself in the fruits of goodness and peace. In all else, we will shut our mouths and with the patience taught us by Jesus wait in silence for your mercy.

Declaration of Forgiveness

This passage from Psalm 9:8–10 gives emphatic voice to the confidence of God's people in divine integrity and mercy: "God judges the world in righteousness, and the peoples with equity. God is a stronghold for the oppressed, a citadel in times of trouble. And those who know your name put their trust in you, for you, O God, have not forsaken those who seek you."

Call for the Offering

One of the startling moments in reading Scripture is to encounter a passage that is so immediately relevant we could almost publish it, unedited, in the daily paper and few would take issue with its premise, even though it is five thousand years old. Take, for example, Deuteronomy 15:10–11: "Since there will never cease to be some in need on the earth, I command you: 'Open your hand to the poor and needy neighbor in your land.' Give liberally, and be ungrudging when you do so, for on this count your God will bless you in all that you undertake." Such instruction requires no elaboration. Let our offering be such that God will indeed bless all that we undertake.

Prayer of Dedication

Take these gifts, you welcoming divinity, and put them to work where you, better than we, know they are needed. So let us be enablers of the ministrations of Jesus and gain a share in the good things that lead to your rule—compassion, and generosity, and mercy—through Christ the compassionate, the generous, the merciful.

Thanksgiving

Author of creation, who strides the galaxies and counts the stars in the palm of a hand, yet marks the passing of the fall wildflowers; Sovereign of history, who calls the nations to task, yet wills to risk the goals of history to our human choices; hear now the list of our gratitude: For common memory and experience that give to all who have been touched by this place a sense of kinship; for the affections that draw us here again and again and warm us with a sense of family and place; for the continuing life and achievements of this congregation, freshly available to each new generation of its people; for the unspeakable privilege of gathering in peace to share our songs and praise and thanksgiving. For all these things, O God, we are profoundly grateful.

Third Sunday after Pentecost
—

Invocation (based on the Prophecy of Joel)

Holy God, whose love burns with zeal for your land, who is moved to compassion for your people, stir us now by your presence here among us; whose authority calls together the nations and instills in them the knowledge that you—and no other—are the Holy One. Then pour out on all humankind a grand epiphany, that our sons and daughters may prophesy, our old folk dream dreams, and our youth see visions; and let all who call on your name know the salvation of our God.

Call to Praise (from 1 Chronicles 16:23–26)

Leader: Sing to the divine Spirit, all earth!

People: Tell of God's salvation from day to day.

Leader: Declare the divine glory among the nations,

People: God's marvelous deeds to all the peoples!

Leader: For great is our Creator, and worthy of large praise,

People: Who is to be held in awe above all gods.

Leader: For all the gods of the people are idols;

People: But God, our God, made the heavens.

Prayer of Praise (from Job 38:4–13)

We proclaim the majesty of God, great sovereign of time and eternity, who laid earth's foundations, settled its dimensions, and stretched upon it a measuring line; who raised its pillars and laid its cornerstone, when the morning stars sang together and all the children of God shouted for joy. We sing the praise of God, who watched over the sea's birth when its flood burst from creation's womb, to wrap it in a blanket of cloud and cradle it in fog, establishing its bounds with the command, "Thus far you shall come and no farther." We shout the glory of creation's Architect, who summons the dawn and shows the morning its place, teaching it to grasp the edges of earth and to shake the wickedness out of it. To you, great and only God, be glory and honor and majesty, in our time and all the times to come.

Call to Reconciliation

The biblical tradition informs us, the apostles admonish us, and Jesus instructs us that only those who come in humility may stand in the presence of God and be declared suitable vessels for God's word. Let us now, therefore, set aside our pride, divest ourselves of any remnant of arrogance, and make common acknowledgment of our need, so that divine affirmation may restore us to wholeness.

Prayer of Confession

God of reconciliation, you call us to be peacemakers; but our history shows how often we are peace-breakers. Faced by actions we deem hostile, we lose confidence in you and transfer it to our weapons. Claiming that we desire harmony among nations, we engage in the rhetoric of violence. Believing that the technology of death can secure our safety, we pay for it by mortgaging our economy, shortchanging our youth, ignoring our poor, and selling our souls. Aware of Christ's admonition that those who live by the sword shall die by it, we fail to see that we need no external enemy; we are sufficient enemy to ourselves. With deep sadness, we acknowledge that we live by fear, not faith, trusting blindly in that which cannot save. Forgive, O God. And forgiving, restore our trust in the power of your love, compared to which the combined might of nations is but pathetic posturing.

Declaration of Forgiveness

In these words from Psalm 27:1, 13, we take courage: "God is my light and my salvation; whom shall I fear? God is the stronghold of my life; of whom shall I be afraid? I believe that I shall see the goodness of the eternal One in the land of the living! Wait for your redeemer; be strong, and let your heart take courage; yes, wait for God!"

Call for the Offering

The psalter of Hebrew Scriptures, the ancient Jewish hymnbook, reflects the full range of human experience—the best and the worst of our human pilgrimage. Our offering call this morning is from one of the more sublime entries, Psalm 112, an ancient hymn of praise. At several points, the psalmist defines generosity as an essential ingredient of righteousness. So we read, "It is well with those who deal generously and lend, who conduct their affairs with justice. For the righteous will never be moved . . . . They have distributed freely, they have given to the poor; their righteousness endures forever." In Hebrew, to be "moved" means to totter, as when an earthquake shakes the land we stand on and throws us off balance. So in stating that "the righteous will never be moved," the psalmist declares that God responds to human righteousness by making us secure. Let us now, therefore, by displaying our generosity, show the world the rock-solid foundation upon which we stand.

Prayer of Dedication

Out of your richness, boundless God, we receive treasure beyond counting. Out of that treasure we now lay before you our gifts and dedicate them to become again your richness. Let them extend through us and beyond us to become bounty to others we have never seen, whose names we do not know, but whom we call neighbor through the mediating grace of Christ Jesus our Savior.

Thanksgiving

Creator God, the abundance with which you bless us is greater than we require and more than we deserve. We yield you thanks, therefore, for all that you give us richly to enjoy: the love and care of home; friendships that rejoice our days; a wealth of knowledge and the skills with which to apply it at work or play; and every gift of health, strength, and happiness. With special gratitude we acknowledge the encouragement of all who have nurtured and sheltered us, advised and instructed us, healed and disciplined us, by whose gift of self we have been helped on our way; and for every vision of truth, and every motive unswervingly to seek it, that you have given to this congregation and all who are a part of it. Let us continue to serve you in this place, O God, in our time and in all the times to come.

Fourth Sunday after Pentecost
—

Invocation

Almighty God, who sent your Child to be the salvation of us all, and calls us in Jesus' name to be agents of reconciliation to the world: impress upon us the full meaning of our incorporation into the community of those who acknowledge Christ's sovereignty, by whatever name called, wherever situated on earth, by whatever language addressed. As you are one God, make us one people. So may the ministry of reconciliation know no division to dilute it, no dissension to weaken it, no despair to drain it of your power.

Call to Praise (from Deuteronomy 32:1–3)

Leader: Give ear, O heavens, and we will speak;
People: Let the earth hear the words of our mouths.
Leader: Let our words drop like the rain
People: Our speech condense like the dew;
Leader: Like gentle rain on grass,

People: Like showers on new growth.
Leader: For we will proclaim the name of the Holy One;
People: Ascribe greatness to our God!

Prayer of Praise (from Psalm 93)

God is sovereign, robed in majesty; God is robed with strength, wearing it like a belt; who made the world firm so that it shall never totter; whose throne, too, is established from the beginning, a seat worthy of One who is everlasting. The rivers rise, and raise their voices. The floods lift up their roaring, the waters their thunder. More majestic than the thunder of mighty waters, more majestic than the rolling combers of the sea, is the majesty of God on high! Your decrees will never alter; holiness will distinguish your house, our God, for evermore.

Call to Reconciliation

In the opening chapter of the first letter of John (vv. 8–10), we are reminded forcefully of how seriously early Christians took the concept of sin, and how important it is, as a precondition to forgiveness, to deal with it openly. Listen: "If we say we have no sin we deceive ourselves, and the truth is not in us. If we confess our sins, God is faithful and just, and will forgive our sins and cleanse us from all unrighteousness. If we say we have not sinned we make God a liar, and the Word is not in us." Since we are called to be people of the Word, let us not make God a liar, but confess our sin and ask for God's mercy.

Prayer of Confession

With haste, we rush to the day's work when personal profit is the reward; with reluctance, we engage the task of ministering to the broken. We are quick to expect apologies, but slow to extend forgiveness. We cheer the misfortune of those we consider our enemies, but drag our feet when it is time to make peace. In many such ways, evident and invisible, we ignore the saving graces that call us to life and pander to the narrow greed that leads to death. Forgive, O God. Do not abandon us, even though we are inconstant; but by the power of your constancy overwhelm our reluctance and sweep us into the delight of obedient love; for the sake of Jesus Christ, whose love for us was so powerful that even death could not prevail against it.

Declaration of Forgiveness

From Psalm 32 (1–2, 5, 10) we take these words of assurance: "Happy are those whose transgressions are forgiven, whose sin is covered. Happy are those to whom God imputes no iniquity, and in whose spirit there is no deceit. I acknowledged my sin to God, and did not hide my iniquity. I said, 'I will confess my transgressions,' and you forgave the guilt of my sin. Many are the torments of the wicked; but steadfast love embraces those who trust in God."

Call for the Offering

The author of the intertestimentary book titled Sirach, with some passion, cautions those who would be God's people concerning their obligation to the needy. "Deprive not the poor of their living, and do not keep needy eyes waiting. Do not grieve one who is hungry, nor frustrate a man in want. Do not avert your eye from the needy, nor give them occasion to curse you; for if in bitterness of soul they call down a curse upon you, our Creator will hear their prayer." Harsh words, but perhaps ones that remind us of how seriously God takes our call to be agents of mercy—and so ought we.

Prayer of Dedication

As your Word sanctifies the words that we speak, Creator God, your compassion makes holy our acts of mercy. Let your will specify the purpose and direction of these gifts that we bring in the name of Jesus Christ; through whom we receive grace to incarnate your love in the flesh of human kindness.

Thanksgiving

You who frame and clothe the universe, whose will for our earth is the all-encompassing shalom, the universal time of justice, the globe-girdling wholeness of human community: thank you for the profligate wealth of life, the sparkle of running and flying and swimming creaturehood, the wonderful diversity of the human family, the fair splendor of being alive. As we gather now in the hope and the possibility of peace for the world, we also thank you for those persons, famous or anonymous, remembered or having no memorial, who have honored your call to be peacemakers. For their gifts, and your blessing of them, we are grateful. Yet let us not be content only to speak words of thanks, but drive us to live out our own lives as makers of peace, that all our actions, like theirs, may compose a living prayer of praise and thanksgiving to you, who are our true peace.

Fifth Sunday after Pentecost
—

Invocation

Covenanting Creator, by whom we are given life, by whose love we are sustained, by whose grace we sense your participation in what we do in this place: speak to us now, that your will may become apparent, your love a palpable fire within us, your grace the impetus that drives us out again into your world, to live as the embodiment of will, love, and grace. So may others, through us, come to you.

Call to Praise (from Psalm 5:11–12)

Leader: Let all who take refuge in you rejoice, O God,

People: Let them ever sing for joy;

Leader: Spread your protection over them,

People: So that those who love your name may exalt in you.

Leader: For you bless the righteous,

People: Your favor covers them like a shield.

Leader: Through the abundance of your steadfast love, we will enter your house,

People: And bow in awe before your holy presence.

Prayer of Praise (from Psalm 97)

God is Supreme! Let earth rejoice, the many coastlands be glad! Cloud and thick night surround you, our God; righteousness and justice form the foundations of your throne. Fire precedes you as you go, consuming evil on every side. Your lightning lights up the world; earth observes and quakes. Mountains melt like wax at the coming of earth's sovereign. Heaven proclaims your righteousness and nations see your glory. God loves those who repudiate evil and guards the souls of the devout, rescuing them from the clutches of the wicked. Rejoice in the One who defines virtue, you virtuous, and give thanks to God's holy name!

Call to Reconciliation

Jesus teaches us that confession and forgiveness go hand in hand—but not simply our confession and God's forgiveness. In Mark 11:24–25, Jesus makes it clear that our hope for mercy from God depends partly on our forgiveness of others. Listen as Jesus speaks: "So I tell you, whatever you ask in prayer, believe that you are already receiving it and it will be yours. And whenever you stand praying, forgive, if you have anything against anyone; so that God in heaven may also forgive you your trespasses." In the spirit of Christ, let both our repentance—and our compassion—be evident in our prayer of reconciliation.

Prayer of Confession

God of life, who calls us into the ways that lead to your house of many mansions: we confess the frequency with which we choose the paths that lead to the halls of death. God of light, who surrounds us with knowledge and bids us seek understanding: we confess how often we choose ignorance, so that we can continue to have our own way. God of holiness, who commands that no lesser gods shall command our allegiance: we confess the idolatries of power and wealth and status to which we turn in the vain belief that they give life meaning. God of love, who calls us to lives of redemptive loving: we confess our attachment to petty hatreds and global distrust. Forgive us these our sins and turn us again to the way that leads to life, to understanding, to right loyalties, to true love; for the sake of Jesus Christ, who lived and died and rose again for your love and our life.

Declaration of Forgiveness (from Psalm 103:1–4)

"Bless God, O my soul; my innermost heart, bless God's holy name. Bless God, O my soul, and forget none of the benefits of the One who pardons all your guilt, and heals all your suffering, redeeming your life from the Pit, and surrounding you with steadfast love and tender affection." With such simple eloquence, the psalmist reminds us how fully we may trust in heaven's mercy and forbearance. Thanks be to God.

Call for the Offering

In Matthew 6:19–21, Jesus advises his disciples with these words: "Do not store up for yourselves treasures on earth, where moth and rust consume and where thieves break in and steal; but store up for yourselves treasures in heaven, where neither moth nor rust consumes and where thieves do not break in and steal. For where your treasure is, there your heart will be also." Let this day's offering be an opportunity for each of us to store up a bit of heavenly treasure, knowing that acts of mercy are remembered, enriched, and repaid by God.

Prayer of Dedication
We possess nothing, ingenious Deity, that you are not able to use with greater resourcefulness than we are. So take what we return to you here and wring from it all the goodness it can buy; that someone's pain may be transformed to healing, their defeat to triumph. Then, because of us, they may learn to praise you.

Thanksgiving
God of Holiness, who urges us to journey in the light but accompanies us when we choose the shadowy path; who rejoices with us in our joy but remains to comfort us in our sorrow; who bids us fully to enter into life, but gently receives us in death: hear our thanks for mercies seen and invisible, understood and uncomprehended. For the unparalleled privilege of life in a free land, we thank you. For diversity of faith and opinion that does not issue in terror and bloodshed, we thank you. For our place in communities we call home and the community of this church, we thank you. For mothers and fathers, sons and daughters, sisters and brothers, and all with whom we share blood kinship and family bond, we thank you. Bend to us, Generous One, and teach us the posture of thankfulness that makes of life a seamless act of gratitude, for the sake of Christ Jesus, in whom we both live and pray.

Sixth Sunday after Pentecost
—

Note: The material for this Sunday was composed around the theme of Independence Day and may be traded with that for the Sunday, during any calendar year, that precedes July 4.

Invocation
We acknowledge your presence, O God of times and seasons, in the great events of our history as nation and as global community; make

equally evident to us your presence in our momentary gathering in this room. Our faith has no difficulty perceiving your action in the dramatic events of our day; give us faith now to see it in the gathering of two or three—or dozens or hundreds—in this congregational home. Then, our lives and our liturgy woven together into a whole piece of cloth, we may feel your presence equally in our work and our worship, through Jesus Christ our Savior.

Call to Praise (from Psalm 19:1–4)

Leader: The heavens are telling the glory of God,
People: Whose handiwork the firmament proclaims.
Leader: Day to day pours forth speech,
People: And night to night declares knowledge.
Leader: There is no speech, nor are there words;
People: Their voice is not such as ear can hear;
Leader: Yet their voice goes out through all the earth,
People: Their words to the end of the world.
Unison: Now send we our words to join them, our voices in praise to God!

Prayer of Praise (from Psalm 150)

We praise you, O God! We praise you in your sanctuary; we praise you in your majestic creation! We praise you for your mighty deeds; we praise you in harmony with your surpassing greatness! We praise you with trumpet sounds, with organ and harp! We praise you with percussion and dance, with strings and wind instruments! We praise you with clapping hands and loud clashing cymbals! Let everything that breathes make with us the music of adoration. Praise God!

Call to Reconciliation

From our parents in the community of faith, we learned that if we claim we are without blemish, we simply confirm how flawed we truly are, how consumed by self-righteousness, how little there is to be done for us. But when we acknowledge our need, God is quick to forgive. Indeed, Christ admonishes, God waits anxiously for us to bring our need and lay it before the throne of grace. So let us not keep God waiting longer, but raise our collective voice and seek reconciliation with our Redeemer.

Prayer of Confession

In all of earthly time, Generous Creator, what nation has ever received more in material wealth than ours; or been blessed by the ingenuity of so diverse and intelligent a people; or assembled such awesome power, the envy of nations and the dread of tyrants? And how, Frightful Judge, shall we render a satisfactory account of our stewardship of these gifts? Stung by greed, we despoil the land, abuse the poor, and forget your law. Lusting for fame and success, we squander precious genius on the manufacture of useless things and consume vast wealth in the production of waste. Drunk with power, we throw our weight around like the neighborhood bully, fearing to trust the community of nations to solve global problems. Remind us, our God, that nations rise and fall to suit your purpose. Then make of this nation a holy people, fit for holy duty, in service to a beloved world.

Declaration of Forgiveness (from Psalm 103:8–14)

God is merciful and gracious, slow to anger and overflowing with steadfast love; who does not harbor indignation forever, whose resentment lasts only a short time. We are not treated as our guilt and sin deserve. No less than the height of heaven over earth is the vastness of divine love for those who fear God's holiness; as far as east is from west, God removes our sins from among us. As a child receives the tenderness of a compassionate parent, so we receive God's mercy, who knows our frame and remembers that we are dust.

Call for the Offering

The closing passage of the Gospel According to Matthew (28:19–20) consists of words we have come to title "the great commission." According to Matthew's account, Jesus charged the disciples to span out across the earth, spreading the good news of God's reconciling love in Jesus Christ and baptizing all who desired to become a part of it. One of the church's continuing stewardship tasks is to provide the wherewithal to pursue that commission. Our job is to underwrite works of love, by which suffering humanity gains tangible evidence of God's purpose. We invite you now to claim this task as your own, by bringing your gifts to Christ's table.

Prayer of Dedication

The privileges that we possess become even more evident, O Giver of peace, when we witness the plight of your people in nations torn by war, or hunger, or social chaos. We are indeed blessed by advantage. We turn, therefore, in obedience to your Word, to share the benefits of privilege. Direct their use to your purpose, that our obedience may be complete.

Thanksgiving

With hearts overflowing, great Sovereign of history, we prepare again to observe the founding of our nation; to recall, with misty eyes and wondering hearts, the outrageous courage of those splendid men and women who dared to risk all, even to stand and die for liberty—theirs and ours. As our first act, we kneel to acknowledge our debt to these ancestors of our commonweal. We proclaim, as well, the divine providence on which they rested their faith, their trust, and their sacred honor. Then we mean to celebrate, with picnics and giddy games, family outings and startling, brilliant, erupting showers of wondrous explosions, the joy of political freedom. Be present in our thankfulness. Be present in our memories. And be present in our silliness and mirth, by which we mean not only to savor our good fortune, but to sing your praise because of it.

Seventh Sunday after Pentecost
—

Invocation

Come to us, eternal Spirit, and show yourself to us as tangibly as we are aware of one another. For if you are not here, our gathering is without meaning; and if you are here and we do not recognize you, our gathering is in vain. So teach us to recognize you, that we may become able to recognize one another, and thereby enter into the true worship of the community that is in Christ Jesus our Savior.

Call to Praise (from Psalm 24)

Leader: The earth is God's and all that is in it,
People: The world, and those who live in it.
Leader: For God founded it on the seas,

People:	And established it on the rivers.
Leader:	Who shall ascend the hill of God,
People:	And who shall stand in the place of the Holy One?
Leader:	Those who have clean hands and pure hearts and do not swear deceitfully.
People:	They will receive blessing from God.

Prayer of Praise (based on Amos 5:8-9)

You who made the Pleiades and Orion; who turns deep night into morning and dims day into twilight; who summons the waters of the sea and pours them out on the surface of earth; who rouses flashing destruction against the strong, devastating the fortress: you who do all this: your name is "I Am." We cry then your praise, Creator God, for your great power. We cry your praise, most high Sovereign, for your inerrant justice. We cry your praise, Soul of compassion, who dispenses judgment and mercy, and bids us be just and merciful; that all the earth, seeing how equity and charity prevail among us, may join the universal anthem in praise of our God.

Call to Reconciliation

If the biblical record is to be believed, no one who ever came to Jesus in sorrow and repentance, seeking forgiveness and healing, was ever turned away. By the same token, no one that we know of was ever offered forgiveness until the need for it had been clearly stated—if not by the sick or suffering person, then by Jesus himself. Let us therefore come in humility, to speak our need to be forgiven and our desire to be healed.

Prayer of Confession

Fountain of infinite imagination, you create a world and challenge us to discover it. Our discovery, however, awakens in us the stunned realization that you mean for us to help create it, to transform it into the garden of your intention. At one moment, seeing the achievements of which we are capable, we think you inspired beyond comprehension. At others, witnessing the stupidity at which we are equally proficient, we think you must have made a terrible mistake. Worse, we doubt you altogether and retreat into uncertainty and fear. Grant us the courage, O

God, not to doubt, but to embrace your vision for the world. And as you do, grant us also the wisdom that discriminates between information and truth, so we can tell when our efforts complement, and when they subvert, your intention. Make insatiable our desire to reach the end-dream of Creation which, as yet, is known only to you.

Declaration of Forgiveness

To the ancient Hebrews, salvation was not a question of securing life after death. It possessed a powerful sense of immediacy, a quality of "here-and-nowness" that moved the author of Psalm 118 to write these words: "God has punished me severely, but did not give me over to death. Open to me the gates of righteousness, that I may enter through them and give thanks to the Holy One. This is the gate of God; the righteous shall enter through it. I thank you that you have answered me and become my salvation. The stone that the builders rejected has become the chief cornerstone. This is God's doing, and it is marvelous in our eyes." Sharing the psalmist's wonder at divine mercy, let us also claim a share in giving thanks.

Call for the Offering

In the Gospel According to Luke 12:32–34, the evangelist quotes Jesus in one of those delightful phrases that grab our attention and oblige us to rethink what we hear Jesus telling us. "Do not be afraid, little flock," Luke's Jesus chides his disciples, "it is God's good pleasure to give you the dominion." That much is easy to take. The catch is in the next line: "Sell your possessions, and give alms. Make purses for yourselves that do not wear out, an unfailing treasure in heaven. . . . For where your treasure is, there your heart will be also." When we give our offerings, Jesus insists, we do not lose, we gain. Giving is our way of making purses that do not wear out. So bring your possessions and carry away your heart's true treasure.

Prayer of Dedication

God of all generosity, the history of your people teems with examples of liberality, where kindness enlarged to sacrifice and sacrifice gave birth to redemption. In bringing these gifts, we seek to practice such generosity and, by practicing it, to transform the conventional into the extraordinary; that through us some one of your suffering humanity may know their torment ended and their misery redeemed, and turn again to praise you.

Thanksgiving (inspired by Habitat for Humanity)

Thank you, merciful God, for homes that are warm in the cold and dry in the rain, pleasant to see and a joy to live in. Thank you that, because we have been given more than we need, we are free to share our surplus with the discouraged, the unfortunate, the exploited—and thereby fulfill the law of Christ. Thank you for the sensitivity of the church wherever it makes tangible the robust love of Christ, reaching out to the poor, the homeless, the hungry, and frightened of the world. Thank you for the substantial commitment of those who practice what they preach, and back their words, not only with their money, but with muscle and mind, modeling for the rest of us a vivid portrayal of love. And thank you for their hope and ours, which refuses to be extinguished and believes against all odds that the job can be done and the goal achieved, because we hope in you.

Eighth Sunday after Pentecost

—

Invocation

Eternal God, speak to us now the word that we need and let that word unfold within us until it becomes for us a light to enlighten us, courage to empower us, a compass to show us the way. Purify, quicken, and refresh us; direct and enlarge our faith; and enable us by this worship to "know you more clearly, love you more dearly, and follow you more nearly," through this and all our days.

Call to Praise (from Psalm 29:1, 10–11—also suitable for use during Epiphany season)

Leader: Ascribe to God, O heavenly beings, ascribe glory and strength.

People: Ascribe due glory to God's name, worship the one who is clothed in holy splendor.

Leader: God sits enthroned over the flood.

People: God sits enthroned as monarch forever.

Leader: O God, give strength to the people.

People: O God, bless the people with peace.

Unison: And we will raise our voices in your praise!

Prayer of Praise (adapted from the apocryphal Song of the Three Young Men, vv. 36–67, inserted within Daniel 3:23–24)

Bless your Creator, you heavens and all powers, singing God's praise and high exultation forever. Bless your Creator, sun and moon and stars, singing God's praise and high exultation forever. Bless your Creator, all rain and dew, winds and fire, winter cold and summer heat, singing God's praise and high exultation forever. Bless your Creator, all nights and days, light and shadows, singing God's praise and high exultation forever. Bless your Creator, mountains and hills, springs and seas and rivers, singing God's praise and high exultation forever. Bless your Creator, all birds of the air and beasts of field and forest, whales and all creatures that move in the waters, singing God's praise and high exultation forever. Bless your Creator, all people of God, singing praise and high exultation forever.

Call to Reconciliation

If we are to receive the grace that God offers in Jesus Christ, we must first acknowledge that we have not earned it but receive it as a gift. This is a remarkable assertion—one that flies in the face of much of what our society espouses, namely: that God loves and forgives us, not because of what we have done, but in the very face of it. The only requirement we are under is to ask for God's loving forgiveness. Let us, then, bow before the throne of grace in our common act of confession.

Prayer of Confession

Great Author of mercy, you admonish us to love you with all our heart and soul and mind and strength and to love our neighbors as we love ourselves. The example of Jesus was to feed the hungry, heal the broken, clothe the naked. We cry amen, piously affirming the worth of these tasks; but our lives hint of duplicity and serve a lesser agenda. We allow the indulgence of personal desire to preoccupy us, the fear of obligation to hinder us, the pain of life to embitter us. We are neglectful that in failing to serve these least ones we fail to serve you. We overlook how our half-hearted loving hinders the increase of your dominion and deprives our own lives of spiritual enrichment. Chasten our neglect, merciful Ruler. In the image of Christ, transform us from recipients to servants. So may we, too, be judged good and faithful stewards of the sacred trust of life.

Declaration of Forgiveness

In Isaiah 1:18 this greatest of the messianic prophets speaks God's word to the people, inviting them to reconciliation: "Come now, let us reason together, says God: though your sins are like scarlet, they shall be as white as snow; though they are red like crimson, they shall become like wool." With thankful hearts, we receive forgiveness and rededicate ourselves to lives of holiness and gratitude.

Call for the Offering

Not all of us are able of serve God in the same way—and God knows better than we what those ways are! More than once, the apostle Paul addressed this diversity in the church. In 1 Corinthians 12:4–7, for example, he wrote: "Now there are varieties of gifts, but the same Spirit; and there are varieties of service, but the same God; and there are varieties of activities, but it is the same God who activates them in everyone. To each is given the manifestation of the Spirit for the common good." So the church is served at least as much by our diversity as by our similarities. Nonetheless, there are some things that all Christians can do and are expected to do. Among them is the expectation that each individual will support the work of the many and that the many will support the effort of each individual by financial support when it is needed. Let this offering be a response, in kind, to gifts the Spirit has bestowed on each of us.

Prayer of Dedication

Yours is the greatness, O God—and the power, the glory, the majesty and the victory. For what exists that is not already yours? We cannot add to it, but return to you these reflections of gifts first received from you, as symbols of our devotion and our desire to be fully incorporate in your loving community of saints.

Thanksgiving

Generous Deity, the list of things to compel our gratitude is too long for counting: the bounty of your mercy, greater than our ability to assess it; the love with which you surround and embrace us, richer than we can enumerate. Of necessity, then, we are reduced to partial lists, deficient understanding, incoherent expression. Yet where we do not know what to say, your Spirit intercedes for us with sighs too fervent for words, making perfect our desire and augmenting how we voice it. For this we are also thankful—to know that you know, more than we, both the measure of that for which we ought to be grateful and how to give it voice. Then thanksgivings and exaltations, you God of mercy, for your infinite generosity.

Ninth Sunday after Pentecost

—

Invocation

Note: Unless the minister is exceptionally skilled as a weather forecaster, it may be wiser not to print this one too far in advance for unison reading!

A.   The glory of a sparkling morning is amplified,

B.   The gloom of a somber day is scattered,

O God, by the warmth of friendships newly recharged and our love for this place and all who are part of our associations with it, who will in time future be part of our memories of it, and

A.   make it shine like the rising sun.

B.   make it sparkle even in the rain.

How precious a gift it has been; how precious a gift it continues to be. Enter into the spirit of our meeting here, then, you framer of friendships and guardian of personal and corporate histories, and instruct us in the ways of gratitude. Strip from us the illusion that these good things come of our deserving and free us to acknowledge them as gifts of your grace.

Call to Praise (from Psalm 43:3–5)

Leader: O send out your light and your truth;

People: Let them lead us.

Leader: Let them bring us to your holy hill,

People: And to your dwelling.

Leader: Then we will go to your altar,

People: Who are our exceeding joy;

Leader: We will praise you with the harp, O God, our God!

People: Why are you disquieted within me, O my soul?

Leader: Hope in God, whom we will praise again:

People: Our help and our God!

Prayer of Praise

Everlasting Presence, we praise you for commanding light that shatters the night; for dividing waters where dry land appears; for earth created and declared good. We honor you for making us in your image, to live with one another in love; for the Spirit-driven breath of life, the gift of speech, the freedom to choose. You disclosed your purpose in commandments to Moses, called for justice in the cry of the prophets. Through succeeding generations you are fair and tolerant toward your people. And when you declared that the time was fulfilled for us, you came in Word made flesh to live among us and increase our lives with abundance beyond measure. With people from all times and places, witnesses to you in voice and act, we lift our hearts in joyful praise, for you alone are holy.

Call to Reconciliation

Bearing witness with Christ that God alone is good and that all the rest of us fall short of that measure, let us all, with penitent hearts, acknowledge our shortcomings and seek the comfort and release of our Creator's forgiveness.

Prayer of Confession

How many times in recent days, God of the compassionate touch, have we seen the opportunity to assist but put it behind us for its inconvenience. How many days have we known of some soul's need but did not respond for fear it would require more than we were prepared to give?

How many momentary incidents have filled us with dread, because anxiety about the possible outweighed faith in your promise? And the while, we kept for ourselves what we might have done for another. O we are haunted by our excess and doomed by our greed. How shall we acquire your forgiveness if we ourselves lack mercy? Please, God, clarify our sense of what matters, compel our courage, and pull us back from the other side, to be Samaritans along the streets of our town and the roads of our lives.

Declaration of Forgiveness

In the book of Sirach 2:9–11, one of the intertestimentary works we know collectively as the Apocrypha, we read an eloquent passage of confidence in divine mercy: "You who fear God, hope for good things, for everlasting joy and mercy. Consider the ancient generations and see: who ever trusted in the Holy One and was put to shame? Or who ever persevered in the fear of God and was forsaken? Or who ever called upon heaven and was overlooked? For God is compassionate and merciful, forgiving sins and saving in time of affliction."

Call for the Offering

Because of variations in language, some passages of Scripture lend themselves to wonderful good humor. Such a one appears in Paul's second letter to the church at Corinth, chapter 9, verses 6 and 7. Paul writes, "The point is this: the one who sows sparingly will also reap sparingly, and the one who sows bountifully will also reap bountifully. Each of you must give as you have made up your mind, not reluctantly or under compulsion, for God loves a cheerful giver." In the Greek, the next to last word in that passage—cheerful—is *hilarion*. What a charming conception is this: give with joyful exuberance, for God loves a hilarious giver! Let your gifts this day bring the laughter of generosity to the table of our Sovereign.

Prayer of Dedication

We thank you, God of our covenant, for the sacred trust that you bestow on us by calling us to be your people; and we dedicate these gifts, as a part of this day's stewardship, in fulfillment of that trust. Let both the value of our gifts and the zeal of our giving multiply in your service.

Thanksgiving

With thankfulness, Creator God, we acknowledge the gift of life and all that sustains it; the love of families and all that they mean to us; the companionship of friends and the support that they give us; the opportunity afforded us by this congregation and the rich promise of its future; and communities that are peaceful and secure, affording us well-being in a world too much torn by hatred and stained by bloodshed. Keep us alert, O God, not alone to the richness of our lives, but to your mercy that provides it; that gratitude may be the hallmark of this people, so that others, seeing both our plenty and our humility, will find cause to thank you as well.

Tenth Sunday after Pentecost
—

Invocation

At your call, Holy One, we come to this place; at your word we shall learn who we are and what we are to do; at your command, we will scatter out again into our neighborhoods. Take away our desire for baskets under which to hide and fashion us into lampstands to hold out your light before this community we are called to serve; that through us your saltiness may be tasted, your yeast begin to brew and multiply, your loaves and fishes be broken and distributed to feed the multitude that is your people.

Call to Praise (from Psalm 46:8-10)

Leader: Come, behold our Creator's works;
People: See what desolations God has brought on the earth,
Leader: Who makes wars cease to the ends of the earth;
People: Who breaks the bow and shatters the spear,
Leader: And burns the shields with fire.
People: "Be still, and know that I am God!
Leader: Exalted among the nations,
People: Exalted in the earth."

Prayer of Praise

Holy One, inexpressible majesty, maker of all things, judge of all beings, redeemer of life: how shall we find sufficient language to speak your praise? If we turn to Scripture, we soon exhaust the supply. If we seek the counsel of poets, their eloquence proves inadequate to our theme. If we seek expression in song, our melodies fade to frustrated silence. How shall we praise you then, dear God? By lives that are lived to your glory, our thoughts a verse to your love, our words a melody to your splendor, our actions a scripture of living witness that you indeed are God and we are indeed your people.

Call to Reconciliation

Our relationship with God brings us to the realization that we human beings are good, because we were created with the rest of the physical order and declared good by our Creator. At the same time, we know that we use God's gifts—intellect and will and freedom—to betray the very traits of character that God bids us embrace. It is this contradiction that leads us to our need for correction; and it is to address this need that I invite you to join me in our prayer of confession.

Prayer of Confession (based on Psalm 15)

O God, who may abide in your tent? Who may dwell on your holy hill? Those who live blamelessly, do what is right, and speak truth from their heart; who speak no slander, do no evil to friends, nor mount a reproach against their neighbors; who despise wickedness, but honor all who fear their Creator; who keep their word even when it hurts; who do not lend money at interest, and do not accept a bribe against the innocent. Whoever do these things shall never totter. Holy One, we would make this our way. When we fail to do so, chastise us. When we stray, correct us. Where we abide in your way, affirm us. Plant us again among the people of righteousness, who are accounted your people.

Declaration of Forgiveness

From the Wisdom of Solomon (3:1, 5–7, 9), one of the intertestimentary works we know collectively as the Apocrypha, comes this poetic hymn of confidence in divine love: "The souls of the righteous are in the hands of God, and no torment will ever touch them. Having been disciplined a while, they will receive great good, because God tested them, trying them like gold in a furnace, and finding them worthy. In the time of their visitation they will shine forth, and will run like sparks through the stubble. Those who trust God will understand truth; those who are faithful will abide in love, because grace and mercy are upon these holy ones, over whom our God keeps watch."

Call for the Offering
In 2 Corinthians 9:8, the apostle Paul, writing to urge that young congregation's financial help for starving Christian in Jerusalem, makes this remarkable claim: "God is able to provide you with every blessing in abundance, so that you may always have enough of everything, and may provide in abundance for every good work." The implication of Paul's assertion is that, by blessing us generously, God intends two things: first, that we ourselves will want for nothing; but equally, that we have at our disposal the means to become, in a palpable way, God's love when others are in need. Is a greater invitation required?

Prayer of Dedication
Note: Because of its play on words, this prayer will make sense only if read in unison.

To all of us who worship in this place, O living God, grant grace to present both our material gifts and our undivided loyalties in living tribute, wholly to you, holy to you. Make us fit dwelling places for your energizing Spirit. So may others, seeing our gratitude and our commitment, give you gratitude and praise.

Thanksgiving
In awe-full love, holy God, you create us and call us to be a holy people. In loving awe, we discover that in shaping us, you intend to share your creative power with us: that we may imagine things that are not and bring them into being. When we consider our worthiness to be entrusted with so potent a gift, we are overwhelmed; for in your power of creation resides the power of destruction and we are not a people of wisdom. Desire threatens to outpace restraint, ambition to overwhelm prudence. Our thanks, then, you trusting Deity, for the love that dares to risk the future to our hands even in the face of our unworthiness; that anticipates the possibility that we may yet participate in holiness, even as we fail to justify it; that continues through time to call us to holy priesthood and partnership in destiny. Thank you for keeping faith with

us, God infinitely trustworthy, and grant us the wisdom—and the resolve—ever more fully to keep faith with you.

Eleventh Sunday after Pentecost

—

Invocation

Tender and compassionate Deity, whose strength is made perfect in our weakness: overcome our reluctance to believe that you receive us as we are. More than that, help us—imperfect though we be—to become more perfect carriers of the message of your love, earthen vessels chock full of treasures to be distributed to others who also long for your promise. May we, consonant with the admonition of Jesus, worship you now in spirit and in truth.

Call to Praise (from Psalm 47)

Leader:	Clap your hands, all you peoples;
People:	Shout to God with loud songs of joy.
Leader:	For our sovereign, the Most High, is awesome,
People:	A great ruler over all the earth.
Leader:	God has gone up with a shout,
People:	Our ruler with the sound of a trumpet.
Leader:	It is God who has authority over all the earth;
People:	Sing praises with a psalm.
Leader:	For the shields of earth belong to God;
People:	Who is highly exalted.

Prayer of Praise

All the voices of heaven and earth are insufficient to sing the fullness of your glory, O God; all the verse of humanity and rhythm of the stars may not capture your splendor. For when, by the lyrics of their being, they have sung their songs, shouted their acclamations, and executed their cosmic choreographies, they have done nothing more than you intend them to do. Help us then, infinite Majesty, to find richer voice with which to praise you, finer song with which to proclaim your wonder, poetry and symphony and dance appropriate to our theme, a new song to sing to the One who is our creator, our redeemer, our sanctifier. And let all earth join us in the mighty Amen!

Call to Reconciliation

We gather to engage in worship, the drawing in of the people of God to praise, to hear, to petition. We are reminded, by Scripture and tradition, that only those who come in humility can worship as God intends—in spirit and in truth. So let us come as honest persons, willing to name our weaknesses and own our shortcomings; not as fools who think it possible to dissemble in the face of God. To that end, I invite you to join your voice with mine in common confession.

Prayer of Confession

Dear God, our lives are filled with misgivings. Anxiety and dread hedge about us. We shun our neighbor, fear the stranger, mourn the lost community that we ourselves abandoned, and seek security in weapons and violence. Quickly we forget your promises: that you mark the sparrow's falling, more so what we require; that physical harm is trivial measured against the loss of our souls; that no shadowed valley is too deep for your mercy's reach, even though death itself dog our steps. Rebuke our doubts, Wellspring of courage. Chastise our ambivalence. Deride our gloom. Do not abandon us to our despair or the sin that clutches at us because of it, but certify us for fearless living, as free and loving as Jesus Christ, who remains our true model of hope.

Declaration of Forgiveness

In the portion of the Sermon on the Mount that we call "the Beatitudes," which means "blessings" (Matthew 5:8–10), Jesus assures us that when we genuinely are poor in spirit, God's realm becomes our possession; that when we are meek, the earth shall be our inheritance; that when the focus of our appetite is righteousness, we will be satisfied; that when our hearts are pure, we will see God; that when we are makers of peace, we shall be called God's children. Rejoice in this confirming proclamation of faith and know the forgiving grace of our Creator.

Call for the Offering

The apostle Paul was gifted at illustrating the relationship between the way we approach generosity and the rewards for doing so. In 2 Corinthians 9:11–14, as part of a broader essay on compassion and generosity, Paul makes this bold assertion: "You will be enriched in every way for your great generosity, which will produce thanksgiving to God through us; for the rendering of this ministry not only supplies the needs of the saints but also overflows in plentiful thanks to God. . . . You glorify God . . . by the generosity of your sharing with them and with all others, while they . . . pray for you because of the surpassing grace of God." Let us now provide for the needs of the saints and earn gratitude for God in prayers of thanksgiving.

Prayer of Dedication

Out of your richness, Source of Bounty, you provide the foundations of our welfare. Out of our richness, we want now to establish such foundations for someone else. By our sacrifice, therefore, we return part of your gift, asking that it become gift again for some others that you also love, who—like us—need your mercy.

Thanksgiving (Traditional/Adapted)

O God our Sovereign, author and giver of all good things, we thank you for all your mercies and for your loving care for all your creatures. We bless you for the gift of life, for your protection around us, for your guiding hand upon us, and for the tokens of your love within us. We are grateful for friendship and duty, for good hopes and precious memories, for the joys that cheer us and the trials that teach us to trust you. Most of all, we glorify you for the saving knowledge of your Child; for the living presence of your Spirit; for your church, the body of Christ; for the ministry of word and sacrament and all the means of grace. In all things, O God, make us wise in the right use of your gifts and make of our lives, through all our days, an acceptable thanksgiving.

Twelfth Sunday after Pentecost
—

Invocation

We are such creatures of habit, O God. The rhythm of life is so reliable, and we grow so accustomed to calm, dependability, routine. So we confess: we are not entirely prepared to handle the disruption that your presence among us promises always to create. Remind us, therefore, whose place this is and whose people we are; that we did not call you here, you called us; that we have no business being here except you set the agenda. Take command then, you Holy Guide of life and fortune, and let the business of this day—your business—now begin in earnest, to carry us where you will.

Call to Praise (from Psalm 57:8–11)

Leader: Awake my soul! Awake O harp and lyre!

People: We will waken the dawn!

Leader: We will give thanks to you, O God, among the peoples;

People: We will sing praises to you among the nations.

Leader: For your steadfast love is as high as the heavens;

People: Your faithfulness extends to the clouds.

Leader: Be exalted, holy Majesty, above the heavens!

People: Let your glory be over all the earth!

Prayer of Praise

We take time out, Creator Spirit, from daily routine—the meaningless clatter, the stale chatter, the jockeying for power—to seek again the ground of our being. Silence our carping and our clamor and teach us to drink from the living spring that wells up in us. Then we will breathe praise for calm spirits and turn to honor you for real blessings: for days and seasons that give rhythm to life; for this place that teaches us how to live; for every human love that fortifies us when we least expect it, dissolving the illusion of isolation; for new ideas that catch us by surprise like crocus blossoms emerging from melting snow, rekindling the mind's affection; and for this congregation of friends, among whom we may both give and receive the graciousness you entrust to us as agents of your love. For these genuine bounties, O Source of all bounty, we honor your name.

Call to Reconciliation

In the apocryphal book of Esdras 16:53–54, 64–65, we read this stinging admonition: "Let no sinner claim not to have sinned: for God will burn coals of fire upon the head of one who says, 'I have not sinned before God or the divine glory.' Behold, God knows all the works of humanity—their imaginations, their thoughts, and their hearts. Because God will strictly examine all their works, and will make a public spectacle of us all. We will be put to shame, and our own iniquities will stand as our accusers on that day." Knowing the truth of this claim, both as regards the majesty of our judge and the fine impartiality with which we are judged, let us respond by joining in confession.

Prayer of Confession

In our soul's deeps we know, Righteous God, that there is no forgiveness apart from repentance; no reconciliation without sacrifice; no resurrection except we submit to the death of self, so that we might be raised with Christ. But it is so hard. We loathe the press of the cross and dread the vale of death's shadow. With the facility of the well rehearsed, we make excuses, postpone the appointment, beg for time. Yet even as we resist, we apprehend your coming mercy that penetrates our souls' murk and promises the healing for which we long. Frightened by the surgery our restoration requires, we yet come trembling before you, O Physician of the human soul, and plead: Heal us. Remove from us the burden of sin; excise our self-deception; and withal, give us your peace.

Declaration of Forgiveness

In his letter to the Romans 5:1–11, the apostle Paul records this view of forgiveness and reconciliation: "since we are justified by faith, we have peace with God through our Savior Jesus Christ, through whom we have obtained access to this grace in which we stand; and we boast in our hope of sharing the glory of God. For while we were still helpless, at the right time Christ died for the ungodly. . . . We even boast in God through our Savior Jesus Christ, through whom we have now received our reconciliation."

Call for the Offering

It is possible, over time, to grow tired of being asked to give away our own wealth to help others. We become especially touchy at times when we'd be pleased to have a bit more ourselves! It is an understandable feeling, but not one that we have the luxury of approving—unless we are prepared to jeopardize our membership in the household of God! Paul understood this when he admonished in Galatians 6:7–10 that we cannot play a shell game with God: what we sow is what we shall reap, for good or ill. If we ignore the world's pain, we will receive the reproof of Christ's pain. But if we respond in love, we add to heaven's joy—and our own. Therefore, Paul urged, "let us not grow weary in well-doing, for in due season we shall reap, if we do not lose heart."

Prayer of Dedication

We bring our gifts to your table, Christ Jesus—the same table from which we receive the bread and the wine that symbolize your tangible love for real people, in real need and real pain. Here we dedicate it, in support of those who work with your people in their need. Through them, let some ones of your children experience, in a form they can touch and taste, the bread and wine of your love.

Thanksgiving

It is easy to be grateful for large things that shape our affairs and sway our lives, the looming miracles of grace that stop us cold in our tracks and shout the mercy of God. Let us now be thankful, too, for small graces that catch us unaware; that occur when we are too busy—or so we fancy—to pause and take notice; or are so subtle, and we so unfeeling, that we disregard them altogether; or so common that we overlook them and miss the patch of heaven they possess. So we thank you, Who fashions all things, for small blessings: the touch of a caring hand when we are ill or disconcerted, a curtain of rain on a scorching August afternoon, a chance meeting of friends along the supermarket aisle, the grin of a child we do not even know. For these little things, gentle God, we thank you and declare: because you came and lived among us, we know the magic of surprise blessings and the joy of small stuff.

Thirteenth Sunday after Pentecost
—

Invocation

At one moment, seeing the sublime achievements of which we are capable, we cry your praise, O God who inspires and defines us. In the next, witnessing the inhumanity of which we are equally capable, we think you must have made a dreadful mistake—or worse, that you are not there at all. Encourage us now, great Intender, not to doubt, but to embrace your vision for our world, instilling in us an insatiable desire to stretch toward the ultimate dream for creation that is, as yet, known only to you.

Call to Praise (from Psalm 66:16–20)

Leader: Come and hear, all you who fear God,

People: And I will tell you what our Maker has done for me.

Leader: I cried aloud to God, whom I extolled with my tongue.

People: Who, had I cherished evil in my heart, would not have listened.

Leader: But truly, God has listened,

People: And given heed to the words of my prayer.

Unison: Blessed be God, who has not rejected our prayer, nor removed steadfast love from us.

Prayer of Praise

The last deep days of summer surround us, you God of times and seasons who ordains the turn of years, and amplifies our joy. Now, before we pass into fall and life returns to the prosaic round of work and shopping, school and commuting, we pause to praise you. Then glory for blue skies and green forests, surf-battered headlands and broad beaches, flower-strewn meadows and maturing fields, days of intoxicating warmth and nights of slumber-provoking coolness. It is a splendid time to be alive, and we thank you for it. We thank you, too, for the clutter of memories that lodge in our brains, this fuel for precious dreams and hopeful plans to temper the short days and long nights of winter. Praise the imagination of God!

Call to Reconciliation

In Paul's letter to the Romans 14:10–12, the apostle issues this admonition, which we adopt as this day's call to confession: "Why do you pass judgment on your sister; or you, why do you despise your brother? For we shall all stand before the judgment seat; for it is written: 'As I live,' says our Sovereign, 'every knee shall bow to me, and every tongue shall give praise to God.' So each of us shall give our own personal account to God." In light of Paul's counsel, let us not delay, but join in making our confession to God.

Prayer of Confession

Into the need of the world you plunge us, caring God, pressing us to live as souls redeemed, through whom grace touches palpably the tortured flesh—gentle as a mother's caress, firm as a father's embrace, bright as a child's grin. But look at us now. Oh we are blighted by our greed, tangled by our fear, a people of little joy and less mercy. Even while you watch, humanity does violence to those you send us to serve and executes the one you send to save us. Forgive us, O God. Restore in us the courage to dare. Teach us again that life is secure only when given away. And brand us with the name of your triumphant child, whose gift of self on our behalf shattered death for all who yearn for life, and waits now for our repentance.

Declaration of Forgiveness

This morning's assurance of pardon comes from Paul's letter to the church at Rome (Romans 10:11–13), where Paul writes, "The scripture says, 'No one who believes in God will be put to shame.' For there is no distinction between Jew and Greek; the same God is sovereign of all, and is generous to all who call upon the holy name. For 'Everyone who calls on the name of God will be saved.'" Receive forgiveness from God and know that restitution, not shame, is our portion.

Call for the Offering

The spirit of generosity that the gospel advocates is summed up in the final chapter of the letter to the Hebrews, where the author notes the behavior that is incumbent on those who claim membership in the body of Christ. In Hebrews 16 we find this brief reproof: "Do not neglect to do good and to share what you have, for such sacrifice is pleasing to God." I invite you now to fulfill the urging of the author of this early Christian letter: to do good and to share what you have, by joining in the morning offering.

Prayer of Dedication

Out of the resources by which our lives are sustained and made bountiful, generous Creator, we set aside these portions to voice to others your love, so that they, too, can know the meaning of lives amply sustained and bountiful. Use our gifts to your own good purpose; then turn and use us, who are the givers, yet again, that the cups of our lives may brim over with the joy that only generosity yields.

Thanksgiving

With gratitude, O God, we affirm that we are the recipients of mystery, into which you now induct us as guardians and partners. How else shall we explain the endurance of love in a world filled with hatred? Or the perseverance of generosity among a people obsessed by self-gratification? Or the stubborn devotion to goodness of those touched deeply by the Word-made-flesh, while the ones they serve continue to heap rewards on those who make a profession of passing by on the other side of the road? Then cheers and celebration, Great Redeemer, for these mysteries of gentleness and humility and self-giving, by which we, like all your saints, may hope to triumph over the very gates of hell. Amen. So let it be!

Fourteenth Sunday after Pentecost

Invocation

Out of the turmoil and confusion, the excitement and tedium, the attractions and distractions that comprise our daily life, Holy God, we come apart to this place of reflection and renewal: to celebrate your presence among us; to hear, afresh, the good news of the gospel of Jesus Christ; to renew our pledge of obedience as his people; to receive your Spirit's empowerment that fires us to be signs and wonders that witness to your redemptive love in our time. Receive us in your mercy; arouse us with your word; and, by your will, commission us to the tasks that will be ours, in your name, at the end of this hour.

Call to Praise (from Psalm 67—suitable for use during Epiphany season)

Leader: Be gracious to us, O God, and bless us

People: And make your face to shine upon us,

Leader: That your way may be known on earth,

People: Your saving power among all nations.

Leader: Let the peoples praise you, O God;

People: Let all the peoples praise you.

Leader: Let the nations be glad and sing for joy,

People: For you judge the peoples with equity, and guide the nations upon earth.

Leader: May God continue to bless us;
People: And let us, with all the ends of earth, revere our Maker!

Prayer of Praise

Stars and planets, galaxies and nebulas, quarks and black holes witness your splendor, you Framer of cosmos. Fire-born skeleton of earth, amended by seismic shift, sculptured by wind and frost, attests to your might. Forests and glades, bogs and brooks, alpine meadows and mist-mantled valleys, confirm your splendid imagination. Teeming swimming flying leaping lumbering profusion of living creaturehood heralds your marvelous mystery of design. And we your human creatures, gifted by consciousness, bearers of moral burden, stewards of technology— shall we not also glorify you, O God who is cloaked in wonder yet revealed in all things, infinitely distant and intimately near, who alone elicits, solely merits, our adoration.

Call to Reconciliation

Where the love of God confronts us, its light is so intense that our lights become shadows in its presence. By this metaphor, we understand that all of us alike are wanting in the presence of divine holiness. Let us, then, confess our inadequacies and give substance to our contrition, that we may know the forgiveness of the One who alone can give us light to overcome our gloom.

Prayer of Confession

By our baptism, God of our common life, we were adopted into the family of the church, to receive its nurture and direction. By our confirmation, we took our place as maturing members of that family, responsible to model before the world what it means to be the body of Christ. The eucharist defines for us, in both body and spirit, the lengths to which you will go to redeem us. Alas, dear God, it is not enough. In fear and shame, we bow to own our sin, confess our failure, and seek your forgiveness. For we are human, given to weakness, unable even to hope unless you help us. Come to us now, baptize us anew with your spirit of commitment, reconfirm us in the task of our calling, and nourish us with the assurance of our adoption as your children, the very daughters and sons of heaven.

Declaration of Forgiveness
In writing to the church at Ephesus (Ephesians 2:17–19), the apostle Paul draws his Gentile audience, whom he termed "those who were far off," within the expanding embrace of a divine mercy previously thought to be the exclusive province of the Jews, whom Paul here labels "those who were nearby." Listen to Paul's description: "So Christ came and proclaimed the good news: peace to you who were far off; peace to those who were nearby; for through him we both alike have access to God in the one Spirit. Thus you are no longer aliens in a foreign land, but fellow citizens with God's people, members of God's own household." This embrace, friends, extends to us as well. Be forgiven, and rejoice.

Call for the Offering
The apostle John, in 1 John 3:17–18, asks this question of his readers and provides a guide to how we are to give of ourselves and of the goods that are placed under our control: "How can we say that God's love dwells in someone who has possession of the world's goods, and sees a brother or sister in need, and yet refuses to help? Little children, let us love, not in word or in speech, but in truth and action." In that spirit, we are invited to make our morning offering.

Prayer of Dedication
Bless these gifts, sanctifying Being, according to the spirit of their giving. By the power of your Spirit, put them to work toward fulfillment of your dominion's goal, which is being realized among us even when we fail to see it; for the ultimate triumph of which we wait and work as partners with Jesus Christ, in whose name we offer both our gifts and our prayer.

Thanksgiving
Nurturing God, ground of our being, by whom our roots are nourished and our life is sustained, we praise you for your presence that never fails, even when we have failed you. We give thanks that by your love we know love and are empowered to love; that by your justice we are able to know what justice requires of us; that by your peace we learn what we must do to become peacemakers; that by your forgiveness we know

both how to give and how to receive the forgiveness that can bind up this world's wounds and heal our divisions. Confirm in us a never-failing trust in your love, your justice, your peace, your forgiveness, which were—and are—patterned for us in our Savior Jesus Christ.

Fifteenth Sunday after Pentecost
—

Invocation

We have long been instructed, God of our lives and circumstances, that it is meet and right that we should praise you at all times and in all conditions. Responding to this call, we gather in adoration. Let there be no grudging obedience to your command; but because our faith and feeling will not be denied, let them rush forth a joyful outburst of praise and thanksgiving. Bless our worship as you have blessed our lives, and constitute us a servant people; then send us into your world, as you first sent Jesus, by whose name we are called to this place and to the task of discipleship.

Call to Praise (from Psalm 103:19–22)

Leader: God's throne is established.

People: God's dominion rules over all.

Leader: Speak blessings, you angels, you mighty ones who do God's bidding,

People: Who are attentive to the holy voice.

Leader: Bless the source of our blessings, you hosts,

People: You ministers who execute the divine will!

Leader: Bless your creator, all created works, in all places of God's dominion.

People: Bless God, O my soul!

Prayer of Praise

Let the people praise you, O God; let all the people praise you, for gifts beyond our discerning and love beyond our deserving. Your will not only creates us but sustains us more richly than we require. Your patience tolerates us even when we turn our backs on you. Your righteousness judges and chastens us and calls us back from the way to oblivion. Your mercy restores and plants our feet on the highway that leads to life. Let the people praise you, holy God; let all the people truly praise you and revere your holy name.

Call to Reconciliation
When we stand knowingly in the presence of God, we are compelled, as was Isaiah in his vision of the Holy of Holies (Isaiah 6:5–8) to wail: "Woe is me, for I am lost; for I am possessed of unclean lips, and I dwell among a people of unclean lips; for my eyes have seen the monarch, the God of hosts!" In response to that confession, Isaiah received the purging restitution of God: his lips were touched with a burning coal from the altar—an act that restored Isaiah's integrity, enabling him to serve as the vessel for God's word. If we would be agents of God's word, we too must stand under judgment and be cleansed and forgiven. Let us speak; God will respond.

Prayer of Confession
You speak to us, Wellspring of being, and the totality of your Word envelopes us: creation and destruction, blessing and curse, judgment and healing. Easily we cry your mercy and proclaim your goodness, asserting the while that you favor us with tolerance unending. With difficulty we acknowledge your other promise—that we especially, with all who are your people, will be held to account for the stewardship of our lives. Then comes the anxious night of our terror and solemn confession: we acquire what we do not need, command what we do not own, demand what we have not earned. God, have mercy. Chasten and correct us, but with wrath tempered, that we may be healed, not destroyed. Restore us to mindfulness that of your grace, not our deserving, there is creation, and blessing, and wholeness.

Declaration of Forgiveness
Paul's letter to the Colossians (2:6–10) contains this affirmative advice that applies no less to us than it did to his first-century audience: "As you therefore have received our Savior Christ Jesus, continue to live your lives in Christ, rooted and built up in him, and established in the faith, just as you were taught, abounding in thanksgiving. For in Christ the whole fullness of deity dwells bodily, and you have come to fullness in Christ, who is the head of every ruler and authority." By the same

authority that Paul signifies, we too may be confident in this: that in Christ, in harmony with divine ambition, God removes our sin and makes us whole.

Call for the Offering

Remembering that Jesus withheld nothing from us, but gave even his life for the sake of all humankind: let us also withhold nothing that lies within our power to give. For when we give, we not only fulfill the admonition of our Sovereign God, but affirm, for those most desperately needing it, the power of Christ's resurrection.

Prayer of Dedication

As your Word sanctifies the words we speak, Creator God; as your approbation makes holy our acts of mercy: so let your will give purpose and direction to these gifts, which are brought in the name of Jesus Christ, through whom we receive grace to incarnate your love in the flesh of human kindness.

Thanksgiving

God of discernment, awash in gratitude we pause to name the deep moments of our lives that teach us to label the trivial and abandon the superficial:

- ⏤ the compassion of family, friends, teachers and colleagues who succor and sustain us.
- ⏤ ideas that grip us and drive us to explore and understand.
- ⏤ the community of faith that teaches us the way and accompanies us as we journey along it.
- ⏤ the light of your Word in statute, prophecy and gospel, a beacon of constancy in a world beset by conflicting values and shabby conduct.

And praise, too, for your confidence in us, which exceeds our confidence in ourselves; for where we shrink to own you for fear of public embarrassment, you risk to our care the goal of history and engage us in the redeeming work of Jesus Christ, who risked all for us and earned our everlasting gratitude.

Sixteenth Sunday after Pentecost
—

Invocation

Open our eyes, God of history, to your movement in and through the times and events of earth and be manifest to us. Open our lives, Holy Spirit within us and among us, to make visible to our town and its people the presence of God in this congregation. Open our arms, Christ of God, to receive your people in need, making clear to them your encompassing mercy. And receive from us now our praise and thanksgiving, who are your servants in the service of humanity.

Call to Praise (based on Psalm 117)

Leader: Praise our God, all you nations!

People: Extol our God, all you peoples!

Leader: Whose great love is steadfast toward us,

People: Whose faithfulness endures forever.

Unison: Again we say, praise God!

Prayer of Praise

In each minute of this hour of worship, Majestic Creator, we will praise you with song and prayer, thought and feeling. In each hour of this day, Christ Jesus, we will conform our obedience to the imperatives of the gospel. In each day of the coming week, comforting Spirit, we will honor you through acts of love and mercy, directed to real people in real need. In all the years of our lives we will continue so to do, making of all life—each minute, each hour, each day—an act of exaltation to your triune holiness, to whom be glory and honor, through this life and beyond.

Call to Reconciliation

There is a paradox in us Christians, a contradiction to how society assigns worth. As a nation, we value power, wealth, and social status. We admire those whose decisions affect many. We envy those who enjoy luxury greater than ours. We dream of how we'd live if we could trade places. We joke about what we'd do if we won the lottery! Yet, while we may feel uneasy, even intimidated, in the presence of those who possess many things, we don't kneel before them, make extravagant claims concerning their goodness, or admit our need for their help. We reserve this for one who was born to a peasant couple, made his home with the poor, and was executed between two criminals. Is it not a wonder? Come bow before this one who is the better way, and confess our weakness.

Prayer of Confession

Spirit of verity, help us to name our sin, for we are accustomed to hiding it from ourselves; and even now, in vain, we may try to hide it from our God. Sightless fools that we are, we suppose you incapable of seeing whatever we ourselves choose not to look upon: our clutching at wealth for selfish intent; our stinginess with the grace that we received free-of-charge; our willful ignorance of the need that roots about the doorsteps of our homes, our church, our town. How shall such an insensible lot as we are see the light, heaven-sent to guide us? God have mercy. Remove the scales from our eyes, that we may see; wash us that we may be clean; heal us that we may be whole. And by the grace that presses upon us even as we cower and turn away, make us such a sign of your transforming power that others, seeing us, will know and adore you.

Declaration of Forgiveness

Let these words from Paul in 1 Thessalonians 5:8–10 serve as our words of assurance this day: "since we belong to the day, let us be sober, and put on the breastplate of faith and love, and for a helmet the hope of salvation. For God has destined us not for wrath, but for . . . salvation through our Savior Jesus Christ, who died for us, so that whether we are awake or asleep we may live with Christ."

Call for the Offering

The gift of Christ to the world calls us to share in the giving, not by obligation but as opportunity. Because the love of God is so ordained that it can never be repaid, except that it be passed along to others. We are encouraged to see the offering in this light: as our chance to embody for others the love that God has given us—and refuses to take back.

Prayer of Dedication

In bringing our gifts to your service, Christ Jesus, we acknowledge your sovereignty before the world and proclaim that you are our Redeemer. By your authority, direct both their use and our lives to your own ends; that we may know the elegant joy of both giving and being gifts in your name, through whom we both live and pray.

Thanksgiving

God of all mercy, receive now your people's thanks for gentle kindness and caring. In moments of spiritual carelessness, we blame you for things we do not understand. In moments of moral laziness, we hold you accountable for events we are unwilling or ashamed to own. Yet, by the miracle of your love, you do not turn against us. As you once entered into human life in the person of Jesus, you continue now to work among us in the person of your Holy Spirit—to teach, to heal, to redeem. So hymns and hosannas, our God, for your love that clasps us even as we strike out to abuse you. And thank you for instructing us in the meaning of thankfulness, that we might finally present to you lives as rich in gratitude as yours is rich in charity, through Jesus Christ who was, and is, the greatest gift of all.

Seventeenth Sunday after Pentecost
—

Invocation

Come into our lives, O intervening Holiness, as palpably as your Word made flesh entered the lives of your people, filling them with grace and truth. Make us alive, as your Word made flesh gave new vitality to your people, kindling in them a splendid resolve. Claim us as your own. Command us as you will. And mold us a holy priesthood, that the Word made flesh, servant to the people of his time, may continue through us to be servant to ours.

Call to Praise (from Psalm 135:15–20)

Leader: The idols of the nations are silver and gold,
People: The work of human hands.

Leader:	They have mouths, but they do not speak.
People:	They have eyes, but they do not see.
Leader:	They have ears, but they do not hear,
People:	And there is no breath in their mouths.
Leader:	Those who make them, and all who trust in them, shall be just like them.
People:	You that fear God, bless God and no other!

Prayer of Praise

Framer of time and eternity, of history and community, we praise you for your wisdom, for it astonishes us; your compassion, for it saves us; your love, for it undergirds us. The gospel of Jesus deeply encourages us, transforming fear to daring and sadness to joy, making tolerable the outrages of life. Your Holy Spirit resides with us, strengthening us to accept the demands of discipleship and revealing to us the redemptive possibilities in the challenges of our time. Wherefore we praise you, who give us being, redeem us from sin and death and sanctify our love and labor.

Call to Reconciliation

If we indulge the deceit that we have no shortcomings and are immune to failure, we provide no proof that we are good, only that we are self-righteous. Jesus made it clear, through many teachings, that there are no rooms in God's house of many mansions for the self-righteous, only for the poor in spirit. That being our understanding, let us summon our humility and boldly confess before our divine Judge.

Prayer of Confession

We know, Compassionate One, that there is no failing so utter that we may not, in candor, reveal it to you. We know, too, that there is no offence so severe that it puts us beyond hope of restoration. But, O God, we dread the face in the mirror as much as we fear the countenance of heaven. For our pride bars us from the honesty which alone makes confession true. Even in moments of self-disclosure, we fancy that our feeble judgment is as penetrating as your own. Then the truth overtakes us and we apprehend your discernment that sunders flesh from bone and heart from soul and sees our innermost selves more clearly than we can see one another. God have mercy, and let your first mercy be to grant us the power both to see our sin and to realize in our flesh the promise of forgiveness.

Declaration of Forgiveness

As John's first letter calls us to acknowledge the reality of sin, it also presses upon us the reality of forgiveness, with this eloquent affirmation (1 John 1:5–7): "This is the message we have heard from Christ and proclaim to you, that God is light, in whom is no shadow at all. If we say we have fellowship with God, while we journey in shadows, we lie and do not live according to the truth; but if we journey in the light, as God is in the light, we have fellowship with one another and the blood of God's child Jesus cleanses us from all sin."

Call for the Offering

Out of the depths of love, God gave us life and sent the Word made flesh to live and die and rise again so that we might become reconciled to our creator and to one another. Out of the depths of our gratitude, let us now demonstrate our grasp of this insight: that the resources at our disposal are truly ours only when we know them to be fully God's. By so doing, we show that we understand the gospel: that Christ becomes manifest not only to us but in us and through us, so that the world's joy might be increased.

Prayer of Dedication

Healer of broken hearts, your mercy is greater than we require; but through it we have opportunity to show that your generosity has borne fruit in us. Take back, then, what you have provided, and spread your mercy anew to some who have been denied it, that Christ's vision may become manifest in them. We ask this for your sake, you who are the greatest gift that is ours both to receive and to share.

Thanksgiving

Let all the world turn to you now in thanksgiving, Sovereign God, to endorse the gratitude that consumes us, who of all people are most in your debt. Not only do you give us life, but the resources necessary to sustain it, the joy of human relationships to enrich it, and useful work to make it productive. Not only do you implant in us a sacred restlessness that will not let us be until we find you; you rush to meet us, to embrace us, to be reconciled to us. Ours now is the frustration of those who, preparing our thanksgiving, discover that we cannot speak eloquently enough, sing fairly enough, shout loudly enough, to satisfy our theme. Let therefore the whole creation come now to our aid and cry thanksgiving to our great and good God; and let all the hosts of heaven support us in the resounding Amen.

Eighteenth Sunday after Pentecost
—

Invocation
Free us now, attending Transcendence, from the distraction of our individual agendas. Silence the clamor of obligation and the din of demand. Drain us of anxiety about success and preoccupation with reputation, that with minds focused and souls summoned we may enter our worship with that purity of heart that Jesus commended, and see God. Through this time together, equip us to return to the tasks of our days with vision cleared, priorities reordered, and confidence restored that your will is our own, through Jesus Christ our Savior.

Call to Praise (from Psalm 145:1–4)

Leader: We sing you praises, God our sovereign,

People: We bless your name forever,

Leader: Blessing you day after day,

People: And praising your name forever.

Leader: Can anyone measure the magnificence of God, the great?

People: Can anyone survey the inexpressible grandeur of the Holy One?

Unison: In celebrating your acts of power, you wherein power arises, each age will praise your doings to the next.

Prayer of Praise
Eternal One, who inhabits both time and eternity and prepares our way in life and beyond, praise for all that makes earth and its seasons glorious, enchanting our senses and rejuvenating our spirits. Praise for homes and schools—the nurturing matrix that shaped beliefs, defined

sensibilities, honed aptitudes, and would not let us take the easy way out. Praise for those who loved us when we were least loveable, had faith in us when we had not yet found faith in ourselves, and welcomed us home even when we had worn out our welcome everywhere else. And praise, too, for the forming and informing presence of the church, our larger family in faith, that attests to the transcendent dimension of our being and fits us for service in both time and eternity. Praise, Sovereign God, for these very present emblems of your mercy.

Call to Reconciliation

In confessing our sins, we acknowledge in a self-conscious way the reality of where we stand in relation to God, by witnessing that God alone is truly good and that each of us individually, and all of us collectively, fall short of that goodness. And by confessing our shortfalling, we acquire that humility in response to which God's compassion is all encompassing. In that light, let us now join in unison confession.

Prayer of Confession (based on Isaiah 50:1–3)

Your judgment is our dread, most righteous God, who through the prophet spoke words that chill our hearts: "Where is your mother's bill of divorce with which I put her away? Or which of my creditors is it to whom I have sold you? No, because of your sins you were sold, and for your transgressions your mother was put away. Why was no one there when I came? Why did no one answer when I called? Is my hand shortened, that I cannot redeem? Or have I no power to deliver? By my rebuke I dry up the sea and make the rivers a desert; their fish stink for lack of water, and die of thirst. I clothe the heavens with blackness, and make sackcloth their covering." Let it not be our lack of confidence in your power of restitution, merciful God, that hampers our confession; but let us wait with chastened hope for your strong arm to save us and your love to deliver us. For you alone, O God, can redeem.

Declaration of Forgiveness

In the very facing of the inner turmoil against which we all struggle, we are made more effective in dealing with it. Because the act of confession, this agonizing about our fragmented spirits and disobedient wills, frees us to recognize, as few other things can, God's readiness to intercede and to help us to overcome. What we cannot do for ourselves, God does through us. The more we attune ourselves to this reality, the greater becomes our ability to draw our wills into line with God's will and to know we are forgiven. Thanks be to God!

Call for the Offering

One is tempted, in viewing the organization of society, to conclude that life's resources are distributed among us individually: each of us has a piece of the pie with which to secure the necessities of life. This is certainly the American way of looking at it. From a biblical standpoint, however, it is too narrow a view. Even a casual observer can see that wealth is not distributed equitably. Some have vastly more than they require, and some have too little to subsist. If it is true, as our faith professes, that God provides all things and that God's concern is for all humanity, then resources are furnished not to serve private wealth but community welfare. So what we possess beyond personal need is excess. It is not ours to hoard, but to share, according to the necessities of all. The offering is one avenue for such sharing, our chance to ensure that God's mercy *is* evenly distributed.

Prayer of Dedication

In thanksgiving, Christ Jesus, we acknowledge the sacred trust you share with us in calling us to be your people. In fulfillment of that trust, we dedicate this offering as confirmation of our stewardship of this day. Let both the power of the gifts and the power of our spirits grow and multiply, O Christ, in your service.

Thanksgiving (Traditional/Adapted)

Almighty God, author of all mercies: we, your unworthy servants give you most humble and hearty thanks for your loving kindness to us and to all humanity. We bless you for our creation, preservation, and all the blessings of this life; but above all, for your inestimable love in the redemption of the world by our Savior Jesus Christ; for the means of grace and for the hope of glory. And, we entreat you, give us that due sense of all your mercies that our hearts may be genuinely thankful, and enable us to exhibit your praise, not only with our lips, but in our lives, by giving up ourselves to your service and by abiding with you in holiness and righteousness all our days. Through our Savior Jesus Christ, to whom, with you and the Holy Spirit, be all honor and glory, world without end. Amen.

Nineteenth Sunday after Pentecost

Invocation

You summoned us to this place, Sovereign Majesty, so we come: to rejoice in our summons, to be reunited with the family into which we are called; to marvel that you do not call us casually, but invest yourself, an effervescent presence, in our work and worship. Give us here the gifts of love, mercy, and peace; then scatter us again, energized to employ your gifts as ambassadors for Christ to an anxious people.

Call to Praise (from Psalm 145:13, 17–21)

Leader: All your words are faithful, O God;

People: All your deeds are gracious.

Leader: You are just in all your ways,

People: And kind in everything that you do.

Leader: You are near to all who call on you,

People: To all who call on you truly.

Leader: Our mouths will speak your praise,

People: And all flesh will bless your holy name forever!

Prayer of Praise

Praise, you Architect of Nature, for the rhythm of seasons that brings us to fall. Praise for the glory of trees shedding transparent flame to litter the landscape and ring our ankles with swirling glory. Praise for the sure passage of birds with inborn discernment of flight paths and destinations never seen. Praise for the chill promise of winter splendor windborne from arctic storehouses. Praise for fall games to swell the lungs and flush the cheeks, for companionship in contest and the spirit of teamwork. Praise for hard work and mental challenge, for the day's duty and the night's repose. Praise for all the common mysteries of life, O God, by which we know you, in which we see you, through which we serve you.

Call to Reconciliation

We come to this place with varied motives and expectations: the joy of celebration; a desire to hear, and to learn from, the Word; to experience companionship with those of kindred mind and spirit; the hope of peace in the middle of life's demands and disruptions. All of us, however, ought also to come in poverty of spirit, to acknowledge that our lives are less than God means them to be and that each of us individually—and all of us as community—stand under judgment. Let us, then, seek God's mercy and forgiveness.

Prayer of Confession

Against the intent of Creation's purpose, O God of honor, we drive the weight of our willfulness, trampling and trashing your word in law and prophecy, gospel and tradition. Clutching the shadows reserved for the truly ignorant, we scorn the pain of Eden's children and shoulder for ourselves the authority to define good and evil. With supreme avarice, we grasp for ourselves whatever it pleases us to think good. Alas, it is a burden too heavy, a task too grand. Bumbling fools, we stumble over our insufficiency and earn the contempt of the humble and wise. Great God, could we not have learned the first time? How often must we be judged before we know the scope of chastisement? How many times forgiven before we stand redeemed? We do not even know how to answer our own questions. In humility we turn again, and beg your forgiveness, who alone are our healing, our answer, our restoration.

Declaration of Forgiveness

The altogether remarkable assertion of Scripture is that where we willingly confess our need for God's forgiveness, even when we go on again and again to struggle with the negative side of our intellect and will and freedom, God forgives us and urges us to try again. It is this rhythm that brings us, time and again, to the need for confession. It is this rhythm that allows us, again and again, to affirm the love of God in Jesus Christ and to declare in Christ's name, as I now declare to you, that our sin is forgiven, our life restored. Thanks be to God!

Call for the Offering

Among the opportunities that are ours as ones who take seriously the witness of Jesus Christ, none is more easily grasped than the call to share our love, in tangible form, with others who desperately need it. If we intend to be faithful to the vision of Christ, to give substance to our recognition of who Jesus is, we should view the offering not as an inconvenience, or a troublesome chore unjustly laid on us, or an effort to take what is rightfully ours, but as an opportunity to make substantial our devotion to Christ, to put flesh on our gratitude. By so doing, we ourselves become agents of that mercy.

Prayer of Dedication

There is no gift we can bring, gracious God, that begins to match the generosity of all that you have given us, except that we, in our turn, give ourselves wholly for you. Let this offering betoken a new beginning, wherein we increasingly devote ourselves to your service, who serves us without reservation.

Thanksgiving

God of grace unbounded: we thank you for the light of another day, for work we are given to do and the strength and skills with which to do it. We thank you for your truth, that both conveys your will to us and lights the path we are to follow. We thank you for your Spirit that moves in and among us, energizing us to fulfill the tasks of servanthood even when our resources seem insufficient or have been consumed to their lowest ebb. We thank you that in your generosity you continue to supply these things when we do not deserve them or when we accept them but do not use them. Your way is wonderful beyond explaining, and for that we are most thankful of all: that because it is your way, we need not try to explain it, but may be content to rejoice in it.

Twentieth Sunday after Pentecost

—

Invocation

The world is filled with voices, God of the intentional word, a confusing jumble of sound. Some desire to serve you, others aspire to privilege. We need to be reminded, from time to time, that you are not constrained by our limitations, but hear it all and understand it as well. Only grant, Holy One, amid this flood of sound, that ours voices will give no support to those who seek privilege, but will be joined to those who mean to spend themselves on behalf of Jesus, at whose summons we come, in whose name we pray.

Call to Praise (from Daniel 2:20–23)

Leader: Blessed is the name of God, from age to age,

People: To whom belong wisdom and understanding;

Leader: Who gives wisdom to the wise,

People: And knowledge to those who have understanding;

Leader: Who reveals deep and hidden things,

People: And knows what is hidden in shadows, with whom light dwells.

Leader: To you, who were the God of our parents in all ages, we give thanks and praise;

People: For you make wisdom and power your gift to us.

Prayer of Praise

By the power of speech, great God of the Word, you summon from chaos the ordered wonder of this physical universe that is our home—in scope bewildering, in glory staggering, in beauty enthralling. Would that we could command even the echo of so astonishing an authority over speech; but language fails to capture the awe we know in your presence. Words express feeling, but do not capture its richness. We speak the word of love, but its full expression eludes us. Even our word of obedience lacks the conviction we mean it to convey. It is enough. If speech is not sufficient, let silence be our messenger, while your interceding Spirit, her sighs too deep for words, conveys to heaven the full scope of earth's adoration and praise.

May be followed by a time of silence.

Call to Reconciliation

The composer of Psalm 14 reminds us forcefully of the presence among us of a God who weighs the quality of our conduct: "God looks down from heaven on humankind to see if there are any who are wise, who seek after God. Have they no knowledge, the evildoers who eat up my people as they eat bread, and do not call upon God? They shall be in great terror, for God is with the company of the righteous." We do well to remember the impartiality of this holy Judge, who weighs us in the balance along with all the rest. Wherefore, indeed, let our confession speak both our contrition and our need of God's redeeming mercy.

Prayer of Confession

Merciful God, because we carry the name of Christ, we are signs of your presence. By call, by faith, by baptism, we are commissioned to be lights to the shadowed world and salt to an undernourished people. Yet we are shadowy guides and bland witnesses. We abandon your children to their pain and fail to lead them to healing waters. Discouraged by divided minds and fragile loyalties, we disqualify ourselves as signs of hope and good news. Your Spirit calls, but we are heedless. We prefer comfortable familiarity and facile security. We are not Christ to our neighbor. Help us, Christ of courage, to let go—to risk everything we have, everything we are, to become a radiant and salty people, confident in your sustaining power, you true light for the world, true salt for the nations.

Declaration of Forgiveness

Has it ever occurred to you that we are willing—indeed able—to offer our confession to God in large part because we know it will be heard with compassion? If Jesus' coming among us symbolizes anything at all, it is this: that we confess not to an angry and punitive God, who can hardly wait until the words fall from our mouths before lashing out at us, but to one whose principal qualities are loving compassion and unfailing faithfulness. What a contrast this is to just about any other to whom we might turn; and how brightly it shines before us in the mystery of love at once close by and transcendent.

Call for the Offering

Many of us, one suspects, view the offering as an act we undertake at our own initiative. Supposing ourselves thoughtful and generous, we prove it by sharing our resources in support of the work of the church. A thoughtful assessment may require us to reconsider. We are not born generous, after all. We acquire altruism by imitating our caring elders. They, in turn, learned from those who taught them. So where does it all begin? From a scriptural viewpoint it always begins with God. Human love and generosity reflect divine love and charity. The offering does not originate with us. We employ it in imitation of God's liberality, and so signal the world whom it is that we serve. Come, let us be imitators of God.

Prayer of Dedication

Holy and eternal One, receive our gifts as if they incorporated our hearts, our souls, our minds, and our strength, as indeed they do; for through them all, and with them all, we mean to love and aid you, in the name of Jesus Christ our Savior.

Thanksgiving

Merciful Creator, the things for which we have cause to thank you are so numerous that we lose count: that you emptied yourself to assume our substance, not because you could not live without us, but because we cannot live without you; that by calling us into the fellowship of the followers of the way, you encircle us with heartening friends, our sisters and brothers in discipleship; that you accommodate us with the unfinished work of the faith, so that we can learn, by our success, the joy of completed tasks; that when the work is hard, you do not send us unprepared, but supply all that is needful, whether knowledge or skill, courage or endurance. Grant, gracious One, that our effort to serve you serves those you love, and draws them, rejoicing, into the community of thanksgiving.

Twenty-first Sunday after Pentecost
—

Invocation
Holy Spirit of God, make evident to us now your presence among us. Arouse our minds, kindle our imaginations, instruct our decisions, shape our conduct. Be evident in our arriving and our leaving, in our worship and our fellowship, in our corporate liturgy and our personal meditation. And give us grace, through it all, to embrace your will for us as persons and as congregation.

Call to Praise (from Joel 2:28–29)
Leader: After those days, says the Holy One, I will pour out my spirit on all flesh;

People: Your sons and your daughters shall prophesy;

Leader: Your old people shall dream dreams,

People: And your youth shall see visions.

Leader: Even on those held in bondage, in those days,

People: I will pour out my spirit, says the God of hosts.

Unison: And my people shall never again be put to shame.

Prayer of Praise
Going agreeably to their rest, O God, the unpretentious leaves now blanket the world in subdued splendor, foretelling the hush of winter soon to overtake us; beneath whose snows their substance will be reclaimed to nourish the rising of another spring. In wonder, we watch and admire, and turn again to proclaim your sovereignty over the physical universe, from the substance of which we, like the leaves, are stitched together. Still more we proclaim your governance over the spirit/breath of life and the mystery by which it engages us who are made sacred through your constituting Word, by which you not only frame us, but redeem our mortality. So praise and laud, merciful Creator, whose name we exalt as no other.

Call to Reconciliation
The author of Psalm 53 issues a brutal assessment: "God looks down from heaven on humankind, to see if there are any who are wise, who seek after God. They have all fallen away, they are all alike perverse,

there is no one who does good, no, not one." Does this seem too harsh? Remember that Jesus chided someone for calling him good. How will we receive this challenge? By understanding that the psalmist did not intend simply to castigate the entire human race, but to castigate those who believe that God's righteousness is no need for concern—that it doesn't matter. It does matter, because it clearly matters to God. Come then, people of faith, and honor our sovereign's holiness by giving voice to the evil that lurks in all of us, seeking divine help to overcome it and affirming the authority of God to purge and heal us.

Prayer of Confession

Our sin is no greater, O God, than the sin of those who ignore you, for they take of your great richness and give you no thanks—just like us when we claim personal credit for that which we received as a gift. Our sin is no worse than those who are hateful toward human sisters and brothers, breaking your heart and drenching heaven with tears—just like us who retreat from mercy, then excuse ourselves because we committed no violence. Our sin is no greater than those who breach the peace, nailing Christ again to the cross and shattering the lives of innocents—just like us when we fail to build the peace, then congratulate ourselves for having disapproved the tyrant. O we are a lackluster lot. Doing nothing, we fail you by failing to advance your dominion. Forgive, God who engages us in the pursuit of mercy, and goad us into action, who cannot serve you by doing no harm but only by making a difference.

Declaration of Forgiveness

An attentive reading of the Gospel makes it evident that reconciling forgiveness was central to Jesus' ministry. On each occasion, when approached by anyone ill, or troubled, or frightened, his response always included a clear pronouncement of forgiving acceptance and reaffirmation. Even on the cross, he asked forgiveness for those who hung him there. In coming in faith to Christ to disclose our own need, we also receive that word of compassion. Rejoice, friends, in our Redeemer's mercy.

Call for the Offering

After all is said and done, stewardship does have its tedious side. Week after week, we give a little here and a little there, sometimes wishing there could be an end to it. How much simpler it would be if God would simply issue an executive order vanquishing misery and want! Or at least that a few of the world's impressive supply of new millionaires write a few checks to cover the cost and get it behind us. Do we need to be reminded that it does not work that way? Do we need to be told that a purpose is being served here, for our own spiritual growth? The offering is part of our stewardship. Through it, we demonstrate our readiness to commit knowledge, labor, and resources to our Savior's work. If we claim the name of Christ, this is part of who we are. It is our work, not someone else's. Let's keep the good work going.

Prayer of Dedication

Everything we have is already yours, Creator God, and comes to us by your mercy. So we have no gift to bring that is able to enrich you, save that we give ourselves. Receive these offerings, we pray, in token of the gift of self that we intend, through our gifts, to devote to you.

Thanksgiving

Into the vast deeps of your liberality, O Source of all that is generous, we pour our meager thanksgivings like brooks that vanish into the sea, leaving no trace on the sweep of the tide. For what weight of gratitude is there that equals the burden of our obligation? It presses upon us in the sacred story of your coming among us. It is recalled in a thousand moments when grace showered upon a perplexed people and ten thousand found tongues of gratitude. And we are among them, whose lives have been touched by the gospel of Jesus Christ; who have shared the miracle feast of a few loaves and fishes and felt in our own lives the impact of the empty cross and the abandoned tomb. For this redeeming story, we thank you. For the love it generates among us in this family of faith, we thank you. For the daring it instills in us to model, before the world, what it means to be the people of God, we thank you.

Twenty-second Sunday after Pentecost

—

Invocation

We know, ever-present One, that to call you now to meet us in this place is an act of foolishness, not faith. For surely you were here before we arrived, as you always are one step ahead of us, patiently urging us to catch up and join you in the day's work. Help us, rather, to make our worship a drama of recognition: in the act of meeting one another, to meet you; in the joining of our hands, to feel the touch of your own; and discernably to see your Word in our spoken, sung, and silent language. Then shall our hour be an event of grace, as are all our times when they are shaped by you.

Call to Praise (from Galatians 4:3–7)

Leader: Before we were adopted by God, we were slaves to the elemental spirits of the universe.

People: But when the time had fully come, God sent forth the divine Child, born of our sister Mary, born under the law, to redeem those who were under the law, so that we might receive adoption as sons and daughters.

Leader: And because we are daughters and sons, God has sent the spirit of Christ into our hearts, revealing how intimately God loves us, and we may love God.

People: So through God we are no longer slaves but children of God, and if children, then heirs.

Unison: As heirs, we celebrate the intimacy of the love that both liberates and binds us.

Prayer of Praise

What wonders are ours to name, great God of endless surprises; and how shall we enumerate them: this dazzling universe littered with galaxies in splendid profusion; the arid-moist, warm-cold wonder of earth that bids us be at home and draw life from her sustaining breast; the sparkling gay profusion of intimately known and not-yet-discovered life forms who share our planet home; the diversity of arts and sciences proceeding from fertile imagination, to charge our minds, exult our souls, and satisfy our wants; families biological and spiritual, who embrace us with affirming love and plant in us the grace to love others. For all these we praise you; but for none more than the astonishing wonder who is Jesus Christ: Word in our flesh, redemptive light in our world, image among us of the God-love that possesses us and that we possess—your gift to us, our offering to the world.

Call to Reconciliation (from Isaiah 66:1–2)

In a brief but stunning essay that compares the vast reach of divine authority with the limits of human ability, the prophet we call Deutero-Isaiah, or second Isaiah, sets the stage for our act of confession. Listen to the prophet's words: "Thus says God: Heaven is my throne and the earth my footstool; where do you presume that you can build a house for me, and where is my resting-place? All these things my hand has made, and so all these things are mine. But this is the one to whom I will look: to the humble and contrite in spirit, who trembles at my word." Let us, after the manner of Deutero-Isaiah, name our shortcoming and tremble before the supremacy of God.

Prayer of Confession

Forgive us, heaven's Majesty, for we are poor stewards and lazy servants. Our days dawn in exuberance and close in lethargy. The sun rises upon our hope and sets on our disappointment. Each morning we promise ourselves that this day will be different, then set about to make sure it is the same. Each day we have your work before us—we know what it is: to love the unloved and unlovable, to share the burden of the freighted and encourage the fearful, to provoke mercy and demand justice. Yet weeks pass by and still we do not take Jesus down from the cross where greed and desperation nail him; while the time of servant-hood slips away, the opportunity squandered. Remind us again, dreadful Sovereign, that if we do not serve you, your household has no room for us. Then rouse us again to faithful stewardship of your gift of life.

Declaration of Forgiveness

The promise of Jesus is that poverty of spirit opens heaven's door; that meekness earns title to the world; that compassion earns mercy; that purity of heart yields visions of God. Be comforted, therefore; only a God of consummate compassion—like ours—would make such promises; as only a God of consummate authority—like ours—is capable of making good the promise. The promise is made. Let the gift be received.

Call for the Offering

Among the foundation motives upon which Christianity thrives is charity. Stingy people are incapable of being loving people. People who are turned in on themselves are unlikely to respond to need, regardless of how it is defined. Our entire faith, in fact, rests upon a presumption of *divine* charity: that our very being is possible only because of God's generosity; much more is it the ground of Christ's redemptive intervention in human history. There is a lesson here: it is the nature of charity that it cannot exist in the abstract but must have a tangible out, a way to clothe itself in the flesh of action. The offering is our opportunity to do just that—to let charity shine, not as an idea, but as a fact of life among the people of God.

Prayer of Dedication

Your love constrains us, Generous Majesty, because you have given so richly to us and hold out now the opportunity for us, by our liberality, to mimic your charity. With glad hearts we do so; for our mimicry is your praise, and your commendation our rich reward.

Thanksgiving

We thank you, God of our days, for seasons when life is serene and we are content with who we are, where we live, and what we achieve; because tranquillity floods our souls with nourishment and strengthens us against the days of despair. We thank you for times when life is difficult and we struggle for balance and feel our way haltingly along the road, because times of difficulty forge strength out of weakness and acquaint us with the scope and limits of our endurance. And we thank you for days of sadness, when our eyes brim liquid sorrow for life badly lived or dearly lost; because in sadness we sense the depth of our compassion and chart the boundaries of mortality. And, yes, we thank you for times of affectionate ramblings with dear friends and dearer family, when life is all giddy silliness and our sides ache with laughter; because in joyful play we apprehend the elation that awaits the family of God when we gather, at last, around your festal table to break the bread of salvation. In all the stations of life, wondrous Deity, and now at this day and hour, our souls overflow with thanksgiving.

Twenty-third Sunday after Pentecost

Invocation

Spirit of God, descend upon my heart; wean it from earth, through all its pulses move; stoop to my weakness, mighty as thou art, and make me love thee as I ought to love. Let the awareness of your presence so wrap our attention that the day's distractions fade and are recognized to be as insignificant as they truly are. May we then find our liberation in worshiping you with our whole heart and soul and mind and strength.

Call to Praise

Leader: Gather in, you people of God

People: We have heard the divine invitation, and we come.

Leader: Lift your hearts, you people of Christ.

People: We have heard the good news of Jesus, and our hearts overflow with joy.

Leader: Raise your voices, O people of the Spirit.

People: We will sing in the Spirit's power, exulting our divine redeemer.

Unison: We cry the praise of God!

Prayer of Praise

We praise you, O God, constant Father of creation's family, whose faithfulness secures us an earth-home at once sustaining and sure. We adore you, O God, strong Mother whose breath gives life to all that lives, whose vitality is our strength, whose constancy our assurance. We rejoice in you, O God, childhood's playmate and mentor, who fosters our maturing and excites us with growth and learning. We extol you, O God, ancient of days, who shapes in your secure hand the twilight of our years and promises to bring us home. We honor you, O God, whose name is beyond our knowing and yet is named in every people's tongue and at every family's table. We laud you, O God, architect and monarch of eternity, who drives us by the vision of abundant life in our time and new life beyond time. May we, Holy Friend, never be wanting your glory, nor your glory be wanting our praise.

Call to Reconciliation

The ancient Hebraic creation stories tell us that God had barely planted human feet on Eden's soil before the trouble began. Some label this Original Sin, a concept with which Jews have some difficulty—and these were, after all, their stories first. The very act of creation, they note, is an act of alienation. Creation cannot become Creation without first being separated from God, just as parents cannot birth a child except the child becomes physically separate from its parents. Just as an artist cannot create a work of art except artist and art become independent of each other. What then of sin? Oh, it is real enough! It consists in our failure to acknowledge that God created us in order that we might be in relationship *with* God, who alone possesses the wisdom and the authority to define how the relationship is to work. In our confession, we have opportunity to admit to God, and to ourselves, that if we remain alienated, it is not because God wills it but because we do.

Prayer of Confession

How do you continue to forgive us, patient Deity? We do not understand your measureless tolerance; nor are we able, for we are a people given to hasty judgment but meager insight. Stingy at forgiveness ourselves, it is difficult for us to envision it in others, and even more difficult to receive it from tender hands. Singed by Jesus' proclamation that we can be forgiven only as we forgive, we hesitate, clinging to our sin's pestilence rather than endure the scorching humility of pardon. Merciful God, what is to be done for us? We are not like you, who accept us in our unacceptability and love us in our lovelessness. Yet pry open our miserly hearts and pour into us the purging flame of holiness, first to purify our hearts, then to fire us to forgive, and to seek the forgiveness of, our neighbor.

Declaration of Forgiveness

It is the scandalous assertion of the Gospel that there is no sin so great, no arrogance so consummate, no evil so profound, that God has not already overpowered and defeated it on the cross of Jesus Christ. We human beings, in our dealings with one another, may prolong judgment, shun forgiveness, and seek revenge. God will have none of it, but rules, in a single, transcending command, that guilt be gone and reconciliation inherit the day. Our sin, friends, is overwhelmed—period!

Call for the Offering

The concept of the tithe is a more confusing one than most Christians have been led to realize. While the practice is frequently cited in Hebraic law, it was common throughout the near-eastern world. Generally, the rule held that one-tenth of the yield of earth, whether crops or livestock, was to be given in tithe. But its purpose was not consistent. At some times the tithe was required to support the temple and the priesthood. At other times, it was a political tax to support the monarch and fund public administration. Also, the tithe has always been subject to abuse, as when Jesus chided the overly pious for tithing not just crops and livestock, but even their spices, while neglecting more important parts of the law. For Christians, the point is this: our giving ought to be substantial and represent in real terms just how important God's work is in the world. Let us give, then, not to satisfy a formula; but to demonstrate the height and depth and breadth of our faith.

Prayer of Dedication

Mighty Sovereign, of what value are our gifts if they fail to please you? How shall they work for good if you do not receive them? How shall they accomplish their purpose, except you order them? In grateful humility, we lay them before you. In compassion receive them. But most of all, put them to work as only you are able, not for our purposes, but yours; not for our glory, but yours.

Thanksgiving

God of many mercies—whose glory is nowhere more visibly displayed than in the brilliance of autumn now ending or the promise of winter new borne on chill breeze and lowering sun; whose earth cannot help but praise you both in its living and its dying—hear our prayer of thanksgiving. We remember with gratitude the many daily blessings that sustain us:

- a remembered melody, long-silent, that took us by surprise, renewing fond memory.
- a petty argument concluded and put behind us at last.
- an idea that struck fire in our imagination.
- food and to spare on our tables and in our pantries.
- the privilege of living in a nation where we may ask probing questions or propose unpopular answers without fear of oppression and reprisal.

By your love and mercy, O God, may it be that all our sisters and brothers, everywhere on earth, will know these blessings and have cause, with us, to voice their thanksgiving.

Twenty-fourth Sunday after Pentecost

—

Invocation

Majestic Creator, be present to us in the cosmic events of our universe. Judge of the world, let your hand be visible in the events of our global history. Rescuer of peoples, reveal yourself in the flow of national events. Shaper of communities, show yourself to us in the times and events of our town and our congregation. Author of life, closer to us than the hairs on our individual heads, make evident your presence among us now, in this room. Then shall we celebrate your presence among us in all the ways that announce your attendance upon Creation, from microscopic life to galactic systems, proclaiming for all to hear that you, only, are God.

Call to Praise

Leader: Sisters and brothers, why have we come here?

People: We come to celebrate the presence of transcendence among us.

Leader: Who has called us to do this?

People: The Holy Spirit of God, who prompts us to come together, rejoices in our coming, and admonishes us to consider our calling.

Leader: Then let us begin by singing the praise of this transcendent
           One, who summons the community of faith—in all genera-
           tions—to live as a holy people.

People: We will sing to God our joy-filled song!

Prayer of Praise

Your majesty, Creator God—cloaked in holiness and shrouded in wonder—taxes both imagination and verbal facility. As your eternity
exceeds the scope of our time, the immensity of your holiness beggars
our imagination. Yet we must seek both to envision and portray it, for
the very mystery that dazzles us summons our praise. Help us, infinite
One. Where speech fails, let song replace it. Where prose is mundane,
let poetry take flight. Where verbal claims are inadequate, teach us the
power of doing. Withal, wherever we are sent, whoever we serve, let
both word and deed so ably portray your love and your longing that
your name is truly glorified in us; through Jesus Christ our Savior.

Call to Reconciliation

Are you content—fully content—with the manner in which you have
acquitted yourself in God's service since last you worshiped in this
place? Is there nothing you would change, if you could? No word that
you'd retrieve, were the power given you to snatch it back and swallow
it before it could again escape your lips? Is there any kindness you left
undone, or truth you amended, or love you withheld? The act of confession is an opportunity to amend these things. Not that we can turn back
the clock and undo them, but that we can give them to God, who will
receive and judge them and, if we truly desire it, grant remission from
them. The opportunity for reconciliation is now.

Prayer of Confession

With humility, our God, we confess the sadness you wear as a burden
because of our failure to live up to the measure of Christ. A people of
plenty, who want for nothing with which to sustain life, we waste our
days grasping for more, scratching to amplify our over-housed, overfed
overabundance, while the silent suffering of the world's poor accuses

us. Driven by lust for things, we become their slaves, devoting our energies and resources to servicing technological idols. Then we posture and whine when they fail us, or when others, who covet them even more than we, steal them from us. Through it all, we omit any admission of how artificial was our need of them in the first place. Remind us again, you who alone defines what is timeless, that we are children of eternity, molded for a holy business, requiring no security greater than your protection, no possession greater than your Spirit, no wealth greater than your love.

Declaration of Forgiveness

Into the abyss of our sorrow, God sends a shaft of purifying light to dispel our gloom and convince us that divine mercy is both proximate and efficacious—that is, it is now, and it is real! My friends, rely on the good news of the gospel: in Christ, God has overcome both sin and death. So long as we embrace this promise, we have nothing to fear.

Call for the Offering

The testimony of Scripture is clear: those who shun the poor, turn their back on want, and ignore suffering have no place at God's family table. Do not mistake what this means. It is not that our failure to do these things in life will exclude us from that table in the life to come, although the biblical witness certainly supports that conclusion. But our mandate is closer to home: if we behave in so stingy a fashion here, we have already excluded ourselves. Our own attitude accuses us and our conduct testifies against us. Once again, let us remember: Christ focuses on the spirit of our giving, not its magnitude. Be of a generous heart and the rest need not concern us; it will follow.

Prayer of Dedication

Your gentleness and generosity, O God, defy our powers of portrayal. There can be no meaningful comparison between what we give you and what you have already given us—and continue to give with each breath of our lives. Yet, by receiving our gifts and adding them to the immeasurable wealth of your kindness, their value is compounded and our joy multiplied. Receive them, great Sovereign, with our thanks and praise.

Thanksgiving

The power and the majesty are yours, Eternal God; but ours the surpassing joy of living under their protection. Yours are the wonder and the mystery; but ours the fascination and excitement of unveiling and exploring them. The powers of redemption and resurrection are yours alone to give; but ours the elation of receiving your love most tenderly present in Jesus, our brother according to the flesh, our savior by the power of the Holy Spirit. With hearts so full that words cannot do justice to feeling, we applaud the splendor of this life that is your gift to us and press with our whole beings to waken the global hymn of gratitude. All wonder and praise and thanksgiving be to our God!

Twenty-fifth Sunday after Pentecost

Invocation

Engage us, Maker of bounty, in the rich rewards of this harvest season, when both the profusion and the frailty of life are starkly evident to us. Through plenty, we learn to loose our lips in joyful thanksgiving. In frailty, we descry the signs of our own mortality. In both, we mark your loving presence that invites us to seize life abundantly and face death hopefully, in the likeness of Jesus Christ, whose name we cry, whose faith we proclaim.

Call to Praise (from Psalm 92:1–4)

Leader: It is good to give thanks to God,
People: To sing praises to your name, O Most High;
Leader: To declare your steadfast love in the morning,
People: And your faithfulness at night,
Leader: To the music of stringed instruments,
People: To the melody of the organ;
Leader: For the abundance of earth makes us glad, generous God;
People: At the work of your hands we sing for joy!

Prayer of Praise

The span of heaven praises you, Sovereign Being, her galaxies parading in glad review; the frame of earth exults you, yielding reliably the provisions of life; the histories of nations serve you, even when rulers nor peoples are sensible to what is wrought. Now we who are your servants add our glory shout; for your word summons us, your will directs us, your righteousness judges us, your love redeems us. And for all this, we mean our praise to outshine the stars, our faithfulness to be more solid than rock, our histories to advance your intent. Grant only the blessing of your approval, O God, and our praise will be complete.

Call to Reconciliation

Note: This call to reconciliation, and the accompanying prayer of confession and declaration of forgiveness, are based on the apocryphal Prayer of Manasseh.

"The Prayer of Manasseh," a tiny but classic work of penitential devotion in the Apocrypha, provides all the material requisite to today's office of confession—our call to reconciliation, prayer of confession, and declaration of forgiveness. From verse 7 we take these words: "you are the God Most High, of great compassion, long-suffering and very merciful, who repents over the evils of humanity. According to your great goodness, O God, you have promised repentance and forgiveness to those who have sinned against you, that they may be saved." Let us now read on together, in unison acceptance of God's "gift of repentance."

Prayer of Confession

God of the righteous, you appointed repentance not for the righteous, but for us, who are sinners. For the sins we have committed are more in number than the sand of the sea; our transgressions are multiplied, O God, they are multiplied! We are unable to look up and see the height of heaven because of them. We are weighed down with them as if by iron fetters; we are rejected because of our sin, and have no relief. For we have provoked your wrath and done what is evil in your sight, and now we bend the knees of our hearts, beseeching you for your kindness. We have sinned, O God; we know our transgression. Earnestly we beseech you to forgive us. Do not be angry with us forever, or lay up evil for us, and do not condemn us to the depths of the earth.

Declaration of Forgiveness

Almighty One, God of our forebears and of their posterity, you made heaven and earth with all their order and shackled the sea by the word of command. Before your power all things tremble, for your glorious splendor cannot be borne and the wrath of your threat to sinners is irresistible; yet immeasurable and unsearchable is your promised mercy. For in us you will manifest your goodness; unworthy as we are, you will save us in your great mercy; and we will praise you continually all the days of our lives. For all the host of heaven sings your praise, and your glory is forever. Amen.

Call for the Offering

At a meeting of United Church of Christ national officers and conference executives, called in the wake of regional disasters that struck the United States in 1995–96, discussion centered on the role of the churches. How can we best respond? The group soon realized that there are three levels of response. We are not equipped to mount a first response, to establish shelters to house and feed those driven from their homes. The Red Cross can do a far better job. Nor can we undertake the second level: removing shattered trees and buildings, repairing roads and bridges, restoring communications. This work requires the full power of government and public utility industries. Uniquely, however, we are best able to provide the third level of aid: to stay with people for the long haul, as they count their losses and struggle to restore their lives. Our strength is not in our speed, but our endurance. The offering is just that: an opportunity to provide help over the long haul. When everyone else has packed up and gone home, we can still be there, saying to those affected, "No, you are not forgotten: we are still with you." In this, perhaps as much as anyplace, we have opportunity to mimic the endurance of God, who never gives up.

Prayer of Dedication

Our gifts are wholly yours, gracious God, but are ours to dedicate, who are stewards of your household's wealth. Knowing that an account of our stewardship will be required, we offer some of what has been earned by the resources you entrusted to us and pray that we may be judged good and faithful servants.

Thanksgiving

Into the unsurveyed reaches of your universe, majestic Creator, we pour our words of thanksgiving, while cynics smirk and laugh that they will be lost in a black hole of cosmic indifference. What a wonder is this, that we send them in confidence still, sure that One who speaks creation out of chaos will also hear the small voices of the children of earth. Against the common wisdom, therefore, we proclaim your majesty that ordains our existence, your goodness that provides our sustenance, your mercy that strives for our reconciliation. With ascending speech, we thank you for the body of testimony which, across thousands of years, flows to us and through us, and—our testimony adjoined—moves on to generations not yet born, proclaiming that our God lives! Thanks be to God!

Twenty-sixth Sunday after Pentecost

Note: The prayers for the twenty-sixth Sunday are composed to be used on the Sunday before Thanksgiving Day.

Invocation

Our forebears gathered in the fall of the year to thank you, God of their deliverance, for a harvest that we would judge marginal, but they declared abundant; for it made plausible the hope that their life would be secure through the harsh winter ahead. We gather in their example, impelled to voice even larger thanks for blessings so profuse they defy enumeration. Will you, in whose hands a few loaves and fishes proved sufficient for the needs of multitude, speak to us here the true meaning of plenty, that our abundance may serve you no less than did our parents' sufficiency.

Call to Praise (from Psalm 145:15–21)

Leader: The eyes of all look to you, O God, and you give them their food in due season.

People: You open your hand, satisfying the desire of every living thing.

Leader: You are just in all your ways,

People: In everything that you do.

Leader: You fulfill the desire of all who are in awe of you,

People: Hearing their cry, you save them.

Leader: Our mouths will speak your praise, mighty Provider,

People: And all flesh will praise your holy name forever.

Prayer of Praise

In sacred congregation, God of grace, we rise to praise you, by whose mercy we are given more than enough and to spare, and bid the words of our mouths proclaim the esteem of our hearts. May our gratitude, awakened by the bounty of earth, praise you. May the yield of our harvest, brought in by the labor of human hands and the resources of technology, praise you. May our pain at the plight of others, who know only spareness and want in this season of plenitude, praise you. May the spur to share our abundance with your children in need, wherever we have power to reach them, praise you. May everything we do in this season of your thanksgiving praise you, O God—our God—forever.

Call to Reconciliation

Everything in our tradition, not least the admonitions of Jesus, encourages Christians to assume a posture of thanksgiving in all facets of life. We are to be, if nothing else, God's thankful people, because we, of all people, comprehend and acknowledge the divine source of life and all that makes it rich and meaningful. And of all people, we know something else, too: that these gifts come to us even though, and even when, we do not deserve them. Our thanksgiving for God's generosity, therefore, is always coupled with expressions of sorrow that we are not more truly responsive to God's grace. Join me now in common confession, so that the voice of our thankfulness can rise from consciences fully cleansed and restored.

Prayer of Confession (from Jeremiah 2:4, 7–8)

You who loosened the prophets' tongues, your word in Jeremiah's mouth stings us with rebuke: "What wrong did your ancestors find in me that they went far from me, after worthless things, and became worthless themselves? I brought you into a plentiful land, to eat its fruits and its good things. But when you entered you defiled my land, and made my heritage an abomination. Those who handle the law do not think of me; your rulers transgress against me; the shepherds of the people rebel against me; and all chase after things that do not profit." We lament, our God, the evil in our nation, the profane pursuits of our people, our failure to keep the covenant of Jesus Christ. We are a people lost, who will find our way only as you lead us. We are a people broken, who will find healing only as you purge us. Acquit us of our evil, impartial Judge of nations; make us fully your people and our nation your glory.

Declaration of Forgiveness

Our forbears in our nation's pilgrimage viewed the tenets of Christian faith with great seriousness. The very first holy day observed in the New World, still observed on a national scale, was a day devoted to Thanksgiving. But they also, at regular intervals, declared days of fasting and penitence, during which they reflected upon their calling and took stock of their stewardship. As we prepare, after them, to observe a day of thanks, let it include celebration of the mercy of God who, for the love of us, adopted human flesh and embraced and defeated sin and death. The very reach of divine reconciliation is a thing of wonder. Let us rejoice in it!

Call for the Offering

Like most holidays, Thanksgiving means many things to many people, but is observed, one way or another, by Americans of every religious persuasion and none at all. It is, after all, a national holiday, over which no religious community any longer has a unique claim. For Christians, however, the day reminds us, in a palpable way, that true thankfulness is not a periodic gesture, much less an annual excuse for gluttony. It is a posture, a bearing, which defines how we move in the world. We conduct ourselves as God's grateful people. Let today's offering demonstrate that realization. Give, this day, in gratitude for God's excellent mercy. There is no motivation to equal it.

Prayer of Dedication

By your love, Christ Jesus, we have been bought back from all that would enslave and destroy us. Knowing ourselves to be among the most blessed folk who have lived, at this or any other time, we are constrained to employ both giving and thanksgiving to scatter across earth the seeds of redemptive love. By our words and music of appreciation, may we show ourselves worthy servants of the living God, to whom is owed the acclaim of a grateful people.

Thanksgiving

Blessed Creator, you appoint us a world where many suffer more than we are likely to experience and want more than we can comprehend. Why are we so favored? The wealth of earth rises to meet us with but little of our labor. The prosperity and freedom we take for granted are the envy of nations. We are flooded by opportunities to work, to acquire, to study, to travel, to enjoy. O God, may the scope of our thankfulness never fall short of the vastness of our blessings. May it be as dependable as seedtime and harvest. May it be as vast as the breadth of our land. But most of all, may it be the occasion for our confession that everything we have that is good and beautiful and joyful is the product of your love. Then we will know to acknowledge: were our entire lives devoted to acts of thanksgiving, your generosity would be infinitely greater still.

Reformation Sunday

Last Sunday of October
Liturgical Color: Red

Reformation Sunday is not truly among the liturgical days of the church calendar. It is not observed by the largest and most global of Christian communions, the Roman Catholic Church—not least because it was the centralized Roman authority against which the Reformers of the sixteenth century rebelled! This is not to argue that the Roman Catholic Church ignores reformation and renewal. Clearly it does recognize these concepts, as illustrated by Vatican II—the most dramatic event in recent Roman Catholic history. Had the Roman church been incapable of change and renewal, no matter how glacial its pace, it would not have survived, much less thrived, for two millennia.

Reformation Sunday, however, is a celebration peculiar to the Protestant traditions. It is a time to recall the truism that the Church of Jesus Christ must ever and always be about the business of renewal if it is not to sink into staid traditionalism. One need not formally be a student of history to list some of the world's great movements which began in revolutionary zeal, acquired power and respectability, and degenerated into corruption or irrelevance. It is a truism in church history that the gospel of Jesus Christ is, and of necessity must be, highly adaptive. If it cannot be retold in ways that are meaningful to each new generation, it will die.

The achievements of the early Reformers are dramatic: the decentralization of church authority from the monolithic Roman model to congregational and representative forms of government; articulation of the "priesthood of all believers" as opposed to the traditional model of the preeminence of clergy; ordination as a functional responsibility, not an indelible order; the elevation of preaching and teaching to a level of importance equal to that of sacramental celebration; the mass publication of Scripture and recognition of the right—indeed the obligation—of all Christians to read and weigh; the conduct of worship in each congregation's native language, so that all have equal access to its intellectual, as well as its mystical, rewards; and a dramatic increase in congregational participation in the act of worship, especially in prayer and song.

Reformation Sunday is an opportunity to remind ourselves that these are gifts. It is a time both to remember our history as reformed and reforming denominations and congregations and to assess the degree of our faithfulness to the task of renewal as a central and ongoing concern. It is also a time to celebrate those who, with particular devotion, contributed in ways both large and small to the historic process of which we are the most recent beneficiaries, many of whom suffered distress, dislocation, persecution, and martyrdom as the price of faithfulness. Consider: how we praise God—even to some extent *that* some of us have come to praise God at all—is a direct consequence of their actions. It ill-behooves us to ignore their sacrifice.

Prayers and Liturgical Readings

Invocation

Author of our faith story, playwright of our tradition, composer of our Reformation lifesong: we hear your praise on a thousand thousand lips now stilled by time, yet audible to our expectant ears. They are the voices of our forebears in faith, who call to us to hold fast their memories, honor their pilgrimages, redeem their labors. In our hour of remembering, transfuse in us their depth and breadth of faithfulness, by which your Word was glorified, the Word-made-flesh became more vividly present in the world and their lives were justified.

Call to Praise (from Psalm 31:1–3)

Leader: In you, O God, we take shelter.
People: Never let us be disgraced.
Leader: In your righteousness, deliver us.
People: Turn your ear to us and rescue us.
Leader: Be a sheltering rock for us,
People: A walled fortress to save us.

Leader: You are indeed our rock and our fortress.
People: We will sing your praise in hymns of adoration!

Prayer of Praise

In a thousand ways, in a thousand nations, you have raised up witnesses to yourself, majestic Divinity, and brought the faithful to light. We who are the beneficiaries of their constancy now rise, in gratitude and admiration, to praise you because of them. We glorify you for the gift of the church, reformed and reforming, this new and renewing light to each generation. We exalt you for the agitating presence of your Spirit in our histories, prodding and stimulating us to dream new ways to worship you and serve your people. We marvel before the profuse wealth of form and expression that your children have imagined, all of it a witness to encounter with the one child of God who is Jesus our Christ; for whom many suffered, many died, many triumphed, many are glorified. Because of your love so evident in their witness, we offer ourselves as authors of new songs to your praise, new witnesses to your glory, new agents of reconciliation to the world.

Call to Reconciliation

Each of us knows, in our secret selves, the pain of shortcoming—the failure to answer, to our fullest ability, the call to obedience to the gospel of Jesus Christ. In this, we are not alone. We are, in truth, part of a great company of sisters and brothers in God's household that transcends both time and place. Be mindful, therefore, as we express our personal needs, that we stand in company with myriad other saints who share our humility, our disappointments, our uncertainties—and our Reformation hope. Let now the sound of our common voice be in unison with theirs, as together we seek divine reconciliation and renewal. Let us pray.

Prayer of Confession

Eternal God, who calls your people to newness of life and your church to the ongoing work of reformation, we concede our reluctance to think beyond stodgy methods, to shatter exhausted symbols, to abandon outmoded ritual. We are friend to those whose social standing matches our own and covetous to be friends with those we envy; but we recoil from the shabby poor, the grossly ill, the social outcast. We prefer the ceremony that comforts to the hard work of tending your Word. We sanctify what is and declare it your will. We screen ourselves from the scandal—and the transforming power—of the cross, neglecting to see that the very ones we abhor are sought by our Christ as wedding guests. Touch us, shake our lethargy, let the power of reformation restore the way of Christ in us and teach us such newness of heart and soul as alone can bring us to the way of salvation.

Declaration of Forgiveness

Leader: In his second letter to the church at Corinth, Paul records this reassuring assertion: "the love of Christ urges us on, because we are convinced that one has died for all; therefore all have died. And he died for all, so that those who live might live no longer for themselves, but for him who died and was raised for them" (5:14–15). Rejoice, dear friends, that in our forgiveness we are freed, both to live for Christ and to be Christ to the world. Is this not good news?

People: This is indeed good news, for which we give thanks and praise to God!

Call for the Offering

In 2 Corinthians 9, Paul seeks to persuade the Christians of Asia Minor that generosity in the name of Christ multiplies and reflects back on those who practice it. Specifically, he states: "You will be enriched in every way for your great generosity; . . . for the rendering of this ministry not only supplies the needs of the saints but also overflows with many thanksgivings to God." It is a theme that plays well among those who hold to the reformed faith, who know how the generosity of those who preceded us prompts us to live God's praise. In this day's offering, we again have opportunity to pass it on, with interest, to others.

Prayer of Dedication

Through this testing of our ministry, generous God, we seek to glorify you, making substantial our obedience to the gospel of Christ. By the generosity of our sharing with all who are in need, may the surpassing peace that you have shed on us become manifest. Thanks to you for your indescribable gift, and for these gifts that we now make yours in the love of Jesus Christ, in whose name we pray.

Thanksgiving

Framer of our tradition and root of our courage, the story of your intercession in our history has been told within the reassuring circle of your family for generations; how much more brave and glorious is its telling when addressed to those who dread and despise it, as well as those who hunger to hear it. We thank you, therefore, for the courage of all who moved beyond the secure walls of church, the sustaining touch of family, the sheltering womb of clan, to proclaim the good news of Jesus Christ to a hostile world. We are grateful, too, for moments when we ourselves have been encouraged by your Spirit to rise above our embarrassment and timidity to speak boldly; to stand proudly in the presence of skeptics and cynics; to be embodiments of love to a society that measures success by the index of personal gain. Empower us further, we pray, to grow to the stature of your apostles of all ages who suffered rejection and humiliation, but refused to dishonor your name. Let your glory be served, your dominion enlarged, by the dimensions of our lives and conduct.

Benedictions

Following are twenty-one benedictions, the first nine of my own composition, the remainder selected from among the most cherished and enduring that appear in Scripture. The reader will note some variation in tone. This is deliberate. Mine were composed while chaplain of Allegheny College, where students expressed an overwhelming preference for benedictions that sent them from the chapel feeling they had been charged with a clearly stated set of responsibilities, i.e., expectations coherent with living as committed Christians on campus.

Some will note the absence of Laban's benediction over Jacob at the pillar of Mizpah (Genesis 31:49). This treasured passage was used, in my childhood, as a Sunday School benediction, because young children can easily memorize it. However, a careful reading of the story will demonstrate why Laban chose the words he did: Jacob had, for all intents and purposes, robbed him blind by cunning and deceit. From Laban's viewpoint, God indeed had better watch between them. It appears that even when physically absent, Jacob's craftiness was not to be underestimated! It never seemed to me a propitious model for closing worship.

1

Go now in peace, being not merely those who tolerate the absence of hostility and disorder, or are content to live in communities where pain and need are kept within tolerable limits; but employing all that you have been given to be peace*makers*. Strive actively and with tireless dedication to achieve that which promotes the common welfare, the merging of those good things, both divine and human, that comprise God's own *shalom*. And the grace, mercy, and peace of that same God, Creator, Judge, and Redeemer, will guide and sustain us all.

2

As we go out now into this good day, let us newly recognize and reaffirm the tasks to which we are called, keeping alive our confidence that the power of our loving god is already out there ahead of us, waiting to sustain and encourage us in our effort to be bearers of that truth that alone will make us free. Go in God's peace.

3

Let us go in peace, knowing that the power of God's grace lives in us and through us, yielding light to guide us, knowledge to empower us, courage to support us, and love to unite us, this day and all the days of our lives.

4

May the shalom of God—that perfect peace that encompasses health, well-being, prosperity, and justice for all people—surround and embrace us; but let us also do everything in our power to be worthy of it, as individuals, as a congregation, as a community, as corporate citizens of God's good earth.

5

Now may the Spirit of the living God, whose mercy brought us here and whose mercy will lead us out again, be manifest in every member of this community that claims the name of Christ, firing in us a vision of what life is being created to be and empowering us to forego everything that may separate us from its realization.

6

Let us go now in God's peace, keeping close to us, at all times and in all circumstances, devotion to personal integrity and scorn for victories cheaply won; ardor for justice and suspicion of personal privilege; abhorrence of war and zeal for peace. Then the knowledge of God's love that we carry in us will truly be the adversary of ignorance and will make us victors over tyranny; in the name, and on behalf of, Christ Jesus our Savior.

7

Let the grace of God that each of us carries already within us now have free reign through and among us, working in us the wonder of rejuvenation that transforms fear into faith; then turn us loose in our stores and offices and neighborhoods, to model before the world what it means to be the people of a God who redeems our time, our labor, and our lives.

8

May the grace, mercy, and peace of God, who is our creator, our redeemer, and our sanctifier, carry us safely through all the days of our lives, and beyond life.

9

Go out from this place in the name of God, who called you here and sends you out again, bearers of the good news of God's redeeming love in Jesus Christ; but do not go seeking signs and wonders. Rather, seek to be signs and wonders. Then we will know, surely, that the rule of God is not far from us.

10 (from Numbers 6:24–26)
May God bless us and keep us; may God's face shine upon us and be gracious unto us; may God's countenance be lifted upon us, and give us peace.

11 (from Luke 2:29–32)
Holy One of history, discharge your servants now in peace, now that your promise is fulfilled. For we have seen your salvation with our own eyes, which you have made ready in full view of all nations; a light that will be a revelation to the Gentiles, and for glory to your people Israel.

12 (from Ephesians 3:20–21)
Now to the One who, by the power that is at work within us, is able to do immeasurably more than all we can ask or imagine, be glory in the church, and in Jesus Christ, from generation to generation, forever.

13 (from Philippians 4:4–7)
Always rejoice in God; I say it again: rejoice! Let our gentleness be known to everyone. God is near; so there is no need to be anxious about anything, but in everything let us make our wishes known to God in prayer and petition, always with thanksgiving. Then the peace of God,

which always surpasses our utmost understanding, will keep guard over our hearts and our thoughts, in Christ Jesus.

14 (from Philippians 4:8-9)

Finally, beloved, all that is true and honorable and just and pure, all that is pleasing and commendable; whatever is excellent and admirable—fix your minds on these things. Keep on doing the things that you have learned and received and heard and seen, and the God of peace will be with you.

15 (from 1 Thessalonians 5:23-24)

May the very God of peace sanctify us entirely; and may our spirits and souls and bodies be kept sound and blameless until the coming of our Savior Jesus Christ; for the one who calls us is faithful, and will do this for us.

16 (from 2 Thessalonians 2:16-17)

Now may our Savior Jesus Christ and God our Eternal Parent, who loves us and gives us eternal comfort and good hope through grace, comfort our hearts and establish them in every good work and word.

17 (from 2 Thessalonians 3:16)

Now may God, the very fount of peace, give us peace, at all times and in all ways; and be with us all.

18 (from 1 Peter 4:10-11)

Like good stewards of the manifold grace of God, let us agree to serve one another with whatever gift each of us has received. Whoever speaks must do so as one speaking the very words of God; whoever serves must do so with the strength that God supplies, so that God may be glorified in all things through Jesus Christ, to whom belong the glory and the power forever.

19 (from Hebrews 12:1-2)

Since we are surrounded by so great a cloud of witnesses, let us also lay aside every weight and the sin that clings so closely, and let us run with perseverance the race that is set before us, looking to Jesus, the pioneer and perfecter of our faith, who for the sake of the joy that was set before him endured the cross, disregarding its shame, and has taken the honored place beside the throne of God.

20 (from Hebrews 13:20–21)

Now may the God of peace, who brought again from the dead our Savior Jesus, the great shepherd of the sheep, by the blood of the eternal covenant equip you with everything good, so that we may do God's will, working among us that which is pleasing in God's sight; through Jesus Christ, to whom be the glory forever and ever.

21 (from Jude 24–25)

Now to the One who is able to keep us from falling and to make us stand, jubilant and above reproach, in the presence of divine glory, to the only God our Savior, be glory and majesty, might and authority, through Jesus Christ, before all time, and now, and forevermore. Amen.

Appendix

Order of Service Based on the Forms of Christian Prayer

Welcome and Introductions

Prelude
Invocation* *(may be spoken in unison)*

The Service of Praise
Call to Praise*
Hymn* *(a true hymn of praise and adoration is preferable)*
Unison Prayer of Praise*
The Gloria* *(omitted during Advent and Lent; see introductory text for section 6 on Lent)*

Office of Confession
Call to Reconciliation
Unison Prayer of Confession
Declaration of Forgiveness

Prayers of the People
Sharing Joys and Concerns *(hearing from the people what is on their minds)*
Prayers of Supplication and Intercession
Prayer of Our Savior

Offertory
Call for the Offering
Anthem, interlude, or special music
The Doxology* *(omitted during Advent and Lent, when the offering is carried to the table in silence)*
Prayer of Dedication* *(may be spoken in unison)*

Service of the Word
Scripture Readings
From the Hebrew Scriptures (Old Testament)

From the Christian Scriptures (New Testament, using Epistle, Gospel, or both) *(congregation may be requested to stand during a reading from the Gospel)*
Hymn* *(a meditative or preparatory hymn is preferable)*
Sermon

Service of Thanksgiving
Unison Prayer of Thanksgiving
A Period of Silence *(real silence, for at least one full minute)*

Announcements
Hymn* *(in general, a celebratory hymn serves best at this point)*
Benediction*
Postlude*

Variations may be instituted for dramatic impact. During Advent and Lent, for instance, the Ford Chapel congregation remained in the back of the chapel until time for the service (the structure of the building accommodated such an arrangement), where we performed the Office of Confession. The people then took their seats during the Prelude. This arrangement both dramatized the season and drove home the fact that no one has earned the right to step into God's presence—indeed, Scripture holds that those who "see" God are consumed by the experience. Rather, we are welcomed into the presence of holiness as an act of grace on the part of a forgiving God—but only after we acknowledge our need and God's mercy.

On days when the eucharist was celebrated, confession occurred during the communion liturgy proper, and the Scripture readings and sermon were moved up to precede the offertory. The Service of the Word concluded with the passing of signs of peace. The eucharist began with the Offertory and concluded with the Thanksgiving. Also, on communion days, the bread and wine were carried in as part of the offering, preceding the collection plates and noted in the dedicatory prayer.

All who are able are invited to stand.

Index of Scriptural References

Material from the following passages is cited in the introductory texts or is incorporated directly in the liturgical material.

Key

BENTN	Benediction
OFRNG	Call for the Offering
RECON	Call to Reconciliation
CALPR	Call to Praise
FORGV	Declaration of Forgiveness
INTRO	Introduction
INVOC	Invocation
CONFS	Prayer of Confession
PRASE	Prayer of Praise
THNKS	Thanksgiving

Old Testament

Passage	*Section*	*Form*
Genesis 1:2	Introduction	
Genesis 1:16–19	2	INTRO
Genesis 2:7	Introduction	
Genesis 12:3	1	INTRO
Deuteronomy 15:10–11	13	OFRNG
Deuteronomy 16:17	4	OFRNG
Deuteronomy 18:15	2	INTRO
Deuteronomy 32:1–3	13	CALPR
1 Chronicles 16:8–11	13	CALPR
1 Chronicles 16:23–26	13	CALPR
1 Chronicles 16:28–34	13	PRASE
Job 38:4–13	13	PRASE
Psalm 1:1–2, 4–6	6	RECON
Psalm 5:11–12	13	CALPR
Psalm 9:8–9	13	FORGV
Psalm 14:2, 4–5	13	RECON

Apocrypha

—

New Testament

—